Reading
Between
the Lips

A totally deaf man
makes it in the mainstream

Lew Golan

Bonus Books, Inc., Chicago

99 98 97 96 95   5 4 3 2 1

Library of Congress Cataloging-in-Publication Data

Golan, Lew. 1933–
   Reading between the lips / Lew Golan.
     p.   cm.
   Includes index.
   ISBN 1-56625-021-8   : $22.95
   1. Golan, Lew, 1933-   . 2. Deaf–Israel–Biography. 3. Deaf–United States–Biography. 4. Lipreading–Israel–Case Studies. 5. Lipreading–United States–Case studies.   I. Title.
HV2848.5.G65A3   1995
362.4'2'092–dc20   94-42477
[B]   CIP

Bonus Books, Inc.
160 East Illinois Street
Chicago, IL 60611

Printed in the United States of America

For Barbara

Contents

Foreword

In 1984, when the Information Superhighway was still an electronic dirt road, Lew Golan and I discovered each other.

He had posted a message on a Chicago computer bulletin board asking for help in finding a gadget with a flashing light that would tell him when his telephone line was in use. He explained that he was deaf, and too often he had sat down to call out with his computer and modem only to discover that his wife was already talking on the phone in another room. The shriek of Lew's modem did not please her.

The same thing irritated my wife, and so I left a message for Lew telling him that I, too, was deaf and asking him to share any information he learned. He did, and quickly we became electronic correspondents. Soon we met in the flesh.

Our friendship was a first for both of us. We each had grown up, worked, married and raised families wholly outside the world of the deaf. Occasionally we had met other deaf people, but never developed friendships with them. For us, deafness has never been a source of pride, a commonality of culture as it is for so many who cannot hear. We have considered it, rather, a genuine physical handicap to be coped with, not celebrated. Although deafness often has made our lives interesting, it has not defined us.

Warily we took each other's measure. Neither of us considered the deafness of the other much of an attraction except, in the beginning, as a curiosity, and later as a minor source of practical wisdom.

Besides lack of hearing, however, we had a great deal else in common. Our childhoods had been remarkably similar. Our playmates had been hearing, and we both had attended public schools long before the term "mainstreaming" was invented. We were both graduates of journalism schools. I was book review editor at the *Chicago Sun-Times*, where years before Lew briefly had been a sports copy editor before finding his calling in advertising and marketing communications. We both were interested in literature, the arts and political events. We both had hearing spouses and had raised hearing families. We each had a child who was a competitive gymnast. We even shared the same birthday, August 17.

And we were single-minded computer enthusiasts. When we got together for the first time with our spouses, they expected an evening of revelation and sharing, for neither had ever met anyone else married to a deaf person. Lew and I never let them get a word in edgewise; we bored them to tears with technobabble about DOS and disk drives.

Other than that, Lew and I are wholly different personalities. I am shy and diffident while Lew is outspoken and aggressive. I prefer solitude; Lew thrives in crowds. I hate to seem dependent on others in any way; it is almost impossible for me to ask a stranger to make a telephone call, even in dire emergency. Lew suffers from no such bashfulness. He is capable of buttonholing someone he has never seen before in his life at the airport and, through him, conducting a complex business phone call. For Lew, that's not a matter of independence but tough-minded necessity. And he's brash enough to make it work.

In the contentious matter of oral communication versus sign language, I have preferred the honey-is-better-than-vinegar neutrality of "Different strokes for different folks." Lew agrees that communication is a personal choice, but he also refuses to allow anyone to denigrate his, as the radicals of Deaf culture have often discovered to their chagrin. Call Lew, as so many of them do, "a poor imitation of a hearing person," and he'll loose a broadside of facts and scorn as enlightening as it is withering.

Because of these differences as well as similarities we became friends. For the last decade we have closely followed each other's lives, mine in America and Lew's in Israel, through the good offices of the Internet as well as during the Golans' yearly visits to their old stamping grounds in Chicago.

During one of those visits, in 1990, I published my autobiography, *What's That Pig Outdoors?* We had talked for years about writing the stories of our lives, and Lew was mortified that I had beaten him to the punch. I followed insult with injury by gleefully inscribing in his copy of my book, "Nyaah! Nyaah! I got here first! (But I'm afraid yours will be better than mine.)"

Is *Reading Between the Lips* indeed superior? Modesty (or embarrassment, take your choice) prevents me from revealing the truth. But I will tell you this:

In reading this book you are in for not only an eye-opening experience but also an absorbing one. For Lew Golan, the English language is a toy as well as a tool; he's a gifted storyteller as well as a consummate salesman. Sit back and watch a master at work.

—*Henry Kisor*

Close your eyes, Benny Goodman

When I was a freelance writer in Chicago, I walked into the reception room of a Michigan Avenue advertising agency. The creative director had called me to pick up an assignment.

The receptionist smiled up at me. "Hello, Lew."

"Hi. Bill's looking for me."

She glanced at her in/out chart. "He'll be back in 10 minutes."

Across the room, a red-faced fellow with a fleshy, veined nose overheard the exchange. "Are you Lew Golan?"

"Yeah."

"My name is Wylie. Bill told me all about you. Want to go down for a drink until he gets back?"

"Thanks, but I don't drink." Besides, it was only 10:30 in the morning.

"Well, I certainly can use a couple. You can get yourself a Coke."

A few minutes later, sitting at the bar, Wylie swallowed half of a double Scotch in one quick gulp. He closed his eyes and waited for the buzz.

Then he peered at me through bleary eyes and shook his head. "Lew, I don't get it. I can't understand why you don't drink."

"Well...."

"If I were you, I'd be the biggest boozer in the world."

"Huh?"

"Even though Bill tells me you're one of the best writers in this business, I feel so very, very sorry for you."

Uh, oh. Here it comes.

"Yes." He couldn't stop shaking his head. "My God, Lew, it's bad enough that you're stone deaf...."

Wylie gave me a mournful look.

"But what's even worse, you're Jewish, too...."

A mouthful of 7-Up went up my nose the back way.

Drifting in a fermented haze, he was oblivious to my coughing and sneezing as I grabbed frantically for my handkerchief.

"Yet you don't drink. I don't get it. I really don't get it...."

Over the course of 61 kaleidoscopic years, through a gamut of pursuits from writing songs to righting wrongs, I have been getting it one way or another. Sometimes I get it right; sometimes I get it in the neck.

This book is a mostly anecdotal and partly philosophical account of making it in a hearing world without hearing anything at all.

If you can see the funny side of the above incident (some people cannot see anything at all comical about bigotry or ignorance), you may get a few snickers at my expense along the way.

For many deaf people, deafness involves a way of life that is heavily dependent on sign language; this all-encompassing way of life extends to school and work, family and friends.

In fact, the September 1993 issue of *Atlantic Monthly* carried a 12-page article entitled "Deafness as Culture." The subhead:

Well-meaning efforts to integrate deaf people into conventional schools and to help them learn English are provoking fierce resistance from activists who favor sign language and an acknowledgment that the world of deafness is distinctive, rewarding and worth preservation.

However, those activists and I are worlds apart.

In India, the Hindus believe that cows are sacred. So if a cow happens to stop in the middle of the road and block a Hindu's way, he waits for it to move.

But in the rest of the world, people simply push the cow out of the way.

Similarly, when Deaf activists say that deafness is something to be revered, all I can say is "Holy cow!"

To me, deafness is nothing more than an obstacle to be pushed aside. And, like a cow, it is often associated with some kind of bull.

Although I have been totally deaf since the age of six, my world has always been that of the hearing. And my deafness is little more than an occasional pain in the ass, because several factors have stacked the deck in my favor:

I grew up among hearing people.

I communicate by speaking and reading lips.

And I married a woman with normal hearing.

This approach isn't for everyone, but it has worked very well for me.

If I had done otherwise, I could very well have been shooting myself in the foot.

The title of this book, *Reading Between the Lips,* refers mainly to speechreading (a more accurate term than lipreading), which has been the keystone of my life in the hearing world.

Speechreading involves more than just looking at the movement of the lips.

To a great extent, it is a mental juggling of several factors. These include the context in which something is being said, plus my inherent knowledge of the world and of English vocabulary and grammar, plus the speaker's body language.

Even the most accomplished lipreader may not immediately get every spoken word in a sentence. But by considering the situation and filling in the _ _ _ _ _ _, it's possible to come up with the missing words without missing a beat.

Speechreaders interpolate and extrapolate information that has not even been spoken—much like reading between the lines.

Someone once wrote about me: "Lew not only reads lips. I am firmly convinced that he reads minds as well." In fact, he was pinpointing the essence of speechreading: understanding what the other person has on his mind.

The title also alludes to the huge amount of reading I have done to make myself as knowledgeable as possible about as many things as possible. The inexhaustible resources of the printed word have helped compensate for what I miss by not hearing.

I feel uncomfortable when I don't have something to read—a book, a magazine, a report, a newspaper, a dictionary, a catalogue, a cereal box— in case I have a moment to spare on a plane, in a waiting room, in a traffic jam, or wherever.

Reading is an indispensable source for deaf people who want to know what's up—and to make their way up—in the world.

These intellectual factors, plus emotional factors such as attitude, show that making it in a hearing world without being able to hear is often a question of mind over matter.

I was born and spent the first 37 years of my life in Chicago, where air raid sirens in the middle of the night signaled that the White Sox had won the 1959 American League pennant.

I now live in Tel Aviv, where air raid sirens in the middle of the night signaled the imminent nearby explosion of Scud missiles from Iraq during the 1991 Gulf War.

Through it all, my world has been a Ping-Pong ball between these extremes of juvenile nuttiness and the deadly serious.

I went to the University of Chicago, and earned my degree in journalism at the University of Illinois. We (wife, four daughters) moved to Israel in 1970. We (wife, youngest daughter) moved back to the States in 1978. We (wife) moved back to Israel in 1986.

The ball has pinged and ponged between some other extremes as well. At America's largest marketing services agency (akin to an advertising agency)—where I was senior vice president, head of creative services and a member of the executive committee—I was responsible for scores of creative directors, writers, art directors, production managers and other people.

At the other extreme, as a full-time freelance writer and producer, I have worked in solitary confinement.

We lived in the Chicago-area megalopolis, teeming with millions of people...and we were members of a small kibbutz for five years.

Today I bounce back and forth between the worlds of business and academia.

I create and produce marketing communications (advertising and sales promotion) for several companies.

I am on the faculty at Tel Aviv University, in a dual capacity as an editor of academic papers and as a computer consultant.

And I write television programs for teaching English in Israel's public school system.

Still, one aspect of my life has remained relatively constant: I'm an incurable protester. In the 1960s I marched for civil rights with Martin Luther King at Selma, and for an end to the Vietnam War with a quarter of a million other protesters in Washington.

Today I march in Israel for religious pluralism, electoral reform and a flexible approach to peace.

And when it comes to some of the current trends involving the deaf today, I march to the beat of a different drummer.

To put things into perspective, the remainder of this introductory chapter gives a brief overview of deafness and deaf people.

Like hearing people, the 20,000,000 people in the United States with significant hearing losses differ in a multitude of factors such as intelligence, ability, education, race and religion.

But beyond these, there are four distinguishing characteristics that are specific to hearing-impaired people: *how much hearing someone lost, when she lost it, how she communicates, and the world in which she has a sense of belonging.*

There is a simple and convenient (but not entirely precise or scientific) dichotomy of hearing losses: *deaf* and *hard of hearing*.

People who cannot hear well enough to understand speech aurally, even with the help of hearing aids, are deaf—although they usually have some measurable residual hearing. About one-fourth of one percent of Americans are deaf—about 550,000 people.

I am totally deaf, with no measurable (let alone usable) hearing, which is a rarity. I'm off the chart.

The next factor is the onset of deafness. The onset is called either *prelingual* (prior to mastering speech, usually around the age of three) or *postlingual* (after three).

A newer term is *late-deafened*, which generally refers to those who became deaf during adulthood—but which can also include those deafened during adolescence.

I became deaf at six, so I am postlingually deaf.

Then there's the principal mode of communication: either *oral* (speaking and speechreading) or *sign language*.

I am oral.

Sign language is further divided into *signed English* (of which there are a number of variations) and *American Sign Language*. Signed English follows the syntax of the English language. The syntax of ASL is substantially different from that of English.

Finally—and here it gets more complicated—there's the world in which one feels the most kinship with others, the most at home.

This brings up communication modes and social norms.

People speak of the *hearing world* (a more-or-less accurate term) and the *deaf world* (a misleading term, since not all deaf people identify with it or even agree on what it is).

It doesn't work to divide deaf people into an *oral community* and a *signing community*. You can't speak of an oral community, because there isn't one.

Oral deaf people tend to identify with the hearing world...feeling more or less at home with hearing people, communicating by the spoken word as hearing people do, and subscribing to the social norms of hearing people. They are just as likely (or even more likely) to have hearing friends as deaf friends.

Although there is no oral deaf community, there is a signing deaf community—but most signers do not belong to it.

Late-deafened people, for example, grow up as hearing people. When they become deaf as adults, they often find it quite difficult to learn speechreading—so some of them learn to sign.

But after decades of belonging to the hearing world, they do not suddenly give up their friends and families and norms and join another world.

This means that there are people who sign but feel closer to the hearing world than to the signing community.

Most people who sign use signed English; only five to ten percent of signers use American Sign Language.

About 30 years ago, an analysis of ASL revealed it to have the characteristics of a distinct language.

Given the current interest in multiculturalism, users of ASL have begun viewing themselves as belonging to a separate culture with its own language.

They refer to themselves as Deaf (with a capital D); most of them are prelingually deaf, and many of them have deaf parents.

ASL is the core of Deaf identity, along with a set of values which has led to an insular attitude toward the hearing world.

Some of the Deaf perceive hearing people as their oppressors, and express no desire to be part of mainstream society.

Authors such as Oliver Sacks and Harlan Lane have written highly favorably about what they perceive as the Deaf culture. But whether the Deaf do, in fact, represent a distinct culture in the usual meaning of the term—rather than simply being a community of ASL users—has been a matter of debate.

More to the point, both Lane and Sacks completely ignore the all-important issue of how non-speaking, non-speechreading deaf people can function in the real world outside the ASL community, especially in the workplace.

William Stokoe of Gallaudet University, who first analyzed ASL as a language, was quoted in the *Washington City Paper* as saying that "ASL is a language of a small group of people, a very tightly knit, very small, closed society."

I do not know any sign language. I belong to and identify with the large, open hearing world, completely and unequivocally.

The fundamental problem of deafness is that it is an obstacle to communication. It quite literally is a sound barrier that separates deaf people from the hearing world.

Deafness can be little more than a nuisance if a deaf person can communicate with hearing people—but a major real-world handicap if he cannot understand what they are trying to tell him, and if they cannot understand what he is trying to tell them.

A number of books have described in heartbreaking detail what the downside of deafness is like. Isolated and frustrated by the barrier, many deaf people lead marginal lives—undereducated and underemployed, with a below-average standard of living.

But this book shows nothing of that picture, because my life has been on the upside.

Therefore, a caveat: although there are quite a few deaf people whose achievements equal or exceed mine, this book is in no way a description of the norm. A lot of deaf people have a lot more problems, or respond to being deaf in ways different from mine.

Furthermore, deafness is not a single, monolithic barrier. It is a more-or-less negotiable obstacle course that presents an extremely diverse assortment of obstructions.

You win some. You lose some. And you avoid some.

Since this book is about what I've done without knowing sign language, I was thinking of calling it *Look, Ma—No Hands!* But this would sound like I'm dumping on signing people, giving the wrong impression of my attitude.

On the contrary, I recognize the value of sign language to certain people under certain circumstances. It is unbeatable for what it is—a fast, efficient and comfortable way for signers to communicate among themselves.

At the same time, sign language does have limitations—and I point these out, as I point out the limitations of speechreading.

Sign language alone, despite its many obvious benefits in making it easier for deaf people to study, work and socialize with each other, is not enough to allow many of them to achieve their full potential in the hearing world.

The trade-off for signing's feel-good environment is that it isolates deaf people even more from hearing people, and it limits their horizons and opportunities.

Few hearing people know sign language, and interpreters are feasible only in isolated circumstances.

So deaf people who can meet the hearing world on its own terms—speaking and speechreading—have many more doors open to them, especially in employment.

Employers say the inability to communicate adequately is the number one problem in the hiring or promotion of deaf people.

Motivated by the Americans with Disabilities Act or by a sense of obligation, some organizations are trying to give deaf people greater access to the hearing world in a number of ways.

These include teaching sign language to hearing people who work with the public; putting closed captions on TV programs; providing interpreters to translate between speech and sign in classrooms, in theaters and other public environments, and on the job; and using computerized technologies for communication.

Nevertheless, in the hearing world there is no completely satisfactory substitute for a deaf person's ability to communicate orally by speaking and speechreading.

Yet some educators want to de-emphasize the learning and use of speech and speechreading in the classroom, or even eliminate them completely.

Their myopic approach has critical negative consequences for the future employability of deaf people.

When it comes to functioning in a real-world job, or dealing with the marketplace, or socializing with non-signers, it's a fact of life that deaf people pretty much have to depend on their own capabilities—at least until society or technology or medical science can come up with a better and affordable way.

Highly educated, highly experienced, highly qualified *hearing* people are having trouble finding and keeping jobs.

Life is tough.

Many of those who find comfort in the shelter of the Deaf community are ill-prepared to deal with the real world.

Since American Sign Language is not based on English, their command of English tends to be poor.

And, because of their inadequate English and their devotion to ASL, many of them are deficient in speaking and lipreading—and the extremists among them actually refuse to speak or lipread, even if they are capable of doing so.

They claim that in a community in which everyone is deaf and communicates in ASL, deafness is not a disability.

But they are sticking their heads in the semantic sand.

The fact remains that in the real world, deafness *is* a disability—and some of their attitudes and actions compound that disability.

Many in the Deaf community—and some hearing admirers—are in favor of *not* trying to eliminate or overcome deafness.

If a child is born deaf, they want to keep him deaf—even if there are medical or technological ways to give him some usable hearing.

And many, backed by Harlan Lane, are, incredibly, advocating that the responsibility for the upbringing and education of deaf children be taken away from their hearing parents and given to culturally Deaf surrogates.

Many advocates of American Sign Language feel that its validity is threatened by the fact that many deaf people are doing just fine without ASL.

So they castigate the deaf who have committed the sin of making it in the hearing world by speaking and speechreading.

The intolerance of their rhetoric comes close to xenophobia. They say that by not using ASL, I am living a marginal life with no identity...that I have no self-esteem...that I'm pretending to be a hearing person...that I'm ashamed of being deaf.

I'm trying to keep an open mind and an even keel about the capital-D Deaf.

They are not a homogeneous group, and the members have a broad range of attitudes; they do not even agree on who belongs to the group and who doesn't.

Yet the extremists among them rub me the wrong way.

The smug, narrow-minded arrogance of the anti-speech militants tars all of the Deaf people with the same brush of intolerance and clannishness.

I think it's fine that the Deaf community has created a supportive social environment for those who need it and want it.

And I think it's really sad that some of them try to lay a guilt trip on those who don't need or want it.

Dependence on speechreading and speaking isn't easy, it isn't perfect, and it isn't for everyone. The early going during childhood and adolescence can be rough.

At times, it can be frustrating, embarrassing and demoralizing.

At the extreme, the experience of trying to be oral has made some people resentful, neurotic or even semi-psychotic.

I do not claim that all deaf people can achieve the levels that I and others have reached; all the pieces fell into place for me.

Nor do I claim that everyone should follow the route I took. Another title I considered for this book is *Speaking for Myself.*

However *desirable* it is for the deaf to communicate by speaking and speechreading, it simply is not *possible* for some of them.

Not all prelingually deaf children—especially those with multiple handicaps—have the requisite combination of factors.

Nevertheless, the fact is that, with early identification and early intervention, significant numbers of prelingually deaf children *are* being taught to speak and speechread.

My point is that for those deaf people who can communicate through speech, speechreading and English literacy, the payoff in expanded horizons and opportunities in the mainstream can be well worth the effort.

This discriminatory situation may not be right.

But this is the way it is today in a world in which most people can hear—despite technological innovations and federal legislation designed to help the deaf.

When my older brother was four years old, my grandmother gave him a toy violin.

He took to music the way a duck takes to drakes, and he went on to solo with the Chicago Symphony Orchestra.

When I was four years old myself and Joe was seven, I had not yet lost my hearing. So my grandmother, deluded by visions of a world-famous brother duo, bought a similar violin for me.

Holding the fiddle, I stood in the middle of the living room as my family waited for lightning to strike for the second time.

Abruptly, I ran to my father's workbench in the basement, picked up a ball-peen hammer, and methodically smashed the tiny violin into tiny bits.

A reflection of sibling rivalry?

A precursory view of my future penchant for breaking down walls, both literally and figuratively?

Or was I just being a brat, as usual?

Whatever it was, my smashing performance did not discourage my grandmother. The following weekend she took me downtown to see Benny Goodman on stage at the Chicago Theater.

To an impressionable four-year-old boy, the King of Swing was irresistible.

With his eyes closed, he pointed his clarinet left and right and up and down as he played to the beat of his tapping foot. He charmed me the way a Hindu charms a cobra.

An hour after the razzle-dazzle ended, we walked out of a State Street music store with a brand new clarinet.

Perhaps thinking of what had happened to the violin, my grandmother took the precaution of buying me a one-piece silver-plated brass clarinet. Unlike a regular wood clarinet, it would *dent* but it wouldn't *break*.

A year later, I entered kindergarten at Horseman Elementary School (which I eventually discovered was really named Horace Mann). When the school's music director found out I could play the clarinet, he asked me to audition.

After eight bars, he stopped me. "Do you have a sailor suit?"

"Sure." It was 1938; sailor suits were *de rigueur* for little boys.

He handed me some sheet music. "Practice this at home, and then bring your clarinet to our next practice on Tuesday."

On Tuesday, I showed up at the gym.

The others in the orchestra were in seventh or eighth grade—12 or 13 years old. I was five years old and small for my age, so everyone towered over me.

Mr. Taylor rapped for attention. "For the Thanksgiving assembly, we are going to play *Bell Bottom Trousers*. The sailor and his girlfriend will be standing in front of the orchestra."

He pointed at me. "Ira Golan will be the sailor. His girlfriend will be played by Harold."

Harold? I looked around. The boys and girls were shouting and clapping and pointing at the sousaphone player.

Harold stood up, his sousaphone wrapped around his torso.

He was the tallest person in the room, taller than Mr. Taylor, and the bell of his sousaphone reached up another couple of feet.

Mr. Taylor rubbed his hands together in delight.

And that is how I made my debut at the Thanksgiving assembly, wearing my adorably cute sailor suit.

Dwarfed by the gigantic Harold in a ruffled pink dress, I blushed furiously as the orchestra played and the chorus sang.

The audience went into convulsions.

I don't remember whether I played well that day. All I remember is feeling like Shirley Temple—and hoping that Benny Goodman wasn't in the audience.

Or if he *was* there, that his eyes were closed.

Still, despite my embarrassment and the hoots of the students, I began seeing the humor of it all—even if it was directed at me—and started hamming it up a bit.

I suppose that's when I started developing some of the assets which later became invaluable in making it as a deaf person in a hearing world:

A thick skin.

A sense of humor.

And an expedient lack of inhibitions about blowing my own horn when the need arose.

Other than that, Mrs. Lincoln...

February 14, 1940, was like most winter days on Chicago's South Side: murky and chilly and windy. In the first-grade classroom at Horseman Elementary, we opened the valentine box to determine the winner of the annual popularity contest.

I was more interested in the trays of heart-shaped sugar cookies. Even at the age of six, I already had an enviable reputation for pigging out on sweets.

So when I told my teacher that I wasn't feeling well, she was neither surprised nor alarmed. She telephoned my mother to let her know I was coming home, made sure I had buckled the ear flaps of my Charles Lindbergh fleece-lined leather hat under my chin, and sent me out into a biting wind.

Six blocks later I pushed open the front door.

"What's wrong, Ira?"

"I don't feel so good. My head hurts."

My mother felt my forehead. It was burning. "Lie down on the couch. I'll call the doctor."

The doctor was a family friend who lived a couple of blocks up the street.

A few minutes later he was taking my pulse and temperature.

"It's probably the flu, Lil. There's a lot of it going around. He's running a high fever. Give him aspirin and orange juice, and keep him off his feet. Don't worry about it."

I went to sleep on the couch. It was early afternoon.

Some hours later, I woke up to find my mother's hand on my forehead. My father was standing behind her.

My mother's lips moved, but no sounds came from her mouth.

"Hey, mom, why aren't you talking out loud?"

My temperature was 105 and climbing. I couldn't hear anything.

The doctor recommended a specialist. My parents bundled me up and drove me over to the hospital.

My temperature went up to 106. I went into a coma.

The diagnosis: spinal meningitis.

In 1940 there was little, if anything, you could do for spinal meningitis. It was fatal in 95 percent of the cases. Of the five percent who survived, most were left crippled in one way or another.

After several days, my fever broke. I came out of the coma.

The doctors found that I had a 100 percent loss of hearing in both ears, and that the loss was apparently permanent.

Other than that, they said, I was fine.

Other than that, Mrs. Lincoln, how did you like the play?

Today, as a parent and grandparent, my perspective of that event is very different from my state of mind at the time.

Today, I can empathize with my parents.

I can imagine the shock and despair they must have felt when it hit them that their little boy would never hear again.

They must have been tormented by painful questions: what will happen to him now? How will he communicate with people? Will he be able to have friends? How will he get through school? How will he earn a living? Will he be able to marry and raise a family?

On the other hand, there was another perspective: *mine.*

How did *I* feel when I woke up from a nap on the couch and discovered that I couldn't hear anything?

How did *I* respond to the shock of my sudden loss?

Uh...what shock?

I was six years old. What did I know about life? To me, despair was something you felt when the White Sox blew a three-run lead in the late innings.

I didn't have the faintest idea of the difficulties that lay ahead for a deaf person. And what I didn't know didn't worry me.

I felt no panic, no fear—unlike the way I'm sure I would have felt if I had suddenly become blind. I felt no sense of disorientation. I didn't get upset or cry.

Something was different, yes; something was missing, yes.

But I accepted it the way I accepted that nine-year-old Joe was bigger than six-year-old me and always got dibs on everything.

It may not have been fair. It may have had its bad moments.

But that's the way it was.

It didn't occur to me to ask "Why me?"

After I came out of the coma, I remained in the hospital for a few weeks. My health improved, but the prognosis didn't.

The doctors concluded that my auditory nerves were irreversibly destroyed. They told my parents that I would be totally deaf for the rest of my life.

They were half right. I have no hearing at all.

But the doctors were wrong about the physical description of my deafness. Half a century later, I found out that there was probably nothing the matter with my auditory nerves.

As with most other people who lose their hearing from spinal meningitis, the problem is in the cochlea—a snail-shaped tube in the inner ear.

Normally, sound waves cause the eardrum to vibrate. Then the vibrations are transmitted to the fluid-filled cochlea and converted to waves, which move thousands of tiny hair cells. The swaying hair cells convert the fluid waves to electrical impulses, which the auditory nerves transmit to the brain.

But my high fever destroyed the hair cells, severing a link in the hearing process. So you could say that I became deaf because of premature baldness.

Those weeks in the hospital were quite easy and pleasant for me. Since television was still a twinkle in Milton Berle's eye, my parents brought stacks of books for me to read.

When the gray lady (precursor of the candy striper) came by with her cart in the morning, I bought the *Tribune;* when she came back in the afternoon, I bought the *Daily News.*

Conversation with the doctors and nurses was minimal, as it would be for any six-year-old in the hospital. They talked mainly to my parents, not to me.

When the doctors did talk to me, it was to ask a simple question that I could easily lipread:

"How do you feel?"

"Can you hear this?"

The nurses, too, had their standard sentences:

"Here's your medicine."

"Time for your bath."

My parents also tended to repeat the same words and sentences:

"We brought you some more books and candy."

"Joe wants to know where you put his mitt."

"Gail keeps asking where you are." I now had a sister, a year and a half old.

A pencil and a pad of paper were by my bed, in case I wasn't able to get what someone said. But people rarely had to use them. Speechreading came easily to me, and there just wasn't that much to say to a six-year-old boy.

Winter melted away, and spring bloomed. I came home from the hospital and spent another few weeks regaining my strength.

In the meantime, the Great Debate raged between the oralists and the signers.

Should I be placed in a school for the deaf and be taught to communicate through sign language?

Or should I stay in the hearing world and learn to communicate solely by speaking and speechreading?

Proponents of the two camps pulled my parents back and forth.

Those in favor of sign language said it would enable me to communicate quickly and accurately without the frustrations and misunderstandings that bedevil those who try to read lips.

They said it would enable me to get a complete education in a school for the deaf without missing any of what my teachers or classmates were saying.

They said it would let me feel comfortable in a community of other people like me, without the problems and tension of trying to fit into a foreign environment.

But, said the oralists: while sign language would give me the freedom to fly with other deaf people, it would ground me in the hearing world.

My options—academic, social and vocational—would be limited by dependence on sign language, since most people do not sign.

Furthermore, the hearing world had been my world for six years. My family and friends were all hearing. The environment was not foreign to me.

In the end my parents decided to go the oral way, and I never learned a word of sign language.

Considering the circumstances, it seems to have been an easy decision for my parents.

I had been talking for four years before I lost my hearing, and I did not lose the ability to speak.

Also, I had been reading and writing for at least three years. By the time I was six, I was reading the morning *Tribune* and the afternoon *Daily News*.

I don't know whether the term "language skills" existed in those days, but I had them.

And my intelligence was quite a bit above average.

What all this means is that I was old enough to have acquired a very good foundation for communicating—yet I was still young enough to adapt quickly and easily to the nuisance of deafness.

I was very, very lucky.

But what about someone who is born deaf, or becomes deaf before mastering spoken language?

In *Seeing Voices,* Oliver Sacks emphasized over and over again how difficult it is for a prelingually deaf child to learn to speak:

> The essential point is this: that profoundly deaf people show no native disposition whatever to speak. Speaking is an ability that must be taught to them and is a labor of years....

> ...her mother devoted hours every day to an intensive one-to-one tuition of speech—a grueling business that lasted twelve years....

> ...years of the most intensive and arduous training, with one teacher working with one pupil....

> ...Teaching of speech is arduous and occupies dozens of hours a week....

> ...poses great difficulties, and which may require thousands of hours of individual tuition to achieve....

It unquestionably is extremely difficult, and takes long hours of dedicated effort by the child and her parents and her teachers. Incredible amounts of work and patience are required to teach speech and speechreading to prelingually deaf children.

Nevertheless: did Sacks mention that prelingually deaf children *are* learning to speak—and that some rely on speech alone?

No.

Did Sacks mention that for many prelingually deaf children, learning to speak has been well worth all that time and effort?

No.

Did he mention the indisputable advantages of being able to speak?

No.

Did he give any encouragement to those parents who have been indomitable in the face of adversity—helping their children learn to speak so they will be able to participate as fully as possible in the hearing world?

No.

One of the most cherished shibboleths of ASL militants and their supporters involves the motivation of parents.

Hearing parents, they claim, want their deaf child to speak and speechread because of an egotistical desire for the child to be like themselves, instead of choosing what is best for the child.

Those who parrot this line cannot swallow the idea that most parents who choose speaking and speechreading as the primary mode of communication for their child are acting in what they honestly believe are the best interests of the child.

So they try to send the parents on a guilt trip—ascribing ulterior motives to the parents' sincere efforts to give their child the best preparation for a happy, fulfilling and successful life.

This shrill rhetoric does nothing to help parents make a rational, informed decision in regard to their deaf child.

There are some good reasons for certain children to learn sign language—but this is not one of them.

Watching the Saturday-afternoon double features at the Avalon Theater on Chicago's South Side, I understood very little of what the actors on the silver screen were saying.

A deaf person cannot get any cohesive sense of the dialogue from a movie or television drama without captions.

Too often the speaker is too far away, or has his back to the camera, or is off-screen. It's impossible to catch more than a few disjointed snatches.

So, as soon as I became deaf, I started making up my own dialogue to go with the on-screen images.

If I knew the plot, fine. If I didn't know the plot, I made that up, too. Action was the name of the game, anyhow, so the plot and dialogue were secondary.

There were horse operas with John Wayne and Randolph Scott...patriotic war movies with John Wayne and Randolph Scott...cliffhanger serials with anonymous actors who thought they were John Wayne and Randolph Scott...jungle adventures starring Johnny Weismuller as Tarzan...slapstick comedies with Laurel and Hardy...wisecracking cartoons with Woody Woodpecker and Bugs Bunny...patriotic newsreels of women riveters building ships.

I didn't have any time to mull over alternative lines for the actors. It was pure on-the-fly improvision.

However, my mind generated only the words—not the sound effects.

I soon became accustomed to seeing movies without the thundering hoof beats of stampeding herds...without the explosions of long guns on the battleships...without the grinding and chugging and wailing of runaway locomotives...without the chattering of chimpanzees and the bellowing of elephants...without the splatting of whipped-cream pies into faces...without the crashing of a ton of bricks atop Elmer Fudd...without the raucous din of metal against metal in the shipyard.

And I didn't even know that there was background music to tell me when to be scared or excited or impressed or happy or sad.

For me, absolute silence was and is the norm. It does not seem strange to me when I see cattle running silently...guns shooting silently...trains rushing by silently...chimpanzees jumping up and down silently...pies hitting faces silently...tons of bricks hitting the ground silently...riveting guns pounding silently.

As I said, I wasn't particularly shocked about losing my hearing.

I had been able to hear all my life, yes—but my entire hearing life had spanned only 6 years, 5 months, 28 days, 11 hours and 2 minutes (but who's counting?).

Children tend to be quite adaptable.

On the other hand, an adult who loses his hearing tends to be disoriented in the silent world.

For 25 or 45 or 65 years, sounds were an integral part of his environment; now he's living in a whole new world.

For a late-deafened adult, an airplane without the high-pitched whine of jet engines is a whole new way to travel. Pneumonia without the wheezing of congested lungs is a whole new sickness.

Where hearing people depend on sound for communication, the deaf can depend on speechreading or sign language or writing.

Where hearing people depend on sound for signals or warnings, the deaf can depend on technical devices or greater alertness.

But where hearing people depend on sound as a reassuring element of their environment, the deaf have nothing that replaces the familiar sounds of life.

These may be as mundane as the wind whistling through the cracks or the hum of the unseen traffic outside...as terrifying as the creaking of a wooden roller coaster or the squeaking of a loose floorboard in the dark...as joyful as the laughter of children in the next room or the twittering of birds in the treetops.

For late-deafened adults, the unfamiliar silence can be awfully depressing. They often feel like aliens in a strange world—a world in which the absence of these sounds of life makes it feel as though everything has stopped. One of the synonyms of "soundless" is "lifeless"; another is "dead quiet."

But children are wondrously resilient.

For me, the perfectly soundless environment was a world in which I quickly became perfectly at home.

For the late-deafened, the sight of a football game without the crash of helmets and the shouts and groans of the crowd is no longer football. It's a whole new ball game.

But for me, the sight of the players butting helmets in absolute silence *is* football—the only game in town.

Filling in the _ _ _ _ _ _

By the time the doctors okayed my return to school after several weeks of recuperating at home, it was almost time for school to be out for summer vacation.

So my parents made arrangements for Mrs. Kinsella to teach me lipreading (which today is called, more accurately, speechreading). Every Tuesday and Thursday morning during July and August, I went to Mrs. Kinsella's home on the southwest side for a one-hour lesson.

Speechreading turned out to have some factors in common with swimming—much as there are similarities between Zen and motorcycle maintenance.

First of all: some people are natural swimmers, and some people are natural lipreaders. (Some people are both, but my swimming coach at the University of Chicago assured me that I wasn't among them.)

Second: the basics are very simple. There really isn't much to learn about how to swim or how to read lips.

Finally: knowing the mechanics of swimming does not make you a swimmer. Although "I know how to swim" has a connotation of "I can swim," these statements are not literally the same.

You can learn everything there is to know about swimming by reading books and watching demonstrations—you can "know" how to swim—but you won't have the ability to swim until you go into the water and start practicing.

And once you can swim, the only way to improve your ability is by keeping at it. The more you swim, the better you might get.

It's the same with speechreading. The "how to" (what little there is of it) is just the starting point. The rest of it you learn the hard way, through experience.

For a couple of hours a week during the summer of that watershed year, I learned "how" to read lips.

After that, I was on my own to sink or swim.

Some lip movements are so obvious you can't miss them.

Most of the vowels look quite a bit different from each other. Everybody can get the "oh" sound, for example, even if it isn't being gasped by Lucille Ball with her eyes wide open and her palm against her cheek. The "ee" sound is just as distinct, even if it isn't being screeched by Lucy when she's frightened by a mouse.

On the other hand, the consonants can kill you. Here's a popular demonstration of how some consonants are indistinguishable from each other:

Have somebody say the following words without using his voice and without exaggerating his lip movements. Or watch yourself in the mirror as you say them silently but otherwise normally.

Bad. Ban. Bat.

Mad. Man. Mat.

Pad. Pan. Pat.

You can't tell the difference?

Neither can I.

Some people try to belittle speechreading by claiming that it's impossible to understand more than 40 percent of what someone says. This is a patently false claim.

The English language has about 40 different sounds; they are called phonemes. About 16 of these (40 percent) are more or less clearly lipreadable without ambiguity.

But there's another vital factor in speechreading: *context.*

Phonemes are embedded in words, words are embedded in phrases, phrases are embedded in sentences, and sentences are embedded in the context of a specific conversation in a specific language (which has specific grammatical structure) with a specific person in a specific situation about a specific subject.

Even if only 40 percent of the individual phonemes are unambiguously lipreadable *by themselves,* the multiple contexts and my own general knowledge and other factors such as body language and facial expressions enable me to read between the lips and fill in the blanks—so that I can understand most or all of what the speaker is saying, not just 40 percent as the naysayers claim.

The nine one-syllable words I listed a minute ago, when spoken by themselves, are guaranteed to confound any speechreader.

But when these words are in the context of sentences, getting them is as easy as taking _ _ _ _ _ from a _ _ _ _. Because speechreading, to a great extent, is a filling-in-the-blanks exercise.

Even without peeking at the list again, you can easily complete the following sentences. Remember that part of the context is the fact that all nine missing words look the same.

Bring your ball and _ _ _ to the picnic.

The weather is very _ _ _ today.

Do you favor a nuclear weapons _ _ _?

Wipe your feet on the _ _ _.

Who is that _ _ _ over there?

What are you so _ _ _ about?

You deserve a _ _ _ on the back.

I need a _ _ _ of paper.

There's another piece of schnitzel in the _ _ _.

Mazel tov! You have just managed to speechread nine key words without even seeing the words being spoken.

It's similar to the way in which hearing people know whether a spoken word is "there," "their" or "they're." For example:

There are three books on the table.

Their books are on the table.

They're on the table.

When the first word is spoken, you may not know which one it is. But after the rest of the sentence provides the context, you easily fill in the blanks retroactively and automatically.

At any given moment, I may be getting anywhere between 100 percent and zero percent of the words someone is saying. But the actual percentage is irrelevant.

The important thing is not what proportion of the spoken words I understand—but whether I get the message.

On one hand, five percent of the spoken words may be enough for me to get the message. On the other hand, 95 percent may not be enough if I don't get a key word.

Suppose I'm finishing up a meeting with a client, and I tell him I can be back the following Tuesday with the first draft.

He pulls out his appointment calendar and says, "Let me look at my calendar. Yeah, I'll be out all afternoon, so we will have to make it in the morning. Can you be here by 10 o'clock?"

If I get only "10," that's all I need to know; I can miss everything else and still get the message.

But if I get every word except "10," it isn't good enough.

It isn't easy to speechread the difference between "eight" and "10" in a rapidly spoken sentence. What helps me is knowing that there's little chance he'll want to meet as early as eight o'clock.

So I ask "10?" and he says either "Yes" or "No, eight."

I made Mrs. Kinsella's task relatively easy. For a six-year-old, I had an extraordinary vocabulary. And I instinctively picked up clues that enabled me to read between the lips.

But what if I had been born deaf, or was too young to talk (let alone have an adequate vocabulary) when I became deaf?

Then it would have been more difficult for me to reach the level of communication on which my life has been based.

The prelingually deaf must learn to make sounds they never heard, and to put them together to form words they never knew.

At the same time, they must learn to recognize these sounds and words visually. Both the chicken and the egg have to come at virtually the same time.

It's difficult, but it's possible.

Prelingually deaf children who learn to speak and speechread despite formidable obstacles...and their teachers and parents who make it possible...are admirable, gutsy, persistent people.

On one occasion, nine years later, I had a taste of what it's like for the prelingually deaf to learn how to speak.

We belonged to a Reform Jewish congregation. Instead of having a bar mitzvah or bat mitzvah at the age of 13, the boys and girls who continued their Jewish education were confirmed at 15.

The textbooks on Jewish history and culture were in English; we studied an English translation of the Torah. Learning the Hebrew language was optional.

But as the big day drew near, I ran into a problem.

My part in the confirmation was to recite the blessings before and after the reading of the Torah. The blessings were in Hebrew.

For Hebrew illiterates, the blessings were transliterated into Latin characters and typed on a 3x5 card:

Baruch ata adonai, elohenu melech ha'olam....

The confirmation was in May. The rabbi gave me the 3x5 card in March, figuring that a few weeks would be enough time for me to get it right.

With a bit of practice, I was able to rattle off almost all of the Hebrew syllables.

However, the Hebrew "ch," as in "chutzpah" or the German "ach" or the Scottish "loch," has no counterpart in English.

Since I had never heard it, I didn't know how to pronounce it.

My father—born in Lithuania and the son of a cantor—was fluent in Hebrew (as well as English, Lithuanian, Yiddish, and I don't know what else). He often sang the *kiddush* at Shabbat services in the synagogue; his natural speaking voice was so deep that I could feel the vibrations in the newspaper I was holding.

But the only language spoken in our home was English.

So, despite my father's multilingualism, I didn't know Hebrew.

I tried every sound I knew that had the remotest chance of being right:

"Tch" as in "chin."

"Sh" as in "Chicago."

"K" as in "chemistry."

"Kh" as in "backhand."

"H" as in "how."

My father tried to explain the sound to me, but failed. So did my mother, my brother, my grandparents, the rabbi, members of the confirmation class, and assorted other friends and relatives.

They tried all the orthodox methods. They showed me how to position my lips and tongue. They put my hand in front of their mouths so I could feel the air being expelled, and on their throats so I could feel the vibrations of their larynxes.

They tried unorthodox methods as well. A teammate on the U of C swimming team persuaded me to sit on the bottom of the pool with him and watch the size and shape of the air bubbles coming from his mouth as he made the "ch" sound.

He meant well, but his idea was all wet.

March became April.

April became May.

The rabbi became nervous.

On a bright, sunny Saturday morning a couple of weeks before the confirmation, my brother and I decided to go up on the roof of our house and do some serious tanning.

We took off our shirts and spread towels on the gravel-covered roof. Lying on our backs, we dozed in the warm sun.

It was a beautiful, breezy spring day. The treetops were swaying back and forth. A few random clouds were drifting across the sky. There was nothing to interrupt my daydreaming.

Nothing except my post-nasal drip. The sun loosened up my sinuses. My head was back, so my throat was filling with phlegm.

I cleared my throat and spat.

Joe bolted upright and stabbed a forefinger at me.

"That's it!" he yelled. "You got it!"

"Huh?"

"That was perfect. Do it again."

I spat.

"No, no—clear your throat."

I cleared my throat and spat.

"Now clear your throat, but don't spit."

I cleared my throat.

"You got it!"

And that is how I learned to pronounce the "ch" sound.

Consider, first of all, that I was a 15-year-old university student, and therefore ostensibly a fast learner. Consider, also, that I had been able to hear and speak perfectly until I was six years old.

Yet it took several frustrating weeks, several would-be teachers, and a severe post-nasal drip to get one little sound right.

Since I am not, despite ample evidence, a complete idiot, this should give some idea of the difficulty of teaching a deaf-born child to speak.

Back to 1940 and Mrs. Kinsella: her regular job was teaching deaf and hard-of-hearing students in a public elementary school.

Most of Mrs. Kinsella's students had some usable hearing and wore hearing aids.

They used speechreading to supplement what hearing they had. Some of them also used sign language while they spoke among themselves, although Mrs. Kinsella never did.

Parker Elementary School, on the southwest side, was one of three Chicago public schools which, in addition to having regular classes for hearing children, also had a separate class in each grade for oral hearing-impaired children.

These classes had fewer students than did the regular classes.

Although most of the students were hard of hearing, there were also a few deaf students who could speak and read lips.

When the oralists convinced my parents not to send me to a school for the deaf, they suggested that I go to Parker. They felt that the small classes in a regular public school environment would ease my readjustment to the hearing world.

At the time, it probably sounded like a good idea for me to go there. For a six-year-old deaf student who wanted to go the oral route rather than use sign language, it offered what today would be called a supportive environment.

But in retrospect, however, it was probably a mistake. The last thing I needed was to have things made easier for me.

My parents read a never-ending flow of books and magazines—partly because there was no TV then, but mostly because they enjoyed reading. It was a natural part of our home life.

My father was addicted to crossword puzzles. The crosswords in the *Chicago Daily News* were fairly highbrow—not up to those in the *New York Times Magazine*, but still very good.

Those in the *Tribune* were not as challenging, but my father bought the Trib more for its politics (he was a Republican, my mother was a Democrat) than for its puzzles.

Most of the time, my father could finish the *Daily News* crossword without using the dictionary. The book was always at his elbow on the lamp table to the left of his armchair, but he resisted the temptation; it was a point of pride with him.

But on the rare occasions when he became absolutely stuck with one or two empty squares left, he would regretfully pick up the dictionary and sneak a quick look.

Then, shaking his head at his stupidity for not having known that a yearling heifer or bullock is called a stirk, he would complete the crossword and toss it aside.

Partly as a result of the example set by my parents, I became both an early reader and an early user of the dictionary. I was incorrigibly curious, and I wallowed in the inexhaustible reservoirs of information contained in the printed word.

In particular, I was hooked on the dictionary. Whenever I was confronted by a word I didn't know, I had to look it up right away. Then I would continue leafing through the dictionary simply for the pleasure of learning new words.

Considering this background, it shouldn't be surprising that I was on a fast track during my elementary school years.

By reading the textbooks and looking up unknown words in the dictionary, I was able to grasp the material fairly easily.

So, in subjects such as math and science and history, the classroom sessions often added little or nothing to what I had already learned from my homework.

With books, I was in my natural element.

Besides, reading permitted me to learn as fast as I wanted. I didn't have to wait while the teacher explained something to classmates who weren't able to get it the first time around.

At first, I thought I was doing something I shouldn't have been doing. If the teacher assigned us to read pages 45 through 49, I assumed it was wrong for me to keep reading after page 49.

Really.

I thought that looking at page 50 would be breaking some kind of rule—akin to starting a test before the teacher gave the word, or peeking at the answers in the back of the book.

But my curiosity always got the better of me. So I kept reading, but on the sly.

Soon enough, Mrs. Kinsella found out what I was doing. It came out when she was giving us the homework assignment.

"I want you to read the chapter about the San Francisco earth-quake in 1906. But first, I want to tell you about a new word."

She picked up a piece of chalk and wrote: *debris.*

A hand went up on the other side of the room. "Deb-riss."

"No, Jimmy," said Mrs. Kinsella, "it's pronounced...."

"Duh-*bree*," I said. "Pieces of something that's been destroyed."

Mrs. Kinsella's head swiveled. "Ira, how did you know that?"

"I looked it up in the dictionary."

"Why?"

"I...um...saw it in the textbook."

"You already read the chapter on the earthquake?"

"Um...yes."

"Ira, I think you better stay after school today."

And that is how I found out from Mrs. Kinsella that I would not be thrown out of school for transgressing the boundaries of the homework assignments.

Mrs. Kinsella looked like J. Edgar Hoover's twin sister, and was tenacious as a bulldog in her commitment to her students.

After school that day, Mrs. Kinsella told me that it was perfectly okay to read ahead of the class assignments, and that there was no reason for me to hide what I was doing.

In fact, it was fine with her if I did my reading in the classroom while she was teaching the rest of the class the material I had already learned.

In the early 1940s, Parker had no formal enrichment programs for overachievers. My teachers winged it, giving me assignments from higher grades to keep me busy. In fourth grade, for example, I was getting eighth-grade English assignments.

I was no genius; I simply happened to be a bright kid in a relatively unchallenging environment.

The basic idea of the special classes was good: to make it easier for deaf and hard-of-hearing children to take the oral route within the public school system.

But in retrospect, I was out of place.

A key factor was my ability to read, understand and absorb the printed word, as well as my appetite for doing so.

A cornucopia of textbooks, novels, newspapers and magazines poured a steady flow of knowledge into my brain—not only about the formal educational subjects I was expected to learn in school, but also about the ways of the world.

It was all there, waiting; all I had to do was read it.

The teachers at Parker were trained to deal with students whose communication problems got in the way of their education. My teachers' problem was that, partly because of my heavy reading, I didn't have a problem.

So they solved their problem by having me skip five semesters; I finished seven grades in five years.

Although my parents were, to some extent, mainstreaming me by having me go to a regular public school in which most of the students had normal hearing, they may have been overly cautious when they put me in the special classes.

Today, there are several degrees of educational mainstreaming. They are differentiated by how much time a student spends actually integrated in regular classes with hearing children, and how much time (if any) in classes for deaf and hard-of-hearing children taught by a trained teacher of the deaf.

In 1940, the oral route meant either special classes for most of the day at Parker, or full integration at Horseman.

Although it eventually became apparent that I didn't need the special classes, they decided to let me finish elementary school there rather than change schools again. At the rate I was going, I'd be out of there soon enough.

Then I went into full integration at the University of Chicago High School, where my brother was a student.

The integration of deaf children with hearing children does not necessarily mean social acceptance.

There is a feeling that even if such integration is educationally successful, the human cost can sometimes be high.

The lack of acceptance by hearing children can mean a lonely, frustrated childhood, which can lead to a negative self-image.

This is one of the main reasons why some people advocate that deaf children be taught in special classes with other deaf children, using sign language in and out of the classroom.

They say it will help deaf children thrive emotionally—because the children will be able to relax and understand everything that is said, thereby feeling good about themselves.

Again, it all depends on the child and the circumstances.

I know that I, for one, certainly did *not* have anything like the miserable, lonely childhood that pro-signers like to impute to oral children in a hearing environment.

Growing up in a typical middle-class family in a typical Chicago neighborhood, I led a fairly enjoyable life with my family and my friends—all of whom were hearing.

It's true, however, that every summer I was made to feel quite inferior for unendurable months.

Joe DiMaggio and the New York Yankee dynasty had a truly phenomenal talent for doing just that to baseball fans (hearing and deaf alike) in less-fortunate American League cities.

3

Sidewalks aren't set in concrete

December 7, 1941:

I am sitting alone at the dining room table reading the Sunday paper. The rest of my family is in the living room listening to the radio.

My brother jumps up and runs over to me.

"The Japanese are bombing us!"

Images from newsreel footage of the London blitz flash through my eight-year-old mind: narrow white searchlights sweeping the blackness...wobbling sticks of bombs raining down on the flaming city...gutted buildings collapsing with hypnotizing slowness.

I rush outside and scan the overcast skies. I see nothing. But in my mind I hear the rumble of unseen bombers passing overhead, hidden by the clouds.

My eyes shift to the eastern horizon. In the distance, above the rooftops, great plumes of all-too-real smoke rise from a flickering red glow on the horizon.

Real smoke.

A real red glow.

I freeze. In my mind, I hear the staccato blasts of exploding bombs.

It is an uneasy moment for a deaf kid with a hyperactive imagination who lives a few miles from the South Chicago steel works.

The curriculum devised by the Board of Education had an item that was, depending on your point of view, either logical and laudatory...or a deliberate attempt to perpetuate sexual stereotypes and discrimination.

Each semester, starting in fifth grade, boys took a class in shop. Girls took a class in home economics.

That's the way it was, and nobody questioned it—until I came along.

I took home economics instead of shop.

Now, I would be delighted to have people applaud me as a precocious pioneer who was gifted with keen social awareness long before society was even aware of the concept...as a crusader for equal rights who courageously challenged the sexist system and smashed the barriers of discrimination.

Well, it wasn't exactly like that.

Probably for reasons of safety, the Board of Education would not allow anyone under the age of 10 to work in the shop. Since I had skipped a few semesters, I was well under the minimum age.

So they sent me to home ec with the girls. I learned to use a sewing machine and made an apron for my mother from an old white sheet. I learned how to cook and bake.

But I coveted the wood nameplates that all the boys made by chiseling the letters in relief on a slice of tree branch.

The shop teacher was a nice, sympathetic man. Every couple of weeks or so he would stop me in the hall or even come into my classroom and ask me whether I was 10 years old yet.

I always said no. And it puzzled me that he kept asking, because I knew that he knew perfectly well when my birthday was.

It wasn't until years later that it hit me what he was trying to do. He wanted me to pretend to misunderstand what he was saying—and to reply "yes" instead of "no."

He was trying to bend the rules for me so that I could work in the shop.

Eventually, when I was older, I became street-wise enough play dumb on the rare occasions when the situation called for it—when it was to my advantage to misunderstand or not understand what was being said to me.

But back then, in my innocence, I played it straight—and blew my chance to make a name for myself in shop.

The boys in my neighborhood usually played baseball down the block in a vacant lot (which we called the emtilot, one word, as in "Lezgo t'duh emtilot 'n' play a coupla innuns"). But sometimes, if there were only four or five of us, we'd play in the street in front of my house.

It was a quiet, elm-shaded street lined with brick bungalows. There was almost no traffic; a car might go by once every 20 minutes or half hour.

We'd be strung out in a straight line in the street, with the catcher and the batter facing the pitcher and one or two fielders. We didn't run the bases or anything—we just hit and fielded the ball.

One particularly hot and muggy August afternoon when I was seven, it was my turn to catch. Home plate was a manhole cover in the middle of the street. The batter was a good hitter, and he was spraying the ball all over the place.

The batter, the pitcher and the outfielder were wilting from their exertion. Finally, the heat and the effort apparently became too much for them; they flopped down on the curb and leaned back with their elbows on the grass.

Without leaving my assigned spot behind the manhole cover, I crouched over and put my hands on my knees in the standard position, waiting for them to come back and resume playing.

Then the front door of our house opened, and my mother came charging out with a grim look on her face.

"Hey," I protested as she headed for me, "I didn't do it."

But she grabbed my elbow anyway and dragged me away. My cheeks burned in embarrassment as the other boys watched.

Then I saw the car that had stopped a couple of feet behind me. The driver had been honking his head off behind my back.

Why hadn't the other boys given me advance warning that a car was coming down the street? And why hadn't they reacted after I didn't move out of the way when the car was standing behind me and honking?

Beats me. Kids can be weird sometimes, especially when they're seven or eight years old. Or maybe, in a preview of adulthood, they just didn't want to get involved.

But that's a minor detail. The fact is that most or all of the blame rested on my shoulders.

When I saw all the boys sit down on the curb at the same time, I should have considered all possible implications of their action instead of jumping to the conclusion that they were tired.

Actually, I should have been more alert in the first place. I was standing in the middle of the street. Streets are for automobiles. Automobiles can squash little boys. Therefore, it was up to me to make sure that I was not one of the little boys who were squashed by automobiles. I should have been looking over my shoulder, like a runner on second base.

The major responsibility for being careful inevitably belongs to a deaf child himself. The sooner he learns to keep an especially watchful eye out for danger, the less chance there is that he'll be picked off by a careless driver or a stealthy shortstop.

A few days after I was born, my parents registered me with the Cook County clerk as Ira Lewis Golan. I went along with their choice for a few years, not really thinking about it.

But when I was 10 years old I decided that whatever an Ira was, I wasn't one.

It happened around the same time that I made an astonishing discovery about the world I lived in: the streets and sidewalks weren't just *there*. They were there because somebody had *put* them there.

I had assumed that they had always been there, and that they would always be there. Like parents, you know?

But then I saw a city crew digging up the sidewalk in front of our house so they could fix a sewer. The pipe had been broken by the roots of a huge elm tree, which had also buckled the side-walk itself. So, after they repaired the pipe, the workmen put in a new sidewalk that curved around the tree a little farther away.

To me, that was an awesome display of power. I had no idea that anybody could have control over where the sidewalk went. I thought it just *went*...and that *you* went wherever *it* went.

My discovery that you can change the path of a sidewalk might have had something to do with my decision to change my name.

"Hey, mom?"

"Yes?"

"My name is Lew now."

"Okay, Ira. I mean Lew."

From the time I found out how easy it was to change my given name, I have been unable to accept the world as given. In finding fault and trying to change the way things are, I have been accused of being hypercritical, hypocritical, judgmental, naive, quixotic, reckless, stubborn and blind.

But that's another story. The point is that when I saw that the sidewalks were not figuratively set in concrete—and neither was my name—I learned that change was possible.

This discovery left me with a nagging sense of dissatisfaction for the rest of my life.

I became incurably aware that there was always some room for improvement...and that improvement was often possible.

From my perspective, the glass was half empty.

One day, I hit the longest home run of my life. It was a lucky shot that soared across the emtilot and across the street.

Suddenly, the emtilot was really empty except for me. Everyone had fled down the alley.

Listening with my eyes, I inferred that I had broken a window.

But I couldn't run away. It was my brother's ball. He'd kill me if I lost it.

Beyond left field, on the other side of my street, stood a home in which a reclusive older couple lived. They had no children, and I rarely saw them.

Hesitantly, I moved closer and peered at the windows. The ball had broken a storm window and was trapped in the space between the storm window and the regular window.

I couldn't reach it.

And there was no way I was going to ring the bell and ask the old man for the ball.

Fortunately, my father didn't make a big deal about the broken window. That evening, he went over and talked to the man and came back with the ball.

Now we come to the stupid part.

I had a paper route, delivering the *Daily News* every afternoon. The paper was offering its carriers a special deal: if you brought in three new subscriptions, you could get a bike for half price.

I had enough new subscriptions, but not enough money.

My mother suggested that I mow lawns in the neighborhood. She told me to look around and see whose grass needed cutting.

Inevitably, the shaggiest lawn belonged to the house across the street from the emtilot.

No way.

"Go on. All you have to do is ring their doorbell and ask them if they want their lawn mowed."

"But what if they're mad because I broke their window?"

"We had it fixed. That's over with."

I crossed the street and walked toward the house.

Then I lost my nerve and kept walking, pretending that I was going to the Kroger or something.

The next day, I did the same thing. And the next. And the next. Each time, I noticed how the grass was getting longer.

Finally, on the fifth day, I psyched myself up. All I had to do was concentrate on ringing the doorbell. Once I had done that, the rest would follow automatically.

As I walked along the sidewalk toward the house, I kept my eyes glued to my destination: the doorbell. I climbed the concrete steps to their front door. The doorbell grew larger and larger. I felt lightheaded.

I pressed the doorbell. The door opened, and the old woman was standing there.

"Doyouwantmetocutyourgrass?"

She stared at me with an astonished look on her face. "Are you out of your mind?"

She stepped outside and pointed to the lawn. My heart sank into my sneakers, and my face burned with embarrassment. The grass, which I hadn't noticed because of my fixation on the doorbell, was short and neat.

"We just had it cut this morning."

Although this incident taught me the danger of letting the grass grow under my feet, the main point is that there's a downside to my driving toward a goal with single-minded determination, blocking everything else from my consciousness.

This intense concentration has a trade-off. Being deaf, I can't afford to have tunnel vision—either mentally or optically. I am heavily dependent on my intellect and my eyesight to compensate for the loss of my hearing. So my obliviousness to my surroundings that afternoon did not bode well for my future.

Once I got the hang of being more observant, however, incidents such as the car behind me in the street and the shaggy lawn story became increasingly rare.

I soon became a disciple of Sherlock Holmes, who had perfected the technique of noticing small details and interpreting them in the light of circumstances.

In fact, I once theorized that Holmes was deaf, had developed his visual and deductive skills in order to compensate for his loss of hearing—and that there was no Dr. Watson.

I claimed that the real narrator of the Holmes stories was the detective's son, who mumbled his words—which is why the deaf Holmes was constantly saying "What, son?"

Once in a while I do something that inadvertently dazzles the uninitiated with my seeming ability to hear. But as Holmes pointed out, it's really quite simple when you know what to look for.

When I left the University of Chicago to study journalism at the University of Illinois, I lived in a fraternity house.

One evening, a group of fellows on the way out of the house asked whether I wanted to go along to a hamburger joint.

I was in the middle of cleaning up the final draft of a paper due the next morning, so I declined.

By the time I was finished, however, they had not yet returned. So I decided to ride my bike over and join them.

Like many campus hangouts, the place was crowded and noisy. The juke box was blaring. You had to shout to be heard.

I spotted my fraternity brothers, wove through the tables, and sat down. They had finished eating and were dividing up the bill.

They obviously would be leaving soon, and I wasn't hungry anyhow, so there was no point in my ordering anything.

A minute later, a waitress came up behind me. She bent down to shout above the din and asked what I would like to have.

I did not see her come over, I did not see her standing behind me, and I did not see her speak to me. Yet I turned my head toward her and replied "Nothing, thanks."

The guy sitting next to me was incredulous.

"Lew, how did you know she was talking to you?"

"I felt her breath on my ear."

"How did you know what she said?"

"What would you expect a waitress to say to me?"

"How did you know it was the waitress?"

"I didn't know for sure, but that's what the chances were."

"But what if it was a girl asking you for a Coke date?"

"Then I would have looked pretty stupid."

Speaking of schoolmates, this brings up an issue that goes back to when I first became deaf: who were my friends in the early years of my deafness, and how did I get along with them?

Most elementary school students go to school in their neighborhoods, so their classmates are usually the kids on the block. Thus, there is no distinction between classmates and neighbors.

But I was a streetcar student in elementary school, since my home was about 45 minutes from Parker. This distance obviously was not conducive to after-school friendships with my classmates, so I had little or no contact with them outside of school.

Also: since I tended to finish a year's work in one semester, I kept moving up into a new group of students each semester. So I had a flow of transitory acquaintances whom I met at the start of a semester and left behind four months later.

There was little or no year-to-year continuity in my classmates.

Also: the more semesters I skipped, the greater became the gap in age between my classmates and me. First it was six months, then a year, then a year and a half. By the time I finished eighth grade, the gap was two to three years.

Also: although my classmates and I were quite friendly with each other and got along well together, I sensed little or no kinship with deaf people. I didn't feel like one. I didn't talk like one. I didn't act like one.

I never had a sense of belonging to their world.

When I was fast-forwarding through the oral classes at Parker, therefore, I felt like an outsider—separated from my classmates by geographical, chronological, temporal and cultural factors.

When I walked out of school at three o'clock each weekday, I walked back into my world.

I felt more comfortable in the hearing world—with the kids on my block and with my family.

By an accident of nature, I lost my hearing. But by choice, I never lost my identity as a hearing person.

So, until I left Parker when I was 11 years old, I shuttled between the two worlds five days a week.

During these grade-school years, my playmates were the same hearing boys on the block I had known before I became deaf.

We lived within a few houses of each other. If you wanted to talk to somebody in those days, you went over to his house and walked in his front door.

Yes, there were telephones in the 1940s.

But the phones in the homes had coin boxes.

You had to drop in a nickel or a slug each time you used the phone. You had to dig into your pocket or ask your mother for a hard-earned nickel before you could call a friend.

That was a strong deterrent against indiscriminate use of the phone. So it was unheard of for one kid to phone another kid on the block. When we talked to each other, we talked face-to-face.

When I was a young boy, therefore, my inability to hear on the telephone was not as much of a barrier to keeping in touch with friends as it is for a pre-teen in today's Touch-Tone society.

Today, a household gets a phone bill once a month. Buried in that phone bill are the unitemized calls the kids make to their friends in the neighborhood.

So it's painless for today's kids to pick up the phone without thinking once about it—unless their parents get on their case.

And it's easy for today's kids to stay in touch phone-to-phone instead of face-to-face—unless they're deaf.

A child's view of the world is somewhat inaccurate.

A deaf child's view is, unavoidably, even more inaccurate.

Col. Robert McCormick was a hard-line conservative who detested President Franklin D. Roosevelt and the New Deal.

His bias was expressed very clearly and forcefully in the newspaper he published, the *Chicago Tribune.*

As an 11-year-old in 1945, all I knew about politics was what I read in the newspapers. The *Daily News* was fairly evenhanded, so it did not influence my opinion of FDR one way or another. I heard no radio commentators. My magazine reading was confined to the *Saturday Evening Post, Life* and *Look*—which were not exactly informative or analytical on political issues.

We did not discuss politics in elementary school, and the kids on the block couldn't have cared less.

And it was impossible for me to follow the heated, high-speed political arguments among my parents and their friends.

By default, my opinion of FDR was shaped by the editorials and slanted articles in the Trib, which portrayed him as a disaster for America.

Perhaps this will help you understand what you may have seen if you happened to be on my block that Thursday afternoon in April 1945, when the news of Roosevelt's death was announced.

Yes, that was me—riding my bike up and down the middle of the street, clapping my hands over my head, shouting gleefully: "The President is dead!"

I still cringe in embarrassment when I think about it.

The spring and summer of 1945 were filled with other historic moments: the dawn of the atomic age...the end of World War II...my graduation from eighth grade.

From then on, my full-time name would be Lew...and my full-time world would be that of the hearing.

4

The Boy Scouts and the whorehouse

It was the best of times, it was the worst of times, it was the age of wisdom, it was the age of foolishness, it was the epoch of belief, it was the epoch of incredulity, it was the season of Light, it was the season of Darkness, it was the spring of hope, it was the winter of despair...
— Charles Dickens, *A Tale of Two Cities*

My adolescence, like those of most young people in the throes of puberty, was a Dickens of a time.

To begin with, I had an almost insurmountable handicap when I entered University High School at the University of Chicago: most of the girls in my class were two years older than I was.

And they were a lot taller, too.

U-High was a progressive private school. But in at least one aspect, the 14-year-old girls there were as conservative as 14-year-old girls anywhere: to them, a 12-year-old boy was the pits. Even if he didn't have acne.

Since my brother was only one year ahead of me, I was hoping people wouldn't know I was three years younger than he was. Unfortunately, I acted my age.

So I had to sweat it out at the sock hops.

Sock hops were mixers at the U-High gym in which we took off our saddle shoes and danced in our socks.

I had no problem with dancing itself. We had learned the basic steps in physical education—fox-trot, two-step, waltz, rumba. Group dances such as the conga line and the bunny hop and the hokey-pokey and the hora were easy to pick up on the fly. The only dance I avoided was the jitterbug.

I didn't have to hear the music or feel the rhythm. I simply picked up the beat from my partner and from watching others out of the corner of my eye.

So the physical aspects gave me no trouble.

But in the beginning, the emotional aspects were something else. The girls clustered in groups like a wagon train in a circle, and it was hard for me to step up to a girl in front of the others.

Although I was thoroughly intimidated by unbridgeable differences between them and me in age and in size, I was eventually able to psych myself up enough to ask girls to dance.

Surprisingly (to me, anyhow), they usually accepted.

For that matter, most 12-year-old boys in those days didn't think much of girls of any age.

So I became preoccupied with other areas of interest. Music, for one.

This may sound like another of my cockamamie ideas, but it wasn't mine. It was my brother's.

Although Joe had already soloed with the Chicago Symphony Orchestra, he still sat in with the U-High orchestra. And he got this bug in his head that it would be nice if we could play together in the orchestra.

I hadn't had anything to do with music for six years. My brass clarinet was tarnishing away somewhere in the basement.

And, as proof that deafness does have a few advantages, I no longer had to endure being an involuntary audience for the hours of practicing that Joe put in at home every day.

Joe told the school's music teacher that I could read music, and that I had a good sense of rhythm, so how about letting me try out on the drums? The teacher readily agreed. He showed me how to hold the sticks and brushes for the snare drums, how to operate the pedals for the bass drum and the cymbals, and which notes in the music referred to which of these instruments.

Although I hadn't held a drumstick since the previous Thanksgiving dinner, I did reasonably well. I bought a pair of sticks and a rubber practice block, and I took a few basic lessons from a bigger kid in the neighborhood.

In a couple of weeks, I was the drummer for both the orchestra and the dance band at U-High. And later, when I joined the Boy Scouts, I was in my troop's drum-and-bugle corps.

There was no trick to it. All I had to do was get the beat from the conductor's baton and play the notes in my sheet music.

I didn't have to hear what I was doing. I monitored the loudness of my playing by being aware of how hard I was hitting the drums, not by hearing the resulting sounds. If the conductor wanted me to play louder or softer, he would indicate with hand gestures—just as he would for anyone else in the orchestra.

Neither did I have to hear the other instruments. In fact, it's probably just as well that I couldn't hear them. When one player went off the beat, others began to follow him instead of following the baton—and if I had heard the cacophony, it would probably have thrown me off, too.

Although I almost never lost the beat, I sometimes lost my place in the music. There are times when it calls for an instrument to rest for several bars; for a percussionist such as a drummer, this may run into an interminable period of counting "*one*-two-three-four *two*-two-three-four *three*-two-three-four" and so on until it's time to play again.

Since I tended to daydream, I sometimes lost count.

Then I would hold up my arms and shrug helplessly at the conductor, who would mouth back: "Fake it." So I would beat out a simple rhythm on the drums in time with the baton, and it usually worked out okay.

Except for the time I was roused from my reverie by the sight of the conductor frantically jabbing his baton in my direction and exasperatedly mouthing the epithet "dumbbell!"

Sheepishly, I started hitting the drums again. The conductor gave an annoyed shake of his head. Looking at my music, I realized that he had said "cymbal."

Quickly, I gave the cymbal a strong blow with the meat end of my drumstick. But it was a few bars too late, and the orchestra had already segued to a softer passage.

As the crash of the cymbal reverberated through the quiet room, every head in the orchestra swiveled in my direction.

And the conductor slapped his forehead, nearly stabbing himself in the eye with the baton.

In the course of reading almost any book I could lay my hands on, I came across the *Handbook for Boys*—popularly known as the Boy Scout handbook.

It immediately engrossed me in a world very different from my urbanized existence up to that time. Camping, first aid, life-saving, knot-tying, signaling and other skills of scoutcraft held an enormous appeal for me.

I told my parents that I wanted to join the scouts. It turned out that our congregation sponsored Troop 529, which met Tuesday evenings at the synagogue.

The chairman of the troop committee tried to dissuade my mother, claiming that my deafness would prevent me from keeping up with the other boys. She ignored his protests and signed me up. Within a few days, I passed my tenderfoot test.

A couple of weeks later, 529 made its annual pilgrimage with other Chicago-area troops to a large scout camp on a lake up in Michigan. We lived in four-man tents equipped with double-decker bunks and kerosene lanterns.

I slept in a top bunk—partly so that I would be closer to the lantern when I was reading in bed, but mainly because the older members of the troop had dibs on the lower bunks. The other top bunk in my tent was occupied by Bernie, who had joined the troop a few months earlier.

The first evening, just before lights out, I was reading the handbook in preparation for my second-class test. Bernie and the other tentmates were swapping lies about their sexual exploits.

Then I felt my body being pushed upward by the feet of the fellow in the bunk below me. I stuck my head over the edge to see what he wanted.

"Hey, Lew, have you lost *your* cherry?"

I didn't have the faintest idea what he meant, but I wasn't going to admit it.

"Holy cow, I hope not."

On the second or third day of camp, Bernie pulled me aside.

"The troop is going to a whorehouse tonight."

"Yeah?" I wasn't sure exactly what a whorehouse was—but I had read James T. Farrell's *Studs Lonigan* and knew it had something to do with sex.

"Yeah. It's part of the initiation rites for new campers."

That night, a couple of the troop's veteran campers led five or six newcomers out of camp via a dirt road to the highway, then down the highway a couple of miles to a side road. There were no street lights, but there was a partial moon that let me barely make out a row of frame houses. The windows were covered, so no lights were visible from the road.

The leaders shepherded us to the middle house, talking as we went along, but I couldn't see what they were saying. One opened the front door and walked in. The others followed. When it was my turn to go in, one of the leaders beckoned me over.

"Do you know what to do?"

"Aw, sure," I lied.

Standing in the doorway, I saw that the vestibule was almost completely dark; the only light came in through the doorway from the moonlit sky. I saw the shapes of the other scouts moving down the hall. I stepped inside to follow them.

But my foot never hit the floor. There was no floor.

I stepped into a yawning chasm. As I toppled into the black space, I threw out my arms. My right arm hooked around something, and I regained my balance.

When my eyes adjusted to the darkness, I saw that I was holding onto a 2x4 stud in an unfinished wall. Below me were bare joists where the floor should have been. As I looked around, I could see nothing except wood framing. The house was little more than a shell.

Ahead of me, the others were stepping from joist to joist in the darkness. A bit shaken by the near fall, I followed them.

Eventually we came to another door. As I stepped out into the moonlit yard, I spotted Bernie a few feet away.

"Hey, Bernie, you call that a whorehouse?"

Bernie looked at me blankly. Then realization dawned all over his face.

"Gee, Lew, I said they were taking us to a *horror* house."

When someone uses a flashlight—when camping, or when the electricity goes off at home, or whenever—he aims the light at whatever he happens to be looking at. So when he's talking to someone else, he naturally points the light at the other person.

But if he's talking to *me*, logic dictates the opposite. He should point the flashlight at his own face so I can read his lips.

However, most people instinctively aim their flashlights at *my* face instead of theirs—which leaves me in the dark about what they're saying.

One of my favorite forms of visual music is a blazing fire. Time passes unnoticed when I stare at the changing rhythms in a campfire or a fireplace—first the dancing fingers of flame from the tinder...then the roaring blaze as all the logs catch...then the steady flickering as the logs burn down...another roaring blaze when new logs are added...more flickering as the logs burn down...then the pulsating glow of the embers before the fire dies out.

It's practically a symphony in six movements.

But the scout campfires and the bonfires at beach parties also had their darker side: they weren't exactly the best environments for me to speechread.

I had no trouble understanding someone sitting next to me and facing the fire—but someone standing and telling a story with his back to the fire would be silhouetted and unreadable. Someone on the far side of the circle, intermittently and unevenly illuminated by flickering flames, was a lost cause as well.

Fortunately, the beach parties in my post-scouting days offered pleasurable opportunities for lipreading in the dark. So don't take this as a blanket indictment of bonfires.

For the next three years or so, scouting was my main interest outside of school.

There was a troop meeting once a week, and a patrol meeting once a week, and weekend hikes and overnighters, and summer camp every year, and occasional jamborees at which troops got together and competed against each other in scoutcraft. My friends tended to be boys from the troop.

I eagerly accumulated ranks and awards as quickly as I could. I made Eagle scout in the minimum twelve months, then kept piling up more merit badges to add three palms to my Eagle badge. I also collected the Gold Quill for journalism, the Ner Tamid for religion, the Order of the Arrow for camping, the Red Cross water safety instructor certificate, and I don't remember what else.

The standard way to display all this stuff was on a merit badge sash, which was worn on formal occasions. Every inch of my sash was covered with 43 merit badges plus a slew of award pins and medals. It would have made the dictator of a banana republic green with envy. It was so heavy that I had to sew a flap on my shirt to keep it from sliding off my shoulder.

The sash was for formal occasions, so I hardly ever wore it. Like a trophy case, it was mainly something to display in my room.

One time I did wear it was at the annual Boy Scout Sabbath, when my troop conducted the Friday evening service.

Like the other scouts in the service, I showed up early at the synagogue in a freshly laundered uniform. But unlike the others, my chest was a blaze of glory.

As I started to walk up the steps to the *bima*, a woman came over to me. I recognized her as the mother of one of the scouts, and smiled at her. She did not smile back.

"Lew, you can't wear that sash."

"Why not?"

"The other boys aren't wearing anything like it."

"The other boys don't *have* anything like it."

Her lips compressed in a thin line. "That's just the point. You're making them look bad."

I sighed. It's tough to be an overachiever.

At that moment, the rabbi beckoned for me to take my seat on the *bima*. I walked up the steps, sash and all.

I saw the woman sit down in a pew next to her husband. He was the man who had told my mother that I wouldn't be able to keep up with the other boys because I was deaf.

The rabbi handed me the text of the service.

"When I stand up and nod at you, you stand up. We will walk to the podium. You read this passage that I marked. When you're finished, you go back to your seat. Okay?"

The entire portion was in English, so it would be no sweat. This was a year or two before the "ch" incident.

Midway through the service, the rabbi rose and nodded to me. I stood up and walked with him to the podium.

The rabbi stood at my side with his hands clasped together, gazing benignly at the congregation. Confidently, I began reading the passage aloud. Every few seconds, I raised my eyes to the congregation. I spotted my parents staring at me. My mother had a tight smile on her face. My father rubbed his forehead with his fingertips.

I glanced sideways at the rabbi. He turned his head to look at me. The benign smile disappeared from his face, and he did a double take. I faltered, but kept speaking.

The rabbi gave me a significant look, then jerked his head backward over his shoulder.

Still speaking, I sneaked a look behind us.

Oy vey. There, behind a lattice partition, the organist was pounding away at her multiple keyboards like the Phantom of the Opera, completely drowning out my voice.

The rabbi hadn't thought of telling me that the organ would be playing as we walked to the podium, and that I should wait until he gave me a sign that it was finished. My lips were moving, but nobody could hear a word I was saying.

Just then, the organist hit the final chord. Unfortunately, I didn't have the presence of mind to start over. So, as the last notes died away, the congregation first heard my voice in mid-sentence, halfway through the passage.

The rabbi closed his eyes and rocked on his heels.

Another time, my troop held an open house for the parents, brothers and sisters of the scouts. The scoutmaster came over to where I was setting up a display.

"Lew, let's give them something to do until we're ready to start the program. Go lead them in a song."

"Who, *me?* I can't sing."

"I've seen you sing with the others."

"I wasn't using my voice. I was just mouthing the words."

"So what? Just get up there and lead them."

So I walked slowly to the front of the room and stalled for as long as I dared before I reluctantly held up a hand for attention.

"Hey, folks, let's sing 'I've Been Working on the Railroad.'"

Hoping that everybody would start singing together from the first note, I raised my arms and waited to give them a good chance to get ready. Then I gave the downbeat and started lip-synching to the nonexistent music.

Everybody just sat there, staring at me in amazement. How was I supposed to know that the leader sings the first few notes himself, and then the others join in?

So there I was, waving my arms and mouthing the words silently and looking like a complete idiot. Somewhere in the audience my mother was smiling a little too brightly, and my father was rubbing his forehead with his fingertips.

Gradually—*very* gradually—people started singing. They were apparently in a good mood and having fun. So, near the end, I pointed to my throat and shook my head and mouthed the words "I'm not using my voice."

In the front row, Bernie pointed to his throat and shook his head and mouthed back at me:

"Neither are we."

5

Asking for the nose

A branch of the Chicago Public Library was located a few blocks from our house. The rules said that kids could check out no more than three books at a time.

But I was going through a novel every day or two, which meant frequent trips to the library—until, finally, the women at the front desk mercifully agreed to let me take out seven or eight books at a time.

I was a heavy reader, but the books I took from the library were not heavy reading. As a pre-teen, my taste ran to humor (Robert Benchley, S. J. Perelman, James Thurber, Ring Lardner, *The Education of Hyman Kaplan*)...westerns and other adventure stuff (Zane Grey, Jack London, Bret Harte, *Two Years Before the Mast, The Ox-Bow Incident*)...war stories (Ernie Pyle, Bill Mauldin, John Hersey, *They Were Expendable, God is My Co-Pilot*)...sports stories (John R. Tunis, Howard Fast)...mysteries (Ellery Queen, Sherlock Holmes, Father Brown, Perry Mason)...animal stories (*The Yearling, Lassie Come-Home*)...and the works of John Steinbeck, Tennessee Williams, Booth Tarkington, Ernest Hemingway, Eugene O'Neill, Mark Twain, Sinclair Lewis, Erskine Caldwell, Thorton Wilder, F. Scott Fitzgerald, Budd Schulberg, Nelson Algren, Meyer Levin,

Ben Hecht, Carson McCullers, Upton Sinclair, William Saroyan, Edna Ferber, Rudyard Kipling, Pearl Buck, MacKinlay Kantor.

For school, I read the classics—Dickens, Dumas, Dostoyevski, and so on.

At home, my mother passed along books that raised my social consciousness. I learned about the black ghetto on the other side of Cottage Grove Avenue, a couple of miles from my home, from Richard Wright's *Native Son*; about juvenile delinquency from *Knock on Any Door*; about war from *All Quiet on the Western Front*; about antisemitism from *Gentlemen's Agreement*.

Along the way, a lot of the vocabulary rubbed off on me. And I learned a lot about life.

Just by reading. And reading. And reading.

One afternoon when I was about 11, I was reading the *Daily News* before my father came home to expropriate it.

My eye fell on the crossword puzzle. I looked at the clues and mentally filled in a few squares.

Then I figured I'd give it a try. I picked up a pencil and started working on it in earnest. To my surprise and delight, I was able to do about half of it.

Stuck, I thumbed through the dictionary for help. Most of the words I had missed were those arcane morphemes found only in crossword puzzles. Eventually, there were only four or five blank squares remaining.

I was enormously pleased with myself, and couldn't wait for my father to get home from his real estate office so I could show him my accomplishment.

Finally, the front door opened and my father walked in.

Brandishing the folded paper, I ran up to him.

"Hey, dad, look—I did the crossword!"

The look of surprise on his face made me beam.

Although my father was proud of his children, he rarely praised us openly. So I didn't expect him to be effusive with approval.

But neither did I expect him to blow up.

His surprise soon changed to anger.

"The crossword is one of my greatest pleasures—and you ruined it for me!"

For a few moments, I was speechless.

Then I had a thought.

"I'll go over to Hermie's house and get their copy of the crossword for you."

"That isn't the point."

He didn't spell it out. But in retrospect, I suppose the point was that if a snot-nosed kid could do the crossword, it was no big deal for my father to do it.

This incident, along with the one about my merit badge sash, illustrated an unhappy fact of life akin to Newton's third law of motion:

If something makes you look good, it can inadvertently make somebody else look bad.

Although I consumed books as if there were no tomorrow, the only writing I had done before I reached U-High was limited to short essays in elementary school.

I found it easy to express myself on paper, but I felt no burning desire to write.

My teachers at Parker had not commented on my writing, other than to give me A's in English. But this wasn't noteworthy, since I had earned straight A's in *every* subject.

The thought of a career as a writer had not yet entered my mind. What I really wanted to be when I grew up was a navy pilot.

This was more than four decades before *Top Gun* cruised across the movie screens, so my inspiration must have come from *Wing and a Prayer* or one of the other wartime morale-boosting films that Hollywood had churned out to keep the home fires burning.

It was my English teacher at U-High who detected the potential in my writing.

He suggested that I join the staff of the school newspaper, where he was the faculty advisor, and get a taste of journalism.

I lapped it up as if it were a double-dip pralines-and-cream cone. I thoroughly enjoyed digging up information, writing articles, taking photographs and making up the pages.

Seeing my words (and especially my by-line) in print was almost as exhilarating as splashing a Zero into the Pacific and making it back to the carrier with half my landing gear shot away.

In the U-High yearbook, the caption under my mug shot said "future journalist."

At U-High, I was just one more bright kid among many—and some of them were a lot brighter than I was.

My straight-A record was shattered when I crashed into U-High's tougher academic challenge—and, in particular, the larger number of students in each class, which made it harder for me to follow what was going on in the classroom.

It was a very educational experience for me—learning what it was like to get B's and C's as well as A's.

The school didn't have anything called Sex Education in those days. But we did have a course called Hygiene, which, for all practical purposes, covered the same area. When it came down to the nitty gritty of the sex act, it provided a fairly accurate picture of what went where.

But I later discovered, to my shock, that one essential bit of information had not been conveyed to me. Perhaps the teacher had mentioned it aloud and I hadn't heard it. Or perhaps, which is more likely, she had never mentioned it at all.

For whatever reason, it took some extracurricular education to fill in the gap in my knowledge.

The revelation took place at a stag party thrown by counselors from the camp where my brother had worked the previous year. He said that they would be showing some movies, and asked whether I wanted to tag along.

I said sure, expecting to see films of canoeing and hiking and good stuff like that.

So I was a bit puzzled when the first film opened with a taxi pulling up in front of a Park Avenue hotel. A man with a mustache and spats alighted and walked through the revolving door.

Then the scene cut to a room where, after a few preliminaries, the chambermaid (clad only in a short apron) and the man (clad only in mustache, spats and shoes) proceeded to dramatize what I had learned in Hygiene.

And that's when I was startled by what I saw on the screen.

Yes, I already knew what went where—but I had absolutely no idea that after you put it there, you were supposed to *move* it.

I thought you just *put* it there, and that was that.

So when I saw the man and woman going at it with gusto, it was a revelation.

Better late than never, I finally learned that action is the name of the game.

Opponents of mainstreaming question the effectiveness of putting a deaf student in a hearing class.

When the teacher or the other students are speaking, how much does a deaf student understand? And how much does he himself speak up—either in answer to a direct question from the teacher, or as a participant in a classroom discussion?

At best, I would follow the teacher pretty well, getting as much as anyone else (or even more) from the presentation. And I'd raise my hand every time a question was put to the class.

At worst, I would sit through an entire class period without understanding what was going on. I might pick up isolated words and phrases, but these were meaningless without the key words and the context. It wasn't necessarily a complete waste of time, however, since I had books with me that I could read—but from a learning point of view, I might as well have been sitting in the library.

Most of the time I was somewhere between the two extremes. It all depended on a number of factors—including:

The balance between show and tell. The more often the teacher showed something visible—a math equation, a chemical formula, a grammatical parsing, an anatomical dissection, a literary quotation, an economics graph, a psychological definition—the easier it was to lipread him and to understand what he was teaching.

Even if the subject itself didn't lend itself to visibility, a teacher who pointed frequently to a blackboard liberally covered with key words and phrases did wonders for comprehension—not only mine, but also that of the hearing students.

The congruence between what was written in the textbook and what was discussed in the classroom. If the teacher explained and elaborated on what was in the textbook, she was easier to follow than if she went off on a tangent.

The quality of the notes taken by students sitting next to me. The better the notes, the better I followed.

Most of my neighbors were willing to let me look at their notes during class. Sometimes I could see the notes from where I was sitting; more often, I had to ask them to hand me their note pads.

I knew I was imposing and breaking their concentration, so I tried to minimize my requests. Sometimes I simply waited until after the class was over.

The sex of the teacher. Women tend to be easier for me to speechread. As a group, their faces are more expressive and they articulate better. This is nowhere near a hard-and-fast rule; many male teachers are easy to understand, too.

It also helped to sit in the front row by the window, so the teacher wouldn't be silhouetted against the sunlight.

The toughest part was following what the other students in the classroom were saying. By the time I found out who was talking, I had missed the first sentence or two.

Since they didn't stand up when they spoke, and often were on the opposite side of the room, I couldn't see them clearly. So, even if I got most or all of what the teacher was saying, I only occasionally understood a classmate's contribution to the discussion.

But a great deal of the time, whatever my classmates were saying was redundant. What I got from the textbooks and the notes and the teacher (in class and afterward) usually covered just about all of the important material.

In the classroom, as in the school orchestra, I sometimes hit the wrong note.

Take the time my social science class held mock sessions of the UN General Assembly, with each student representing a different country. The chair rotated every 20 minutes.

When the teacher called on me to chair the session, I walked up to the front of the room.

From the newspaper articles we had been reading in class, I knew something about what was going on at the UN. But I didn't know the first thing about parliamentary procedure.

With something less than complete confidence, I sat down at the teacher's desk and picked up the gavel.

Six or seven students raised their hands. Arbitrarily, I pointed the gavel at Great Britain and nodded my head. He began speaking. I didn't have the faintest idea what he was saying—but so long as he kept talking, I didn't have to do anything.

When he finally stopped, half a dozen hands went into the air. Again, I arbitrarily pointed the gavel. The Soviet Union started talking. I didn't get a word he said, either.

But it obviously didn't matter whether I really got it, so I relaxed. There was nothing to it. It went on like this for 15 minutes.

Then China was interrupted by Argentina, who raised his hand and called out "Point of order." China stopped talking and looked expectantly at Argentina, so I pointed my gavel at Argentina and nodded my head.

Argentina spoke rapidly for half a minute. I didn't get a word of what he said.

When he stopped talking, everyone turned to look at me.

I shrugged my shoulders. "What do I do now?"

In the first row, Canada said "You're out of order."

"I know I am," I replied. "What should I do?"

"Say 'You're out of order.'"

"Oh." I pointed the gavel at Argentina. "You're out of order."

"Not him—her."

I redirected the gavel. "Not you—you."

I glanced nervously at the clock on the wall. In a few seconds, I would be saved by the bell.

A hand went up. I pointed at Spain. "I move to adjourn."

That one was easy enough.

"All in favor, raise your hands."

A forest of hands went up.

I banged the gavel. "Adjourned."

No one moved.

Canada leaned forward, tapped his nose with his forefinger and said "Nose."

Embarrassed, I took out my handkerchief and wiped my nose.

He shook his head. "Ask for the nose."

"Huh?"

Then I finally got it.

Noes.

"All against, raise your hand."

The Soviet Union raised his hand. "Nyet."

I banged the gavel. "Adjourned."

On the other hand—sometimes I was better than I thought.

In history, for example, we were assigned to draw a series of illustrations explaining the what and why of the Boston Tea Party.

We had read the textbook, and then the teacher had devoted a few classroom sessions to the subject. I got much of what the teacher said, but I knew that I had missed quite a bit of the discussion—especially what my classmates had said.

The chapter in the textbook had six sections. Each section had a subhead of 10 or 12 words summarizing the key points of that section.

I used each subhead as the caption for one illustration. I drew six cartoons illustrating the six subheads, and copied the subheads verbatim under the cartoons.

It seemed like an obvious way to go. I expected the others to do something deeper and more complicated—which they did.

To my delight, I got an A on the assignment. And to my surprise, the teacher held up my work in class and talked about it.

No one else in the class of 35 students had taken the simple, obvious approach I had followed. I had cut to the core of the issue, using the major points as the basis for my illustrations.

That incident helped me crystallize my approach to life and to my career in communication:

Get to the heart of the matter, and keep it simple.

Sooner or later I was bound to start taking a greater interest in girls, if for no other reason than I needed a date for the dances.

My first forays into Asking a Girl for a Date were conducted on the stairways at U-High. I would stand on the first step, which added several inches to my height—making me a little taller than my female classmates.

When a girl who looked familiar approached, I would flash her a smile and say something confident and suave, something that would make her say "yes":

"Hi, Judy, are you washing your hair next Saturday night?"

If I was lucky enough to get a response, it would be something like "My name is Marilyn."

Actually, I was probably not much more gauche than any other 12- or 13-year-old boy in those days. And I did manage to get the necessary dates without too much trouble.

What I lacked in maturity and social graces, I made up for in persistence and luck.

While I probably wouldn't have won any popularity contests, I did manage to get elected class treasurer.

And I did make a few good friends among my classmates—people I ate with at lunch time, conversed with in the hallways, worked with on the school paper, swam with on the swimming team.

I finished high school in three years.

That's noteworthy because I was taking a two-year curriculum.

Those were the days when Robert Maynard Hutchins was the innovative chancellor of the University of Chicago, before going on to head the Ford Foundation.

He believed that students were spending too many years in school—especially if they went on for postgraduate degrees. He wanted them to get into and out of college earlier.

So, to speed things up, the U of C Laboratory School telescoped the curriculum by two years. Elementary school stopped at sixth grade. Then the four-year University High School covered seventh through tenth grades.

This enabled qualifying students to enter the college at the age of 16 instead of the usual 18.

Since I had graduated from eighth grade at Parker, I bypassed the first two years of U-High and started in ninth grade.

After two years at U-High—ninth and tenth grades—I could go on to the college.

But I wouldn't be 16 when I entered college. Since I was two years ahead of my age group, I would be 14.

During my second (and supposedly final) year at U-High, the principal summoned me. I assumed he wanted to talk about my chronic tardiness in getting to my first class of the day.

My daydreaming wasn't limited to orchestra rehearsals. I also daydreamed while getting dressed in the morning.

I would sit on the edge of my bed and pull on one sock...then just sit there, the other sock in my hand, thinking about things.

One thought would lead to another by free association: Maggie wetting her pants in *A Tree Grows in Brooklyn*...Jackie Robinson breaking in with the Brooklyn Dodgers...the Artful Dodger teaching Oliver Twist how to pick pockets...the Cardinals picking off two interceptions in yesterday's game at Comiskey Park (years before the football franchise moved from Chicago to St. Louis, eventually winding up in Phoenix)...cardinals, finches and blue jays darting through a preview of my bird study merit badge test.

My daydreaming tended to be topical, so the subjects changed from day to day.

However, there was one daydream that recurred regularly for a few years:

My rocket ship.

Today you would call it a space ship. But to Buck Rogers, Tom Swift and me, it was a rocket ship.

Buck Rogers in the 25th Century was a comic strip, a radio program and a Saturday-afternoon movie serial. *Tom Swift and His Rocket Ship* was one of the adventure books for boys in the *Tom Swift and His...* series.

The end of the world was at hand. In a matter of hours, the planet would explode.

And I owned the world's only rocket ship. I was the one who decided who could take the journey to safety on another planet.

Now that's what I call an ego trip.

The whole purpose of this fantasy was to get back at people who I felt had done me wrong.

My rocket ship was poised at a 45-degree angle in an underground cavern.

Next to it I was sitting on a golden throne, grinning like Jack Nicholson playing an Egyptian god.

An endless line of people filed past my throne one by one.

Silently, I shook my head at each one.

I can't even remember who they were or why I wanted revenge.

All I remember is that whenever somebody did me dirt—real or imagined—I put him or her in the line of people who were never gonna get on my rocket ship.

And I would sit there on the edge of the bed, holding the other sock in my hand, nodding with satisfaction over the latest additions to the line.

Eventually I would snap out of the daydream, put on the other sock and my shoes, wolf down my Wheaties or Rice Krispies, and pedal my bike furiously to school.

On the way, I would try to think up an excuse for my lateness. My explanations left Miss Wilson exasperated and skeptical.

So when I walked into the principal's office, I took it for granted that I had been summoned because my excuses were becoming inexcusable. He went straight to the point.

"Lew, I think it will be in your best interests if you stay at U-High for another year instead of going on to the college this fall."

I was stunned. "What? Just because I was late a couple of times, you're going to hold me back?"

"This has nothing to do with being late. It has to do with being 13 years old and deaf. That's a heavy combination for a college student."

"I'll be 14 in August."

"Okay, 14. It'll be tough enough with your deafness, but your age will make it a lot worse."

He looked down at my file.

"Your grades are certainly good enough to get into the college. But perhaps they would have been even better if you had made more of an effort to follow what was going on in class. You're missing some of the finer points that are being brought up in the discussions."

True. I did a lot of daydreaming in class, too.

"You need a little more time to grow up. That's why I'd like you to stay here for another year. You don't have to repeat any of the courses. Just take whatever you want, so you'll have a broader background when you go to the college."

He was right: I was immature.

But he was wrong: the extra year at U-High didn't help.

When I entered the college of the University of Chicago two weeks after my fifteenth birthday, I still couldn't take the world seriously.

And I still can't.

6

She trimmed her goat
at the flea market

Paranoia is an occupational hazard for deaf people. What are those people over there talking about? What are they thinking? Are they talking about me? What are they saying about me? Hey, they're laughing. Are they laughing at me? Why are they laughing? Is my nose dripping? Is my fly open?

I found out the answers the hard way at college.

My daily routine at the University of Chicago was fairly constant. When I wasn't in class or playing bridge in the students' lounge, I worked out on the swimming team.

Fortunately, the U of C put more emphasis on strong minds than on strong backstrokes. I was a fairly ordinary member of the team, holding the number one spot in the individual medley, number two in the backstroke, and number three in the butterfly.

One day, as I was sitting on the edge of the pool after finishing my practice laps, somebody came up behind me and pushed me into the pool.

When I floundered gasping back up to the surface, I saw one of our freestyle sprinters looking down and giving me the finger. I returned the gesture.

A few days later, the same fellow came up to me at practice and held up his hands in a gesture of surrender. "Hey, Lew, I want to apologize for pushing you into the pool last week."

"Huh?"

"I was standing behind you and asked you something. When you didn't answer, I figured you were ignoring me. So I pushed you in. I didn't know you couldn't hear me."

"You didn't know I'm deaf?"

"No. I just found out a few minutes ago, when I asked the coach why you always get the outside left lane."

That's when I discovered that of my 11 teammates, some didn't know that I was deaf—even though I worked out with them every day.

I had assumed that the word would spread from one to another: hey, y'know that guy over there is deaf?

But no, they weren't talking about me. Why should they be? There were more important subjects to discuss—girls, cars, grades, movies, sports. They couldn't care less whether I was deaf.

It was a bitter pill for a paranoid to swallow.

I always had the first lane on the left, and the starter stood a few feet to my left. By turning my head, I could watch his finger on the trigger of the gun.

As soon as his finger started moving, so did I. My toes left the starting block almost simultaneously with the sound of the gun.

My major claim to natatorial fame, according to the coach, was that I had the fastest start he had ever seen...and the slowest finish.

False starts are a common occurrence. Sometimes the starter has already started squeezing the trigger when someone jumps the gun—so the gun goes off, and the rest of the swimmers follow the gun-jumper into the water.

Then the starter fires a second shot to signal a false start.

At the start of one individual medley, while I was still in the air, I thought I saw the starter pull the trigger a second time. So when

I hit the water I just glided along with my eyes closed, letting the tension drain out of me.

Then, ready to head for poolside, I lifted my head lazily and opened my eyes—and was shocked to see that everybody else was swimming at top speed far ahead of me.

Oy, I thought, it wasn't a false start—I had blown it.

But then I saw the starter running down the length of the pool, firing his gun frantically again and again as members of both teams jumped into the water to physically restrain the swimmers.

The scene at the far end of the pool looked like something out of a Laurel and Hardy two-reeler.

That was an extraordinary day for my team.

Not because the only one in the race who "heard" the second shot was deaf...but because the other swimmers were so exhausted from the false start that I was able to splash my way to one of the few wins of my career.

My performance in a football game at the University of Chicago was so noteworthy that the old *Herald-American* printed a three-column photograph of me in action, and the *Tribune* devoted a paragraph of its story to my exploits.

Ten years after the former Monsters of the Midway had dropped out of football, some students who had heard awe-inspiring tales of autumns gone by decided to bring back a tongue-in-cheek taste of the glory days.

They formed two ragtag teams and played the Philosophy Bowl in front of 800 spectators on a cold, windy November afternoon.

I did not play on the Platonists, nor on the Aristotelians.

I played on the huge 10-foot drum formerly used by the long-ago marching band.

The drum was so overpoweringly loud that no one who valued his eardrums could bear to be near it.

Since the noise didn't bother me, I took over the drum role—beating it every time someone dropped the ball.

The constant movement kept me comfortably warm.

The spectators got a bang out of it.

And I earned an obscure footnote in the incredible shrinking annals of sports at the U of C.

Speaking of football: there's an analogy for speechreading in the way a quarterback plays pro football. Even though the action is physical, a great deal of the quarterback's job is mental.

First of all, there's all the information that's crammed into his head—the fundamentals of playing football, the rules, his team's offensive plays, the other team's defensive alignments and coverages, what the other team is likely to do in each situation, the strengths and weaknesses of each player on the field, the weather conditions, the score, the time remaining on the clock, instructions from the sideline, and so on.

This database is comparable to my general knowledge of the world, of English grammar and vocabulary, and of the speaker and the context of the conversation.

Then, when the quarterback is crouched behind the center waiting for the snap, his eyes are scanning the defensive players and he's trying to read their minds and anticipate what they're going to do—just as I try to think along with the other person and anticipate what he's going to say.

Then the ball is snapped—and now everything is happening in real time.

The quarterback tries to keep his eye on his teammates and opponents who are moving all over the field—some doing the expected, others doing the unexpected—just as I keep my eye on the other person's lips and eyes and hands and body, as well as on other people who may be in the conversational group.

The quarterback may not be able to see everything that's going on; same with me.

So, with his brain churning like a computer, the quarterback tries to receive new information visually and relate it mentally with his database and analyze it and fill in the blanks (maybe figuring, for example, that one of the outside linebackers is probably hurtling toward him on his blind side) and make an on-the-spot decision: what does all this mean?

Maybe the play will go like clockwork and he'll see his wide end free and clear in the end zone and he'll drill the ball right into the money. It looks easy, and speechreading often is for me.

Or maybe it'll be a busted play and he'll scramble around trying to see what the hell is going on and he doesn't know where his receivers are and the linebacker is clawing at his jersey and he's improvising and he spins to his right and there happens to be a hole in the line and he stumbles through it for a first down. A little luck never hurts in speechreading, either.

Or maybe he reads the defense wrong and it blitzes him and he hurries the pass and it wobbles into the hands of the free safety just as the linebacker blindsides him into the turf where he watches the safety run back the interception for a touchdown. Same thing can happen to me: egg all over my face.

You win some, and you lose some. And there's no substitute for experience.

Some of the troublesome words that come up frequently are negative contractions. It's difficult to tell the difference between "can" and "can't," for example—yet these are often key words in a sentence.

Suppose Barbara says to me, "Gordon _____ go to the Bears game with you." Unless she nods or shakes her head, I wouldn't know whether he *can* go or *can't* go.

It's quite easy for a speechreader to make mistakes, so the process of reading between the lips contains a built-in error-checking routine.

This works in reverse. Instead of using my inherent knowledge and the situational context to determine what the speaker is saying, I check what I think the speaker is saying against my knowledge and the context to determine whether it is likely that he actually said those words—just as I know that a morning meeting is more likely to be at 10 o'clock than at eight.

If it makes sense, I accept my interpretation; if it doesn't, I reject it and try again.

Suppose a friend says what looks like "I trimmed my goat at the flea market last night."

First of all, I know she doesn't have a goat. Second, I know that she wouldn't be caught dead at the flea market. Third, I know that the flea market isn't open at night. So my error-checking routine rejects that interpretation.

"You *what* last night?"

"I ripped my coat at the Philharmonic."

On the other hand—sometimes the error-checking routine itself trips me up.

I may lipread something correctly just from the movement of the lips—but my cerebral computer says it doesn't sound right, so I ask the speaker to repeat his words.

Like the time a new clothing store held a sidewalk sale. I tried on a pair of jeans. As I stood in front of a mirror, pulling in my stomach, a salesman walked by. I turned to face him.

"How's the length?" I asked.

"Fine. How's your sister?"

No way he could have said that. I had never seen him before in my life, and my sister had been living two thousand miles away in California for the past 25 years.

"Excuse me?"

"How's your sister?"

It turned out that 30 years previously, my then-teenage sister had thrown a party and he had been a guest. He had seen me briefly when I came home and went upstairs.

Now I was a lot older, a lot grayer, and 20 pounds heavier—but he recognized me.

Since I hadn't known that he knew me and my sister, I assumed that I had misunderstood his question—but I had actually been right the first time.

During a one-on-one conversation, people break eye contact now and then for a few seconds. It can be uncomfortable to keep your eyes fixed on the other person for an extended time.

But some people carry this to an aggravating extreme: they have an annoying habit of letting their eyes wander all over the place while you're talking to them.

At a party or in a restaurant or on the street, their eyes sweep the area like radar antennae—presumably searching for something more interesting than what I'm saying. They have to check out everything within eyesight or earshot.

Unfortunately, I can't give them a taste of their own medicine—because I *have* to keep my eyes glued to the face of whoever is speaking.

If I'm not looking at someone's face, I'm obviously not paying attention to what he's saying.

Other people can at least give the pretense of listening to me with one ear; I can't even do that.

Barbara says that people are flattered by my concentration on their faces while they are speaking—just as people are put off by those with roving eyes.

Although I'm usually interested in what the speaker is saying, there are exceptions. My eyes may be fixed on his lips, and my head may be nodding at the right moments—but if he goes on interminably, my thoughts may be a million miles away.

Although I do let my mind wander at times, I try not to let my eyes wander as well.

Quite frequently, I inadvertently mix up the names of our four daughters—referring to Laurie when I mean Lisa, or Debby when I mean Julie.

Nobody worries about it or looks for a Freudian explanation.

So it may appear to people that Barbara is being sarcastic when she answers the phone and then says to me "It's your daughter Julie," implying that I don't even know who Julie is.

Of course I know who Julie Golan is. She's our second (or third?) daughter.

That's not the problem.

The problem is that the phone call is just as likely to be from my cousin, Judy Golan.

And there's no way in the world I can distinguish between those two names when they are spoken.

Even the context is often the same: "Julie called today" or "Judy called today." "I went shopping with Julie" or "I went shopping with Judy." "Julie's coming for dinner tonight" or "Judy's coming for dinner tonight. "

So Barbara is reduced to saying "Your daughter Julie."

It makes me feel like an idiot.

But hey, it works.

7

What if I don't raise my finger?

During Christmas vacation in 1952—long before the name was politically corrected to "winter break," and long before the interstate expressway system was built—I and two other college students drove a new 1953 Packard straight through from Chicago to Miami, stopping only to fill the gas tank and empty our bladders.

At two o'clock in the morning, I was driving through the Smoky Mountains while the other two slept.

As a native Chicagoan, I had never seen a mountain—let alone driven down a steep, forested mountainside on a winding, two-lane road in a pitch-black void with a sheer drop inches away.

Rigid with trepidation, I gripped the wheel with sweaty hands and stared blindly at the small pool of light cast on the road by the car's headlights.

The night was completely moonless. The road was completely shoulderless. I was completely shitless.

As the Packard hurtled through the darkness, the fellow next to me suddenly woke up with a disoriented start and frantically tried to pry my fingers off the steering wheel.

I yelled to the guy sleeping in the back seat to get the crazy idiot off me before we all went off the road.

Then I noticed that my thumbs, hooked through the concentric ring inside the steering wheel, were involuntarily squeezing it in terror.

Unknowingly, I had been shattering the still night air with the nonstop blaring of the Packard's deep-throated horn....

My parents were far from being overprotective. Since I have always been quite self-sufficient, their approach to me was one of *laissez faire.*

But where wheels were concerned, they couldn't help leaning toward the old wives' tale that it was dangerous to drive if you couldn't hear the honking of another driver or the siren of an unseen ambulance or fire engine.

When I was a teenager, unfortunately, it was not widely known that deaf people are safer drivers. We tend to be more observant, drive more carefully, and have proportionately fewer accidents.

I learned to drive back in the dark ages of 1948, when stick shifts were the norm. In the interests of public safety, I don't recommend the self-teaching method (monkey see, monkey do) which I undertook in the pre-dawn hours without parental awareness, let alone consent.

Once I had proven to my parents that I knew how to drive (a revelation that evoked disbelief, then anger, then resignation), it didn't take too much persuasion to get my mother's signature on an application for a driver's license.

As soon as I reached my sixteenth birthday, the minimum age for getting a license in Illinois, I passed the exam and collected the holy document.

My parents were willing to let me drive occasionally while one of them was in the car with me.

As my skill improved, so did their confidence in me—to the point where I was finally allowed to fly solo.

Then the car—a 1947 four-door Plymouth—became the focus of arguments between my brother and me over who would get it.

One argument that sticks in my mind, however, didn't involve who would get the car—because both of us were going to the same dance at the U of C. The argument was over who would get to *drive* the car, while the other sulked ignobly in the back seat with his date.

Our father settled the dispute with what he probably thought was Solomonic wisdom.

"Lew," he said to me, "you're a better driver than Joe is."

I beamed with righteous pleasure.

"However," he continued, "Joe will drive tonight."

"Huh?" I yelped. The logic of my father's decision escaped me.

But my father had retreated behind his *Daily News*—which was a good trick, since it was folded down to the crossword puzzle.

Maybe my father still couldn't entirely discount the old wives' tale about deaf drivers.

Or maybe he didn't want Joe to be embarrassed in front of our dates by having his kid brother do the driving.

Or maybe he was trying to teach me that life just wasn't meant to be logical, let alone fair.

After two years of liberal arts in the college of the University of Chicago, I decided that I wanted to major in journalism. So I transferred to the University of Illinois, whose school of journalism was one of the best in the country.

I had gone through U-High and the U of C on tuition scholarships while living at home six blocks from the campus. But now there would be my living expenses downstate, in addition to the tuition.

Fortunately, somebody told me that the state had a vocational rehabilitation program that paid for the schooling of deaf people.

All I had to do was prove two things: that I had been accepted at the journ school (which was easy, since I had a letter from the dean), and that I was deaf (which was more difficult).

The state sent me to an eye-ear-nose-throat doctor for an exam.

"How will you know whether I'm telling the truth?" I asked his nurse as she adjusted the earphones on my head.

"Well, you won't be able to see when I press the button on the audiometer. If you raise your finger at the wrong time, I'll know you can't really hear the tone."

"No, no, I mean just the opposite. What if I *do* hear the tone, but *don't* raise my finger?"

"But why would you pretend to be deaf?"

"Because this means a lot of money to me. Tuition, room, board, books. If the doctor certifies that I'm deaf, I get a full scholarship. If he doesn't, I get hell from my father."

The reception room was empty except for the nurse and me. She glanced at me warily.

"Well, I'll just have to trust you to let me know when you hear the tone."

With her hands hidden behind the audiometer, she looked at me expectantly. I sat there with my hands in my pockets.

She turned up the volume. I didn't react.

She turned it up some more. "Do you hear anything yet?"

"Sorry, no."

More volume. A disappointed look.

More volume. A suspicious look.

She shook her head. "That's as loud as I can make it."

I nodded sympathetically.

The door to the doctor's office opened and the doctor stepped out. The nurse picked up the form and walked over to the doctor. She shielded her mouth from me with the paper and spoke for a few moments, punctuating her words with significant nods of her head in my direction.

The doctor nodded, took the form and extended his arm toward me. "Please come with me," he said.

We went into a very small examination room. The room was so small that the eye chart was on the wall behind the patient's chair, with a mirror on the wall in front of the chair.

"So, you want me to verify that you are deaf?"

"Yes."

"*Are* you deaf?"

"I hope so."

"My nurse thinks you're faking it to get a scholarship."

I gave him an injured look.

He peered into one ear, then the other. Then he picked up a tuning fork about eight inches long, struck it against the table, and pressed the base of it behind my ear. He raised his eyebrows. I shook my head.

The doctor picked up a larger tuning fork about 12 inches long, struck it, and pressed the vibrating bar behind my ear.

"Yes?"

"No."

The doctor sighed, went over to a closet, reached to the back of a shelf, and removed a tuning fork about 18 inches long. He wiped the dust off it, then struck it against the table.

It vibrated so uncontrollably that he had to grasp his right wrist with his left hand like Dr. Strangelove.

He pressed it behind my ear. My head shuddered.

"No?"

"No."

The doctor put down the tuning fork, gazed at the ceiling, and walked around the chair until he was directly behind me.

Looking out the window, he asked: "What time is it?"

I looked at my watch. "Two-thirty," I replied.

Triumphantly, he ran around the chair to face me. "You heard that! You aren't deaf."

"Hey," I said, pointing to the opposite wall, "I read your lips in the mirror."

"Nonsense. You aren't deaf. I'm not signing that form. Get out of here."

"The mirror...the scholarship...."

"No way." He opened the door. "Good-bye."

Eventually, after doing a fast tap dance, I was able to convince him to sign the paper.

Like most other American males of my generation, I registered for the draft when I turned 18 during the second year of the Korean War.

Local board 80 of the Selective Service System was on the second floor over a store on 63rd Street. You could almost touch the El tracks where the trains rumbled by.

Standing at the counter, I filled in the registration form. Toward the end, I paused on a question I hadn't expected:

"In your opinion, is there any reason why you should *not* serve in the Armed Forces of the United States of America?"

After thinking about it for a couple of seconds, I wrote "no."

I signed the form and gave it to the woman behind the counter. She skimmed through it, nodded her head, stamped and initialed it, and dropped it into a basket.

Then she filled in a registration certificate: name, address, date of birth, eyes, hair, complexion, height, weight, race.

The final item: other physical identifying characteristics. She read off the question just as a train thundered by, drowning out her words.

She started to repeat the question, but I was already answering her: "Well, these two small scars on my wrists."

She blinked. "How could you hear me with all that noise?"

I shrugged, not wanting to spoil the illusion by telling her that I could speed-read upside down.

A few days later, I received a card in the mail with my draft classification—1A: available for military service.

The following week I packed a suitcase, said good-bye to my family, and went marching off to the journ school.

Several months later, local board 80 sent me an invitation to come in for my physical exam. I sent back my regrets, explaining that I was in my junior year at the university.

The board responded with another notice of classification, this time making me 2S: deferred as a student for the duration of my studies.

I graduated a few months after the truce agreement was signed in Korea.

But local board 80 was still on a wartime alert. And in those pre-computer days, they had an effective tickler file that told them when I was due to graduate and lose my student deferment.

I soon received a new notice informing me that I had once again been classified 1A.

I put the card in my wallet and forgot about it.

Eventually, my name came up again on the list. By this time I was living in Cleveland, but had neglected to notify the draft board of my change of address.

So the board sent a notice to my parents' home in Chicago, instructing me to report for a physical.

When the card arrived, my mother read it. Since I had never told anyone I was 1A, she assumed the board had made a mistake.

So, instead of forwarding the card to me, she picked up the phone and called the office next to the El tracks.

"This is Mrs. Golan. You've made a mistake about my son Ira."

"Just a moment, and I'll get the file." Pause. "We don't have an Ira Golan in our files."

"Excuse me, I mean Lew Golan."

Pause. "Yes, here's his file. What is the problem?"

"You must be out of your mind to want my son in the army."

"But...."

"Don't you know he's deaf?"

"Deaf? Let me look." Long pause. "No, there's nothing in his file about that. His physical description says nothing about being deaf. And he wrote on his registration form that there was no reason why he shouldn't serve."

"That's Ira, all right. I mean Lew. Believe me, you don't want him—and not just because he's deaf."

At this point, the draft board had several alternatives. It could have insisted that I go back to Chicago for a physical exam by its own doctors. Or it could have had me examined by a Cleveland draft board's doctors. Or it could have accepted documentation from doctors in Chicago who knew me.

But it didn't choose any of these.

Instead, the woman at my draft board simply took my mother's word for it.

Yes, over the phone. I never went in for a physical.

On the spot, the draft board mailed out a new classification notice—4F: not qualified for military service.

Honestly.

I tell people that my mother had a standard way of introducing me:

"You know my son Joseph, the violinist? The one who plays first violin in the Chicago Symphony Orchestra? Well, this isn't Joseph. This is another of my sons, Ira. I mean Lew."

It's not true, but I still like to tell it.

On the other hand, this really did happen to Barbara:

She was browsing in a women's clothing store in Highland Park. Another woman walked into the store.

The store owner greeted the newcomer, then introduced her to Barbara.

"Barbara Golan? Say, I went to the University of Chicago with a couple of Golan brothers, but I haven't seen them since then. Are you related?"

"Yes. One of them is my husband."

"Is your husband the violinist or the...um...?"

"The um."

A couple of times during my teen years, one organization or another would ask me to be a guest speaker or to participate in a panel discussion about deafness.

After one event, a woman from the organization invited me to attend a meeting of their youth group.

I had no contact with other deaf or hard-of-hearing people, and it had never occurred to me that deafness might be a common interest (like stamp collecting or Scouting or alcoholism) that brought people together.

Out of curiosity, I decided to take a look.

Most of the members of the group turned out to be hard of hearing rather than deaf.

They welcomed me quite warmly, introduced me around, and tried to make me feel part of the group.

Although most of them spoke and understood spoken English (either with the help of a hearing aid or by lipreading), there was always a great deal of sign language flying around.

I went to an occasional meeting on and off for a few months, but I felt completely out of place—an alien.

My mother had chosen to keep me in the hearing world when I became deaf. Yet she wanted me to broaden my horizons, to have the widest possible circle of acquaintances.

So when I stopped going to the meetings and told her that I didn't belong there, she called me a snob.

My mother was probably right.

But so was I.

My mother could be very down-to-earth in her priorities, which were determined by the reality of each situation.

Since the reality was that I was deaf, for example, she gave high priority to protecting my most vital remaining sense—my eyesight. She impressed on me the importance of avoiding eye damage from an accident, as well as eyestrain from reading in poor light.

One day when we were teenagers, my older brother did some grievous, unforgivable harm to me—the details of which I have long since forgotten, but which probably had something to do with my being sacrilegious about his violin practicing.

My eyes swept desperately around my bedroom for something to help me offset my brother's superiority in height, weight and reach so that I could retaliate.

Since it was the middle of winter, the handiest object available happened to be a pair of hockey skates tied together by the laces. So I grabbed them.

Swinging the skates like a bola, I set out in hot pursuit.

I chased my brother through the house—down the front stairs, through the front hall and dining room and kitchen, up the back stairs.

As we tore wildly through the kitchen where my mother was scrambling eggs, she glanced at the skates I was brandishing a few inches behind my brother's skull.

Without missing a beat, she leaned backward into my field of vision and called out over her shoulder:

"Lew—watch out for his hands."

8

Getting the picture

The journalism instructors at the U of I tried to create a real-world ambiance, such as in my press photography course. Most of the photographs we were assigned to shoot were simulated, with class-mates pretending to be the Queen of England or whatever.

But the final assignment was to shoot the real thing. It had to be a picture of an unstaged event—a photograph that could actually be published in a newspaper. The grade on that picture would account for a big chunk of the final grade in the course.

In December, as the roads became dangerously slippery with ice, an idea for the final assignment crystallized in my mind: I would take a picture of an automobile accident.

So after dinner on a stormy night I borrowed a car, took my Speed Graphic and film and flash bulbs, drove to the state highway patrol station outside Urbana, and received permission to sleep in one of the jail cells until something happened.

A few hours later, a hand on my shoulder shook me awake.

"There's been a bad accident 10 miles out on Route 10, near Ogden." The officer pointed out the location on a map.

I drove there as quickly as I dared on the two-lane road through open farmland. A few minutes before I reached the accident site, an ambulance with flashing red lights passed me in the opposite direction on its way back into town.

When I reached the wrecked car, I saw that it had crossed the road, rolled over, and smashed into a power pole. It was upside down in a field, its top crushed in. The driver's door hung agape, and bloodstains covered the seat.

I moved around to find the best angle, pressed the camera to my cheek, focused through the vapor from my breath, and shot.

Then I pulled the camera away from my face—and yelled in pain. The back of the camera was frozen to my cheek.

Rocking the camera back and forth, I managed to work it off my cheek along with a few bits of skin. As quickly as possible, I took more shots from other angles.

Then I drove to the hospital. At the front desk, I asked where the patient was. The receptionist gave me the room number.

Camera ready with the aperture and speed set, the shutter cocked, the film cover removed, and a bulb in the flash gun, I walked along the corridor until I came to the room.

Just inside the open doorway, the man was lying motionless in bed. His upper body was enclosed in an oxygen tent. Tubes ran into his arm and nose. On a chair next to him, his wife sat holding his hand and crying.

It was a great Page One picture. I didn't have to move an inch. All I had to do was raise my camera and shoot.

But I couldn't do it. I couldn't bring myself to disturb them with the flash, let alone invade their privacy by publishing a picture of them in such a vulnerable moment.

So I turned around and walked out, my stomach churning with a sinking feeling of having blown an incredible opportunity.

It was now about three o'clock in the morning. I drove over to the *Champaign-Urbana News-Gazette*, gave my film holders to the night editor, and told him what was on the film.

The following morning my photograph of the car appeared in the paper, along with the all-important credit line.

The driver died two days later.

I got an A+ on the assignment, an A in the course, and a very laudatory letter of recommendation from my instructor.

But I never told my instructor about the scruples that had kept me from photographing the dying man and his wife.

Maybe he would have said that I had done the right thing in not exploiting the opportunity. Maybe he would have supported my inaction with some sentiment about ethics taking precedence over the competitive pressures that bedevil the profession.

On the other hand, being a veteran newspaperman himself, he might have dispensed with the ivory-tower lip service to morality. He may well have given me a taste of real-world journalism—by lowering my grade for failing to get the picture.

In my fraternity house, not everything was fun and games. It was also a venue for some serious extracurricular education.

One of my roommates was a pre-med student who liked to share his new-found lore with anyone who would listen.

Illustrating his impromptu lectures by sketching with a bar of soap on the long mirror that ran over the row of sinks in the bathroom, like an instructor drawing on a blackboard, he would discourse on such useful topics as the structural and functional characteristics of the female genitalia.

One morning I pushed open the bathroom door and found four or five fellows surrounding my roommate, who was in the middle of an animated description of some woman he had been with the previous weekend.

For a change, he wasn't talking about sex; he was extolling the woman's cultural sophistication. He paid tribute to her knowledge of literature, music and art, and to her attempts to persuade him to take more interest in these uplifting areas.

I followed his monologue for half a minute or so, and then interrupted with a standard question that was virtually guaranteed to generate whoops of glee from the group.

"Yeah, but does she fuck?"

Immediately, every head swiveled in my direction. There was an uncomfortable silence. When my roommate saw who had asked the question, he gave a weary sigh.

"Lew, I'm talking about my mother."

For some time after that, I was gun-shy about speaking up in a group unless I knew for sure what they were talking about.

Most of my fraternity brothers were nice enough, and I became fairly friendly with some of them. On rare occasions when I had to depend on them for something, they were gracious and helpful.

When the Illini basketball team was playing an away game at Indiana that would determine the Big Ten champion, for example, they relayed the play-by-play to me as we huddled around the radio. Maybe it was because I helped them write their papers.

A few of them, however, were first-class nogoodniks—just like in the war movies, which always had one or two rotten apples in every barracks.

There was one guy in particular who walked around with a supercilious air that you could cut with a spoon. I disliked him at first sight, and an incident soon justified my assessment.

All of the fellows in the house knew that when they wanted to talk to me, I had no objection to whatever method they chose to get my attention.

If I was within reach, they could tap my shoulder or nudge my ribs or jiggle the newspaper I was reading. Farther away, they could wave a hand or throw a pillow or stamp a foot on the floor, or ask someone standing next to me to poke me. If they happened to be in a doorway or at the foot of the stairs, they could toggle the light switch. Whatever worked was fine.

I was reading a magazine in the deserted lounge one afternoon when this guy came in with a visitor. A minute or two after they entered the room, while they were standing 20 feet away from me, the guy stamped his foot. I glanced up.

He didn't want anything. He didn't say a word to me or even nod in acknowledgment. He was simply showing the visitor how he attracted my attention, as a real estate agent might demonstrate a feature of a house. I may as well have been a fireplace with a remote-controlled damper.

Uncharacteristically, I was struck speechless by his insensitive and rude behavior. By the time a suitably contemptuous epithet worked its way to my lips, they had left the room.

The fraternity house was the locale of another notable incident during my first semester downstate. There had been a dance on the campus, and afterward some of us brought our dates back to the house.

I watched nonplused as four or five fellows moved with purposeful precision around the room, turning off lights and pulling drapes to block out the street lamps.

This was in 1952, when we had such Paleolithic curiosities as housemothers and campus rules that confined the opposite sex to the ground floor.

In moments, the room was pitch black. I thought they were kidding, so I waited for someone to turn on a light. Nobody did.

I whispered into my date's ear: "What's going on?"

She traced with her finger on the back of my wrist: "Necking."

So we started necking. With one thing leading to another, I met an intimidating obstacle in the form of an item of feminine apparel indigenous to the 1950s.

After a few moments of frustrating failure, my date traced a word on my wrist: "Wait." I felt the sofa bounce, and then she was gone. A minute or so later, the sofa sagged as she sat down again.

Mirabile dictu, the obstacle had disappeared. We resumed. Time passed unnoticed. The surf pounded in my brain.

Unfortunately, I continued to have a bit of difficulty. Even more unfortunately, I forgot that there were several other people in the room with us.

So, in a normal tone of voice that easily carried the length and breadth of the blacked-out lounge, I said: "I can't reach it."

Too late, the girl clapped her hand over my mouth. Too late, I realized where we were and who was listening.

Mortification drenched me. In a moment, I knew, the lights would go on and my fraternity brothers would be pointing at me and whooping and hollering.

But nothing happened. Then I felt the girl shaking with laughter.

Eventually, she calmed down and patted my wrist. I didn't know what else to do, so I picked up where I had left off...dreading the moment when I would have to face my fraternity brothers in the unforgiving glare of the lights.

But no one said a word to me—either that night or afterward.

Evidently, the other couples must have been similarly engrossed in their own private worlds and had not heard my inopportune progress report.

Nevertheless, it was a memorable lesson for me in the pitfalls of matching the volume of my voice to the situation.

Getting thrown out of an interfraternity softball game is unheard of. Nevertheless, it happened when I was umpiring at first base when a bout with mononucleosis left me too weak to pitch.

Our team was in the field with two out in the top of the fourth when the other side's batter hit a grounder to third. The throw to first was straight, but the runner was fast—so the play was close but routine from my perspective behind the first baseman. I simply muttered "safe" without raising my voice or making a gesture.

To my surprise, the fielders came in and the other team took the field. I assumed I must have blown an obvious call for the third out and nobody had heard me call the runner safe.

Nobody except the runner himself. He whirled and pointed at me and yelled "The ump called me safe."

Everybody froze and looked at me. Our captain rushed over to me with a threatening stride. "Did you call him safe?"

"Yep."

"Everybody knows he was out."

"How do they know?"

"They heard the slap of the ball hitting the first baseman's hands before they saw the runner's foot touch the bag."

Then he grabbed me by the elbow and pulled me off the field.

"You're out of the game."

I particularly enjoyed my senior class in community newspaper management because of the real-world experience. Toward the end of the semester, we spent three days in a small town and put out that week's issue of the local newspaper.

I had four by-lines in the paper—a feature column on the front page, an inquiring-reporter story about attitudes toward daylight saving time, an editorial on the town elections, and a sports story about a baseball game at the high school.

A week after the paper came out, I passed by the instructor's office just as he emerged.

"The publisher of a chain of weekly newspapers called me this morning. He saw what you did in Villa Grove, and wants to hire you as his editor."

"Doesn't he want to meet me first?"

"He's seen your work in the paper. That's all he cares about."

"Does he know I'm deaf?"

"Yes."

"And I still get the job?"

"No. I turned him down. You still have another semester to go before you get your degree."

"Hey, wait a minute," I said. "How much does it pay?"

"Eighty dollars a week." In 1953, that was pretty good money for a first job out of school.

"I'll take it."

"No, you won't. There will be other jobs when you graduate."

I paced his office in frustration. He was right, but I didn't like it.

A photograph on one of his bookshelves caught my eye. It showed a tall, incredibly thin man standing by a tropical tree.

"Who's that?"

"That's me when I got out of a Japanese prison camp."

Since he was built like a pro football player, he was obviously pulling my leg. So I responded in kind.

"I was a sonar operator on a sub in the North Atlantic. A flotilla of German destroyers almost sank us with depth charges. The blasts coming through my earphones destroyed my hearing."

I was only 11 years old when World War II had ended eight years previously, but my instructor believed me and spread the tale.

When the story came back to me from someone else, I returned to my instructor's office.

"Hey, I was just kidding about being on a sub. Just like you were kidding about the prison camp."

"I wasn't joking. I really was on the Bataan death march."

As an elective, I took a course in business law.

The textbook was outdated, so all the information came in the form of lectures.

Fortunately, one of my fraternity brothers was in the class. He was a business major, and took copious notes.

By reading his notes instead of going to class, I was able to understand virtually everything. On the few occasions when I needed clarification, I went to the teacher's office and asked her.

I got an A in the course.

But the focus of this anecdote is not on what I was able to accomplish by using the notes.

The focus is on my fraternity brother, who had heard everything perfectly and had written down everything I needed to know to get an A.

He failed the course.

9

The Humpty Dumpty
School of Definitions

"There's glory for you!"

"I don't know what you mean by 'glory,' " Alice said.

Humpty Dumpty smiled contemptuously. "Of course you don't—'til I tell you. I meant 'there's a nice knock-down argument for you'!"

"But 'glory' doesn't mean 'a nice knock-down argument,' " Alice objected.

"When I use a word," Humpty Dumpty said in rather a scornful tone, "it means just what I choose it to mean—neither more nor less."

—Lewis Carroll, *Through the Looking-Glass*

Even though the technology exists to give usable hearing to deaf children, their parents should not permit this to be done.

It is better to let them stay deaf.

That's the incredible position of Harlan Lane, the hearing author of a number of books about deafness, who echoes the militants in the capital-D Deaf community.

He claims that surgeons and audiologists and hearing parents cannot resist tinkering with a child's ears because of their own neurotic and profit-driven need to "fix" something.

The activists declare: *it ain't broke, so don't fix it.* As far as they are concerned, there's no "if."

According to them, deafness isn't a hearing disorder; it's simply a different culture, and all cultural diversity should be respected. Therefore, efforts to cure or prevent deafness are wrong.

But if the sense of hearing isn't functioning, isn't it broken?

Not within the capital-D Deaf community, they say.

Where everyone communicates in American Sign Language, they say, someone who can't hear is a normal, fully-functioning person in that particular social group.

Never mind that there is a lot more to the real world—and full functionality—than being able to socialize easily and comfortably with other signing people.

Never mind that in the hearing environment, a deaf person has a very real disability that has very real consequences in school, on the street and in the workplace.

Never mind that where the Americans with Disabilities Act is concerned, the capital-D Deaf are quick to identify themselves as disabled people entitled to ADA protection.

Within the sheltered Deaf community where everyone is deaf, they say, deafness is not a disability. So, from the Deaf cultural point of view, nothing is broken.

And never mind that more than 90 percent of deaf babies are born to hearing parents—which means that they aren't even in the Deaf community at all.

Opponents of cochlear implants give several reasons for being against giving a deaf child some usable hearing:

1. *A deaf child should be kept deaf to avoid jeopardizing the future of their culture.*

Since the capital-D Deaf community depends on the existence of deaf people who use American Sign Language, they fear that a reduction in the number of deaf children will weaken the Deaf community and lead to its extinction.

They say that those who try to give hearing to deaf children are committing cultural genocide—even though less than 10 percent of deaf people are culturally Deaf.

I think it's fine for Deaf people to develop workarounds (such as American Sign Language) and mindsets (such as the cultural perspective of deafness) that help them deal with their situation physically and emotionally, so they can be comfortable and happy and have something they can call their own.

But it's something else to say that children should be kept deaf in order to help the Deaf perpetuate their self-perceived culture.

That point of view is grotesque, like a mad-scientist movie.

Lane admits that his major concern is *not* for the individual deaf child, but for the "richly diverse [American] nation."

Even if an implant would "reduce the burdens the child will bear as a member of a minority...even if the devices were perfect," he would not use it to lessen or eliminate the child's disability.

He acknowledges that the deaf child would then be left to face a life "full of challenge" (his euphemism for the burdens, obstacles and deprivations of deafness).

But, apparently, it doesn't bother him that the deaf child will be burdened, blocked and deprived, because Lane considers cultural pluralism to be the greater good.

Besides, he himself doesn't have to face the "challenges," since he can hear.

In trying to legitimize his position that deaf children should be kept deaf, Lane wraps the issue in the banner of cultural diversity—which quite rightly calls for differences in cultures to be respected and accepted.

But he is ignoring the fact that some features of some cultures are simply outside the pale of western civilization.

Female circumcision (in which the clitoris is removed from all girls in a society) and the public slaughter and eating of dogs are integral to some non-western cultures—but that doesn't mean they should likewise be welcomed and tolerated in America.

2. A deaf child should be kept deaf to avoid putting him at risk.

Opponents point to the dangers of any surgery, especially head surgery. Granted, there are risks—but they are comparable to those of a mastoid operation.

It's nowhere near as risky as brain surgery or heart surgery—yet the opponents of cochlear implants don't suggest that parents of a child with a debilitating heart defect forgo the risks of heart surgery, or that parents of blind children keep them blind because of the risk of brain surgery.

Yes, there are risks, and no one says otherwise.

No one has an implant before a risk/benefit analysis is made.

Those who choose to go ahead are not ignorant of the risks, nor do they ignore the risks. But unlike the anti-implant side, they can see that the benefits may very well outweigh the risks.

The FDA—a conservative, slow-moving organization—agrees. After due consideration, it approved cochlear implants in 1990 as being safe and effective for children as young as two years old.

3. A deaf child should be kept deaf to avoid stigmatizing her.

If you try to "fix" someone's aural system, this argument goes, you are rejecting her for what she is. You are implying that there's something wrong with her, and making her feel ashamed.

Those who want to keep deaf children deaf say they want the children to feel good about themselves as Deaf people, rather than viewing themselves as misfits.

A cochlear implant or a hearing aid is psychologically bad for deaf children, they say, because it is a constant implication that something about the child is defective. This perception of a defect, they say, leads to low self-esteem.

However, they don't explain why a child with poor vision should not be deprived of eyeglasses in order to give him self-esteem.

Or why a crippled child should not be deprived of leg braces or a wheelchair in order to give her self-esteem.

Or why a child with a bad heart should not have a pacemaker implanted.

Nor do they explain how I am well aware that one part of me is 100 percent defective without my self-esteem suffering at all.

My deafness is a functional defect. I can't hear anything at all—conversations, music, automobile horns, the radio, Scud blasts.

I unquestionably recognize that in one specific area I am, yes, impaired/disabled/handicapped/deficient/deviant in the real world. This causes me a number of problems—some big, some small.

It's obvious to me that I have a set of completely broken, totally useless ears.

So who's perfect?

I don't dwell on it. I don't bitch and moan about it. I don't let it run my life.

But yes, I recognize and accept it.

Everybody has both positive and negative aspects. What counts is not an absence of negatives (there's no such animal), but the bottom line—making my positives outweigh my negatives, so that the bottom line is that I'm okay.

To deny that deafness is a defect is a self-delusion. Those who try to call a negative a positive for the sake of so-called self-esteem are indulging in newspeak.

I've been hearing, and I've been deaf. I speak from experience (as Lane does not) when I say that the isolated and relatively minor advantages of deafness are far outweighed by its disadvantages.

Yes, I accept and deal quite well with my deafness, but that doesn't mean I can't recognize that having hearing is better.

On the computer network, someone wrote that a seven-year-old child should not have to think of himself as being defective—that he should be allowed to think of himself as a child with a name, not as a child with a defect.

A deaf professor responded:

> When I was seven years old, I didn't just think of myself as defective; I knew for a fact that I was. It was extremely obvious that my ears did not work, and that this was a very serious defect indeed.

The last thing I needed, emotionally or otherwise, was for my parents to pretend that I was somehow "normal." I was not normal, I was deaf, and this presented immense problems which could not be wished or pretended away.

For my parents to love me the way I was, they had to help me deal with these problems—not pretend that they didn't exist or that there was some never-never land where I would be normal. My feelings of being loved 100 percent were reinforced, not diminished, by all the trekking to the doctors and the audiologists and the speech pathologists.

I was David, and my parents loved me. I was deaf, and they were doing something about it because they loved me.

All the Humpty Dumpty definitions of deafness and disability cannot obscure an incontrovertible fact of life:

It isn't how you define the problem that counts.

It's what you do about it.

Some people choose to do nothing about it except stick their heads in the semantic sand.

Who should make the decision on whether a child is given the opportunity to gain some usable hearing?

If the parents are hearing, Lane says, it should *not* be up to them.

Hearing parents are ill-informed about Deaf cultural values, he claims, and will want their child to be like they are—like hearing people—so they will "wrongly" approve an implant.

Instead, says Lane, the decision on the child's fate should be made by a surrogate. But not just any surrogate.

He says it should be made by a culturally Deaf adult—in other words, one of those who believe deaf children should be like *they* are: devoid of hearing.

Yes, Lane would take that responsibility for their children away from the parents and give it to a fringe ideologue whose decision would be a foregone conclusion: *the child must stay deaf.*

The parents, according to Lane, are not capable of making what he considers to be the right decision.

Sounds like a cross between fascism and *Rosemary's Baby.*

Opponents of cochlear implants claim that they are misleadingly promoted as miracle cures and cure-alls.

By the media, perhaps. It's true that newspaper articles and television sound bites often oversimplify and overhype the implants.

But you can't simply go ahead and have an implant just because you read about it in the paper.

Candidates must go through a detailed assessment program to weed out those who are unsuitable for one reason or another.

And the professionals who work with the deaf constantly issue caveats aimed at keeping the expectations of potential implantees and their families down to realistic levels.

I know of four oral deaf people (including myself) who were turned down without even having a formal screening; we were told at the outset that we function well enough without the implant.

The hearing provided by an implant is partial and distorted; the brain has to interpret the sounds and become used to them.

Consequently, the most important factor is the long, rigorous postoperative learning process.

While some people may understand a few spoken words right away, it takes a year or more of intensive self-training to reach a high level of effectiveness.

This is why the screening phase looks for people who are strongly motivated to work long and hard at adapting their brains to make sense of the sounds. The more effort they put into it, the more benefit they are likely to get from their implants.

Although the selection process tries to choose those candidates with the best chance for success, it is not an exact science.

Not all implants are successful, and the degree of success covers a broad range from minimal to major. There is no guarantee of how successful an implant will be, if at all.

Still, most implants do make a significant contribution.

They enable *some* people to understand speech over the phone. They enable *most* people to pick up enough sound to improve their speechreading and speech. And they enable almost *all* people to hear environmental sounds such as doorbells and car horns.

Lane misses no opportunity to slam the professionals for one reason or another—such as for making money on implants and other devices for the deaf and hard-of-hearing.

He makes a big point of the fact that psychologists, audiologists, surgeons, anesthesiologists, hospitals, device manufacturers, speech therapists and others in the field get paid for what they do.

Lane would have us think that, unlike mercenary professionals, he has the welfare of the children at heart in writing his books.

But he is a professor at a university—and, as he admits, "faculty are required to publish research in order to receive promotion, increases in pay, and 'tenure,' a guaranteed job until retirement."

So his books on deafness are in his own self-interest—not only in his academic job, but also as a royalty-collecting author.

Controversy helps sell books and makes papers publishable, and it helps him get speaking engagements which help him sell books. It is in his economic interest to write and say things that conflict with what pro-mainstream and pro-implant people say.

The greater the controversy and the longer it lasts, the more opportunity he has to make money from it. He cannot be said to be an impartial observer with no financial stake in the situation.

Therefore, what he says should be viewed accordingly...along with his selectivity and phraseology.

Consider the following quotes about cochlear implants:

...no one can predict the level of success before surgery...

The risks of implant surgery are the same basic risks associated with any surgery that requires general anesthesia. In addition, there are also a few other potential risks related to operating on that section of the head. They include inflammation or bleeding, numbness or stiffness about the ear, injury to the facial nerve, taste disturbance, dizziness, increased tinnitus, neck pain and perilymph fluid leak, which may result in meningitis.

The presence of any foreign body under the skin can result in irritation, inflammation or breakdown of the skin in the area around the receiver/stimulator, and/or extrusion of the device. Such complications may require additional medical treatment, surgery, and/or removal of the device.

A blow in the area of the implanted components may damage the internal device and result in its failure.

Failure of the components could result in the perception of an uncomfortably loud sound sensation.

The long-term effects of implanting or using a cochlear implant are unknown.

Potential hazards include new bone growth in the cochlea or deterioration of the nerve cells.

Where did this litany of risks, complications, failures, problems, malfunctions and hazards come from?

From anti-implant activists?

No.

The warnings are from a Cochlear Corporation brochure—yes, from one of the "profit-driven" manufacturers.

Yet Lane claims that the doctors and audiologists and implant manufacturers and so on are driven by financial incentives rather than by concern for deaf people, and therefore cannot be trusted to give complete, unbiased information about implants.

Look who's talking.

Actually, there isn't anything wrong with academics and authors profiting from their work.

So why shouldn't professionals likewise get paid for their work with the deaf?

In stretching for such a ridiculous argument, Lane is doing no more than demonstrating the weakness of his position.

In another attempt to denigrate cochlear implants, Lane criticizes the validity of tests that determine the effectiveness of the device in helping someone understand the spoken word:

> The experimenter is sometimes forced to suit the test to the child: for example, to present only those few words the deaf child knows; that's like getting to choose among the questions you must answer on an exam—your score will be inflated.

First of all, how does he expect a child to recognize a word she hasn't yet learned?

Secondly, he apparently forgot that 169 pages earlier, he was complaining that it is unfair to test deaf people with the same personality and intelligence tests that are used for testing hearing people:

> But if [psychologists] do not adapt the test for their deaf clients, the deaf persons' scores do not present a true picture of their knowledge or state of mind.
>
> Since deaf test-takers in America frequently are not fluent in English, they not only fail to understand test instructions thoroughly, invalidating the results, but also fail to understand the test content itself....

Apparently, Lane's stance depends on whose ox is being scored.

Lane admits right at the beginning of *When the Mind Hears* that his book is biased. It glorifies the pioneers of ASL and demonizes oral advocates (especially Alexander Graham Bell).

He calls it a history of the deaf. Actually, however, all 500-plus pages, with 1,200 endnotes and 2,000 bibliographical references, comprise only a one-sided history of deaf *education.*

If there is life after school, Lane doesn't mention it.

Then Oliver Sacks, inspired by Lane's book, wrote *Seeing Voices.* This, too, was a paean to ASL and the capital-D Deaf culture.

This, too, studiously ignored what happens to these people when their education is finished.

Do they find satisfying jobs that take maximum advantage of their capabilities? Do they advance to supervisory and executive positions in the mainstream? Do they earn enough money to afford a decent middle-class (or better) standard of living?

Do they live in comfortable homes in pleasant neighborhoods? Can they afford to travel, to send their children to college, to drive a late-model automobile? Do they buy books, attend plays, have hobbies, go to ball games? Do they socialize with their neighbors and other hearing people?

Neither Lane nor Sacks found it worth mentioning whether these people do anything besides sit around telling each other how good it feels to communicate in ASL.

I would think that this subject is important enough to be in a comprehensive history such as Lane's presumes to be.

I would also think that a culture's notable personalities would include people who achieved a measure of success in various fields, thus serving as role models. Yet the only luminaries in these books are the educators who spread the use of ASL.

For Lane and Sacks, what they call the Deaf culture apparently exists in a Petri dish—with no connection to the real world.

Studying the culture through a rose-colored microscope, they do not concern themselves with such details as how the Deaf will eventually find fulfillment in a challenging occupation that provides them with a good living.

Nor do they mention the documented, all-too-common negative effects of the insulated Deaf environment—especially among those raised in the ultimate isolation and academically unchallenging mileu of a state residential school for the manual deaf.

These include immaturity, naivete, intolerance, lack of attitudes and people skills needed for employment and independent living, dependence on welfare, and lack of intellectual development.

For Lane and Sacks, ASL is the end-all and be-all, and the future apparently will magically take care of itself.

Lane doesn't say a word about the usefulness of ASL in the real world. And the closest he comes to talking about vocations outside the field of deaf education is in a single sentence: he makes a passing reference to a finding that 80 percent of deaf workers were in manual or unskilled occupations.

Sacks, to his credit, does mention the issue in his book (if only as a couple of asides):

> There were, indeed, real dilemmas [in the 1870s], as there had always been, and they exist to this day. What good, it was asked, was the use of signs without speech? Would this not restrict deaf people, in daily life, to intercourse with other deaf people? Should not speech (and lip reading) be taught instead, allowing a full integration of the deaf into the general population?

But Sacks never even *tries* to answer the questions. And he never talks about how signers are expected to make a living after graduation.

His only other acknowledgment that someday signers will have to function in the real world comes when, describing his visit to the signing environment at Gallaudet University, he admits:

> Some of its students were occasionally reluctant to leave its warmth and seclusion and protectiveness, the coziness of a small but complete and self-sufficient world, for the unkind and uncomprehending big world outside....
>
> The students I met seemed animated, a lively group when together, but often fearful and diffident of the outside world....

The thousands of endnotes and references in *When the Mind Hears* give Lane's book an air of academic authority.

But when it comes to actually proving one of Lane's major contentions, the "proof" is apparently made of thin air. He wrote:

> A recent study by Gallaudet College of the scores of some 17,000 deaf students on the Stanford Achievement

Test illustrates how oralism has reduced the educational achievement of the deaf since the days of Laurent Clerc and James Denison. As a benchmark, the achievement of the average hearing seventeen-year-old American student on the SAT is called twelfth-grade level. The achievement of the average deaf seventeen-year-old is sixth-grade level in arithmetic (their best subject), and fourth-grade level in reading (paragraph meaning).

But what were the arithmetic and reading levels of the average deaf seventeen-year-old *a century earlier*, in the days of Laurent Clerc and James Denison?

Lane doesn't say—which is understandable, given that such data probably do not exist.

Without comparable data, what is the basis of his claim that educational achievement of the deaf has declined since then—let alone that the purported decline was due to oral education?

The unquestionable fact that the achievement levels of *today's deaf* students are lower than those of *today's hearing* students does nothing to prove his allegation.

It simply masks his lack of proof.

Alexander Graham Bell's mother and his wife were both deaf. He, his father and his grandfather were all involved in teaching speech.

His father, Alexander Melville Bell, developed the Visible Speech system; its principles have been the dominant influence on the teaching of speech ever since.

Bell's unrelenting advocacy of speech and speechreading, which helped determine the course of deaf education in the United States, was aimed at bringing the deaf into the larger (hearing) society.

He did not want them to be restricted to a community of signers who could communicate only among themselves.

His invention of the telephone evolved from his efforts to create a device that would help deaf people communicate.

Eventually, earphones similar to those in telephones were used in early hearing aids. Bell's experiments in the 1870s laid the groundwork for today's powerful, miniaturized instruments.

Bell also wanted to reduce the incidence of deaf-born children. It is about one per thousand if the parents are hearing—but 50 to 100 per thousand if both parents were born deaf.

This is compelling evidence that a highly significant proportion of infant deafness is hereditary.

From what was known then about genetics, Bell concluded that deaf people should be discouraged from marrying each other. So he was against special schools or classes for the deaf, clubs for the deaf, and anything else that would bring deaf people together and lead to marriage among them.

Despite Bell's dedication to helping deaf people overcome the communication barrier and live in the mainstream, and to reducing the incidence of deafness, Deaf people view him simplistically as someone who tried to eliminate their culture.

Harlan Lane fans these flames of resentment against Bell in his admittedly skewed "history" of the deaf. And Lane told me that he perceives Bell as the devil incarnate, whose immense ego led him to try to use science to make deaf people "normal."

Today, many Deaf militants and their supporters such as Lane claim that doctors, audiologists and teachers are deliberately trying to destroy the deaf culture. This is pure paranoia.

Some of them may be paternalistic, arrogant or incompetent (or all three)—but most of them are conscientiously trying to improve the lives of the deaf.

Few, if any, have ulterior motives.

Because I stress the need for deaf people to develop whatever speech and speechreading capabilities they can, I am often viewed as being against sign language in general and ASL in particular—and, by extension, against the Deaf community.

I deny it, but a lot of people don't believe me.

It is inconceivable to them that I have any motive for promoting oral skills other than to eliminate sign language and, consequently, their culture.

If I'm for speaking and speechreading, so goes their reasoning, I must be against sign.

I tell them that I couldn't care less what mode of communication a group of people want to use among themselves—so long as they develop speech and speechreading to the best of their abilities in order to maximize their opportunities—particularly at work.

Neither do I feel that all (or even most) children should take the oral-only route in school. I agree that it is impossible for many of them, and that many students will benefit from a combination of signed and spoken English.

Nor does this mean that I believe everyone can develop flawless speech and speechreading. Most deaf people will never have world-class oral skills. But that's no reason for them to give up trying to speak and read lips, either. Whatever they *can* achieve will be of good use to them.

Most people who practice music never make it to Carnegie Hall. This doesn't mean that they should stop practicing and forget about music.

By doing the best they can, they enrich their lives with whatever level of music they're capable of producing.

Finally, trying a different tack, I posted the following tale on the Internet discussion group on deafness:

When my mother was pregnant with me, she started getting labor pains during a typical Chicago blizzard.

While my father was driving her to the hospital, the car skidded at an intersection and knocked down a post.

A stop sign flew off the post and smashed into the windshield, where it hung a few inches from my mother.

The shock intensified my mother's labor, and my father had to deliver me right there on the front seat of the car.

When I was a teenager, I spent my summers playing 16-inch softball and bridge at what was officially named the 55th Street Promontory.

It was a man-made park that stuck out like a finger into Lake Michigan—so everybody called it the Point.

One day, as four of us were sitting on the grass playing bridge, the dummy admitted that he went to a fortune teller once in a while.

I told him that only a dummy would believe that baloney, but the idea struck my partner as fun.

"Hey," she said, "let's all go see that fortune teller. We can find out what we'll be when we grow up."

Reluctantly, I went along with them to a small storefront on 47th Street.

The fortune teller was a wizened old Chinese woman who spoke fluent Yiddish.

The guy jerked his thumb toward us and said "These are my friends from the Point."

The old woman looked us over, then asked me to sit down.

She took my palm and asked, "What sign were you born under?"

"A stop sign," I said.

She nodded her head sagely and stroked the whiskers on her chin.

"I see your future very clearly. You are going to be the Point man in the stop-sign movement."

If this tale rings a Bell, that's because it's written with the same scholarly dedication to the truth, the whole truth and nothing but the truth as was a certain "history" of the deaf.

10

Welcome to the real world

Actually, the Point really was my favorite hangout during my school vacations.

The year I turned 18, I had a summer job delivering supplies to bars and cocktail lounges on the far south side of the Chicago metropolitan area.

Driving a battered panel delivery truck, I made the rounds and dropped off cases of napkins and toilet paper, glasses and dishes, soap and bleach.

On my way home the first day, I self-consciously steered the truck down 53rd Street, hoping to be seen by my friends.

I spotted a tanned girl in a tank top and short shorts who looked familiar. Then I remembered we had played softball together at the Point. I stopped the truck and honked the horn.

"Want a ride?"

"Sure."

She climbed in. There was no passenger seat, so she sat on a case of paper towels.

"I'm Lew."

"I'm Barbara."

Trivial as it sounds, it was a major turning point in my life.

During my early and middle teen years, I had been friendly with a number of girls from school or the Point or the synagogue's youth group. Some of them I dated more than once, and three or four I saw more or less regularly.

Sometimes I had a date on which a girl and I really enjoyed each other's company. Sometimes the evening was sort of okay—say, better than staying home on Saturday night. And sometimes one or both of us would have been better off staying home.

I didn't always have the opportunity to ask a girl face-to-face for a date. So I had to call her up and ask her over the phone.

This operation usually involved my sister Gail—who, being only 10 or 11 years old, was not especially versed in the niceties of making preliminary small talk with high school girls.

So a girl on the other end was likely to pick up the telephone and hear a child's voice saying "Hello. My brother Lew wants to know if you want to go to a movie Saturday night."

It wasn't the smoothest approach they had ever heard. But what were my alternatives? Who else would I want to call for me?

My mother? Aw, come on. My father? Fat chance. My older brother, Joe? No way. My younger brother, Guy? A possibility, but he was only three years old.

So, by default, Gail was stuck in the role.

If the girl was someone whom I had dated before, it didn't make any difference that my sister was calling for me.

But if the girl was someone new, she might be somewhat taken aback at first.

When I wasn't on a date with a girl, my socializing tended to be with a group of four or five guys from the neighborhood a year or two my senior. We'd go bowling or play miniature golf or go stag to a party or see a movie or just drive around.

Socially, I sort of drifted through those years. I wasn't especially interested in anyone, and no one seemed to be especially interested in me. I had a number of friends, yes, and we had good times together—but there wasn't any one girl who was my best girl.

I was never preoccupied with the issue. But now and then I ruminated about whether something was keeping me from getting close to someone—or, more accurately, keeping someone from getting close to me.

And if it was my deafness that was the barrier, then there would always be a wall between me and everyone else.

One thought that did *not* occur to me was that everyone goes through periods of self-doubt like this. Especially teenagers.

Then Barbara opened the door of the truck and climbed into my life. She was the right person at the right time. She was open, independent, energetic, sociable, attractive and ebullient.

We started dating. Soon, we were going steady. And we were comfortable and natural with each other in a way I had never been with anyone else.

My deafness meant little more to her than did the Terry-Thomas gap between my two front teeth. It was just part of who I was, something that occasionally called for a bit of compensation—such as when we went to a movie and she filled me in on the dialogue.

We enjoyed simply being with each other. And eventually, we took it for granted that we would get married sooner or later.

Barbara's father was against our getting married, no matter when. He seemed to like me personally, but he was convinced that a deaf man couldn't give his daughter the kind of life she deserved.

A year passed, and another. Barbara started her first semester at the University of Illinois at the same time I began my last semester. By then, she was 18 and I was 20. I moved out of my fraternity house and into a rooming house not far from her dorm.

I finally felt like a whole person.

I couldn't help marveling at my good fortune in finding a woman who actually wanted to marry me. In my eyes, she was one of a kind.

I graduated from the school of journalism and started looking for a job at Chicago's four major newspapers—the morning *Tribune* and *Sun-Times*, and the afternoon *Herald-American* and *Daily News*. But none of them had anything for me.

So I knocked on the doors of the publishing houses. I was finally granted an interview at one of the country's largest educational publishers. They liked enough of what they saw to invite me back for a battery of intelligence, knowledge and aptitude tests.

Then the personnel manager called me in for a third visit.

"Lew, you had some of the highest scores I've ever seen around here. You unquestionably have more than enough ability to be an editor in this company. I wanted to tell you that personally."

I smiled.

"However...." He looked embarrassed.

My smile faded.

"The people who make the final decision have decided not to hire you. That is all I can say about it. I'm very sorry."

I walked out, more stunned than angry.

At the time, I assumed I was rejected because of my deafness. Today, I am more aware of the antisemitism that pervaded some businesses at that time, and I now realize that another possible reason was the fact that I was Jewish. Or maybe I simply lost out to the nephew of one of the vice-presidents.

What the actual reason was—my deafness, antisemitism, nepotism or whatever—I never found out. But the experience wasn't a total loss; at the very least, my skin grew a little thicker.

I had written a letter of application to the editor of the *Sun-Times*. Eventually, I received a reply asking me to call Budd Gore, assistant to the executive editor, for an appointment.

I went in to see Budd. He told me that there were no editorial jobs for beginners at the moment, but my letter had been passed along to him and it so happened that he could use an assistant.

Would I be interested in a temporary job on the administrative side until something opened up in editorial, with no promises that I would get any openings?

I would.

So my first job out of school was as assistant to the assistant to the executive editor. My title was bigger than my salary, which was $40 a week.

My first task was to measure the space each of the four Chicago papers had devoted to articles on violent crime during the past months. Budd led me to a room piled high with back issues, gave me a ruler and a pencil and a pad of paper, and asked me to do as much as I could during the next three days.

By the time he came back from lunch on the first day, I had finished measuring every newspaper in the room. From then on, it became something of a game as he tried to find something else for me to do before I finished an assignment. I wrote his letters, edited the newspaper's internal house organ, the *Tiny Sun-Times*, and did other odd jobs.

After a month, he conceded defeat—just as a copy editing job opened up on the sports desk. I got it.

My pay more than doubled, to the guild rate for beginners in 1954: $88 a week. The hours were 3 p.m. to midnight, with Tuesdays and Thursdays off. I was on three months' probation.

I sat with three or four other copyreaders around the rim of a semicircular table. Facing us in the slot was the copy chief (who was usually the assistant sports editor). Everything came to him first—articles and columns written by *Sun-Times* staffers; news and features from the Associated Press and the United Press wires; local stories from the City News Bureau; press releases from sports teams, promoters and related organizations; and photographs from all of these sources.

Only a tiny fraction of the mass of words and pictures ever made it into the newspaper. It was the job of the man in the slot to choose what to use; the rest was thrown out.

In a matter of seconds he made his decisions. If he picked a story, he scrawled a code that indicated the type of headline to use—typeface, size and number of columns. This was also a guideline for cutting the story; the smaller the headline, the shorter the story. Then he tossed the story to one of the editors on the rim.

As he saw what was available, the assistant sports editor drew a layout of the pages—showing where each article and photograph would go, and how much space it would get.

The sports pages had a distinctive, raucous flavor of their own that set them apart from the rest of the paper. The sportswriters turned out colorful, opinionated, finger-pointing copy intended to entertain the readers as much as to inform them. There was no pretense of disinterested objectivity.

Working the sports desk was fun. The hardest part was coming up with headlines that weren't trite (which, because of the severely limited space and time available, most headlines tended to be).

We used puns, rhymes and topical allusions in the headlines to help liven up the pages. Once in a while the man in the slot cracked the hint of a smile when he read a head I tossed to him.

We corrected spelling mistakes, tightened up sloppy sentences, and watched for factual errors. The flood of stories across the copy desk, and the constant reading of sports pages in all the Chicago papers, left a residue of sports lore in the mind of each editor against which he checked the accuracy of the writers' work.

When it looked to me as if Cookie Lavagetto's name had been misspelled in an article, I asked the guy on my left how to spell it. His version didn't look right either. So I looked it up.

Then, being a cocky 20-year-old punk with no discernible social graces, I put the almanac under the guy's nose and pointed to the spelling and said "That's the way the cookie crumbles." Justifiably, he wouldn't talk to me for a week.

The sports copy desk had an involuntary sideline: answering telephoned queries from fans, such as "Has Mantle hit more home runs batting left-handed or right-handed?"

We had staff columnists such as Gene Kessler and syndicated columnists such as Red Smith. We usually didn't cut or change their copy much, if at all, in deference to their exalted status. However, sometimes I couldn't resist. Like when Kessler opened his column with a sentence about 75 words long. I cut it up into four or five sentences to make it clearer and easier to read.

When Kessler saw it in print, he came storming over to the desk. Luckily for me, the copy chief said he couldn't remember who had edited it.

We cropped photographs to eliminate unnecessary detail and create a stronger image or a better composition. And we wrote the captions for the photographs.

Down in the composing room, the Linotype machine operators set the copy into metal type and the engravers turned the photographs into etched plates. Then the make-up men arranged the type and plates according to the layout drawn by the assistant sports editor.

The elements never fit perfectly without some changes. If a story was too long, some of it was cut. If it wasn't long enough, a short item was added to fill the extra space.

The make-up men themselves did not make these decisions on what to cut or add. As press time neared, a copy editor from each desk (news, features, sports) would go down to the composing room and stand across the waist-high tables from the make-up men, telling them what to cut from a story or what item to use as a filler.

My second week on the job, I went down with another editor from the sports desk to see how the make-up was done. The next day I did it myself, with the other editor hovering in the background.

On one page, one column was too short and the next column was too long. I saw that by moving a short item from one column to another, the problem would be solved.

So I tapped the paragraph of type with my forefinger and asked the make-up man to move it over one column to the left.

Immediately, he cupped his hand to his mouth and shouted for the shop steward (the union representative in the composing room) to come over. The make-up man yelled agitatedly at him and jabbed his finger at me.

The other copy editor hurried over, listened for a moment, then held out his arms wide and spoke apologetically. I nudged him.

"Hey, what did I do?"

"You touched the type."

"So?"

"It's against union rules. Editorial people can't touch anything in here. You can point, but you can't touch."

One of our jobs was to look over each edition for typographical errors as it came off the press. Then we'd mark them and send them down to be fixed for the next edition.

But correcting the errors meant resetting and recasting an entire line of metal type even if only one character was changed. In doing so, the typesetters sometimes made new errors.

Once I edited a story about a boxing match between Ezzard Charles and Tommy "Hurricane" Jackson. In the first edition, one of the paragraphs appeared like this:

> *When Jackson stepped into the ring,*
> *he was booed. Why? who knows?*

The "w" after the first question mark wasn't capitalized. So I marked it and sent it down.

When the next edition hit the streets, it read:

> *When Jackson stepped into the ring,*
> *he was boozed. Why? Who knows?*

That was the summer that Barbara and I made our de facto engagement official.

I'm not sure what triggered the announcement.

Maybe it was because I had a big-league job and was able to take on the financial responsibility of marriage. Or maybe it was because my older brother was getting married in August, and I was being prodded by the pitchfork of sibling devilry.

Barbara and I didn't set a date—just some unspecified time in the near future.

My mother was delighted. My father was satisfied.

Barbara's mother was quiet. Her father was upset.

I was on top of the world—the *real* world.

Everything that counted was coming my way.

At the end of my three-month probationary period, the sports editor called me into his office.

"Your work has been very good, Lew."

Finally—I get a raise!

"But you don't handle the phoned-in questions, so the other fellows have to shoulder a greater burden. That isn't fair."

My stomach started churning.

"I'm sorry, Lew, but we'll have to let you go."

The only problem with this explanation was the fact that we didn't get more than a dozen phone calls a day, if that, spread among four or five people on the desk. What burden?

I know that I did my work well and quickly. I had been told so on more than one occasion.

So the only logical reason had to be that my brashness rubbed too many people the wrong way.

But the brashness was my protective coloration. It was supposed to keep people from thinking about my deafness, and it usually worked.

This time, though, it must have worked too well.

It was a major blow to my career hopes. I had been exactly where I wanted to be, on a major metropolitan newspaper, doing the kind of work I enjoyed.

And it was a blow to my ego. I needed solace.

Barbara was downstate for the fall semester, and the following weekend was homecoming.

I called her and told her I was coming, so she could get me a ticket for the football game.

She could easily switch seats with someone else so we could sit together.

We're loyal to you, Illinois
We're orange and blue, Illinois...

As the Illini marching band came streaming out between the goal posts and onto the field at Memorial Stadium, led by the hopping Chief Illiniwek looking as though he was trying to stamp out a brush fire with his bare feet, the Illinois fans stood and clapped their hands.

The Wisconsin fans sat on their hands.

I leaned over and put my head in my hands, trying to figure out why I was sitting on the opposite side of the field from Barbara.

I hadn't even known there was a hint of a rift between us—let alone a chasm the width of a football field.

The first I heard of it was when I drove up to her dorm that morning and walked across the lawn to where she was basking in the September sun.

She rose from the blanket and met me halfway.

"Hi, Barbara. Want to go get a Coke or something?"

"Can't. I have a date." She nodded toward three other people on the blanket—one female, two male.

"You have a what?"

She nodded. "I think we should be seeing other people."

My stomach reeled from the blow. "But...why?"

She shrugged. "That's what I think we should do."

"So what am I doing here?"

"You said you wanted to see the game. Here's your ticket. You'll be sitting with Shirley. I couldn't get you a seat next to mine."

My stomach threw in the towel.

I figured that as long as I was there, I might as well go to the game.

I have no idea who won or what the score was.

I spent two and a half hours staring blankly at the blurred mass of humanity on the other side of the field, wondering which one was Barbara.

Then I drove back to Chicago, stunned by the one-two punch. In a single week, I had lost the perfect job and the perfect mate.

Twenty days after my twenty-first birthday, my life was in ruins forever.

```
Dear Barbara:
   On a September afternoon 39 years ago,
I was sitting in Memorial Stadium,
wondering why I was on the opposite side
of the field from you. I'm still
wondering.
   You may have told me the reason at the
time. If you did, it's been blanked out
of my memory (perhaps understandably).
Now I'm trying to fill in the blanks.
   If I may be so uncouth as to invade
your privacy, would you be good enough to
spell out, as uncompromisingly as you
can, why you decided to split? I'd
appreciate knowing both what you were
thinking at the time...and how you would
analyze your heartless cruelty today.
                                    Lew
```

Dear Lew:
   I'm glad you wrote. It brings back lots
of warm, wonderful feelings and memories.
   I am convinced that my actions that
weekend had more to do with who I was
than with who you were. I was very young
and much too scared to leave home. I was
still very dependent on the approval of
my parents in all aspects of my life.
   My father was very much against my
marrying anyone before I finished

college, and was convinced that I would not continue my studies if I got married.

I must admit that he was also not particularly enthusiastic about my marrying a deaf man.

However, I know now that had I been ready to marry, my parents could have done nothing to prevent me from doing just that. Furthermore, I would have married you because I loved you.

I guess it just was not meant to be.

Through the years I have thought about you, asked about you, and often have regretted that you couldn't wait.

(Heavy sigh.)

Barbara

Dear Barbara:

If I understand your letter correctly, here's what happened 39 years ago:

I thought you meant "I don't want to marry you."

But you actually meant "I don't want to marry you *now.*"

This seems to have the makings of a Gilbert and Sullivan operetta.

Lew

Dear Lew:

I'm glad you finally got it.

What took so long?

Barbara

11

Shooting myself in the foot

```
Budd Gore
Director of Advertising & Promotion
The Halle Bros. Co.
Cleveland, Ohio

Dear Budd:
   When you left the Sun-Times and went to
Cleveland, you told me to keep in touch
and let you know what's happening with me.
   I lost my job and I lost my girl.
                    Despairingly,
                                    Lew


Dear Lew:
   Come on over here. You haven't got
anything left to lose.
                    Expectantly,
                                    Budd
```

I packed a suitcase, put a new ribbon in my Royal portable and took the train to Cleveland. Halle's turned out to be a fine old department store comparable to Marshall Field's in Chicago.

Budd gave me a cubicle in the advertising department and a copy of the *Cleveland Plain Dealer*. I looked through the ads and found a room in the area around Western Reserve University.

I had taken a basic advertising course in journ school, so I knew a little bit about the subject. Budd piled my desk high with tear sheets of ads from men's clothing, women's fashions, furniture, housewares, cosmetics, sporting goods, the downstairs store, and so on—and told me to study them.

Then I started writing ads.

The information came from the departmental buyers—features, benefits, colors, sizes, prices. Often, the information was less than adequate; then I'd go downstairs and bug the buyers for more.

Department stores were training grounds for new copywriters. Mainly, what the writers learned was not creativity, but discipline—writing to fill a precise amount of space designated for the headline and body copy.

Since the most important consideration was to show what the merchandise looked like, illustrations took up most of the space—leaving room for only a minimal amount of copy.

Some writers tried to write meaty, benefit-laden copy. But these rarely got into print without being emasculated.

In general, the copy tended to be sketchy and lightweight, with women's fashions, perfume and cosmetics having a nonsensical non-language of their own.

As on the *Sun-Times*, Budd tried to keep me busy in all of the domains under his authority—advertising, public relations, window display, in-store signs.

I spent most of my time in advertising, but I also wrote a weekly PR column that appeared in the Sunday paper and another one that appeared in a weekly magazine (for which I was paid a munificent bonus of $5 each).

The sign shop printed cardboard signs that slipped into metal holders. These described merchandise, or promoted special events, or gave directions.

There isn't much that a writer can do with the signs, so my job was mainly to make sure that the spelling and punctuation were correct.

Still, I tried to add a little punch to them whenever I could, such as this sign I wrote for the lingerie department:

For a quick pickup—
Perma-Lift bras

The departmental buyer not only refused to put up the sign; she called Budd and complained. He choked on his cigar and asked me to keep a low profile for a while.

I made a pest of myself with my questions. I wasn't satisfied with knowing the way things were done; I wanted to know *why* they were done that way, *why* they weren't done some other way.

Quite often, there was no good reason.

Eventually, Budd wrote an article for a trade magazine in which he said, in part:

> That's what we too often lack: the questioning mind, the objective approach, the persistence so necessary to complete the assignment with skill and success, the pride of achievement.
>
> Where do we get this choice mind? We keep looking and we keep training. Sometimes maturity comes walking in the door. More often it flourishes from careful teaching and encouragement.
>
> We've got one on the vine at Halle's—a young man in his early twenties, totally deaf since illness struck him at the age of six, an honor graduate from a midwestern university's school of journalism.
>
> He's been fired from one job. He's been a little spoiled, perhaps, by his friends, as the handicapped so often are. He's been brash and full of beans. He drives a red roadster and I suspect pinches the girls.
>
> But he's got a magnificent mind...inquisitive, curious, agile, uninterrupted by outside noise. And he reads like a

demon. Now he's starting to write persuasively, with grace, with substance.

Don't disturb him. Don't steal him from us yet.

Just write me periodically and inquire whether he's working for me or I'm working for him.

I certainly hadn't graduated with honors, and my six-year-old Pontiac convertible was green, not red.

But Budd's comment about writing persuasively made me think, for the first time, about making a career out of what I had assumed was a temporary interlude in advertising.

I didn't know it yet, but my embryonic career in journalism had been aborted.

Some people are never able to understand that I cannot hear anything at all. Like the woman who worked in the window display department, next to the advertising department.

On my way downstairs for lunch one day, I stepped out of our department on the eleventh floor and into an elevator going down. The elevator was already crowded with noontime traffic from the twelfth floor, where the executive offices were.

Just before the doors closed, the woman ran out of the display department and squeezed into the elevator next to me.

We were jammed together shoulder to shoulder.

She turned her head so that her mouth was a couple of inches from my ear, and shouted at the top of her lungs:

"HELLO, LEW!"

The stares of the executives burned into the back of my neck.

On the other side of me, the elevator operator wrinkled her brow sympathetically and smiled.

She was no more than five feet tall, and looked about 14 years old. I smiled back, momentarily forgetting my discomfort.

Just then, as the elevator doors opened to a crowd of people on the tenth floor, the woman stuck her elbow into my ribs and screamed:

"*HOW ARE YOU?*"

Unfortunately, I did not have the presence of mind to bolt from the car and take another elevator or the escalator.

So I endured the longest and most agonizing elevator ride of my life as

we
stopped
at
every
single
floor
on
the
way
down.

One of my jobs was to baby-sit celebrities when they came to the store for a personal appearance.

One day, Cary Grant was the commentator for a fashion show in the tea room. I took him in hand from the time he stepped out of his limo until he stepped back in a couple of hours later.

I didn't have much to do. He was a pleasant, undemanding person who didn't ask for anything more than a glass of water.

As he was leaving, he shook my hand—just as the photographer from PR snapped a picture. An hour later, the photographer handed me a print.

There wasn't any point in having a picture of Cary Grant shaking my hand unless I showed it to someone.

So, on the way up to my office, I showed it to the elevator operator.

She was the same diminutive girl who had sympathized with me when the screamer yelled in my ear. She was quite attractive, with short-cropped dark hair and a perky smile.

"Look—Cary Grant and me."

She studied the picture for a moment—then looked up at me with innocent eyes.

"Which one is Cary Grant?"

The elevator reached the eleventh floor. I didn't get off.

"My name's Lew. What's yours?"

"Barbara."

"Can I drive you home after work?"

"Yes."

Four months later, we were married.

Driving Barbara home that first evening, I found out that she was four years older than she looked. She had graduated from high school a few weeks earlier, was working at Halle's that summer, and would be entering Ohio State University in the fall.

It was almost a year since I had found myself on the wrong side of the football stadium. I had finally accepted reality: that chapter of my life was closed.

Barbara was not only opening a new chapter; she was starting a whole new book. She proved how colossally naive I had been in thinking that Barbara from the Point was the only person who could have the desire and the ability to share my life.

She soon made me realize how much I had underestimated both myself and other people.

It was a revelation I never forgot.

Looking back, neither Barbara nor I can remember how or when she learned I was deaf—so, apparently, it was an insignificant factor between us from the beginning. We saw each other almost every day at the department store, so making contact was no problem.

Barbara's father was pleasant and easygoing; her mother tended to be more birdlike and wound up.

Both of them seemed to accept me for what I was—a relatively nice Jewish boy on the way up, maybe a little bit different from the other boys Barbara had been dating. I had a college degree and a professional job and a car, which wasn't a bad start.

Like most young people in the relatively low-key Eisenhower years, neither of us was into political or social awareness, let alone activism; the turbulent '60s were yet to come.

Perhaps it was sheer chance that we later turned out to hold, on a wide range of subjects, similar views that we didn't even know we had.

Or perhaps we developed them together.

Neither of us had any taste for the pomp and circumstance of a formal wedding, nor did we want to open the door to arguments with either set of parents about the dubious wisdom of Barbara getting married at the age of 18.

So one day we decided that the following month we would get in the car and drive to Chicago—stopping in Indiana (where the minimum age was 18) to have a justice of the peace make it legal.

On the appointed day, I rang her doorbell at 9 a.m.

No answer.

I rang again.

No answer.

Had she changed her mind and gone to work?

Had her parents discovered the plan and locked her up in her room, where she was shouting for me to rescue her?

Was the doorbell out of order?

I couldn't hear what was happening, and my imagination was working overtime.

There was a pay phone on the corner, but no one was outside on the quiet residential street to make a call for me.

It was a very, very inconvenient moment to be deaf.

Expecting her parents to come charging out with fire in their eyes, I tentatively rang the doorbell again.

At last, the door opened a crack and pair of bleary eyes peered through the opening.

"Oh, it's you. What time is it?"

"A quarter after nine."

"Sorry. I forgot to set my alarm. Come on in."

We finally made it across the state line and went to see a justice of the peace.

He was about a head shorter than I was, and had something wrong with his neck; his chin rested on his chest, and his face pointed straight down at the floor.

Since I couldn't see his face, I couldn't read his lips.

No problem. When the time came, Barbara poked me in the ribs with her elbow. "I do."

Meanwhile, back in Cleveland, Barbara's parents came home and found the note she had scribbled on the way out: "We went to get married. We'll call you from Chicago."

By the time we reached Chicago, they had tracked down my parents by phone and the four of them had decided that Barbara and I should get married all over again the following weekend, this time in the synagogue by our rabbi.

No problem. When the time came, I recalled how to pronounce the Hebrew "ch" sound. I still had my postnasal drip.

A week after getting remarried, we returned to Cleveland and rented a two-room apartment. We stayed with Barbara's parents while I painted the walls after work.

One evening, as I started to paint, I realized that I had forgotten to take newspapers to spread on the floor. So I picked up the phone and dialed the number of Barbara's home.

I imagined the mechanical relays clicking into place at the phone exchange...the phone ringing...Barbara walking over to the phone and picking it up...Barbara saying "Hello."

"Hello, Barbara. Please bring some newspapers for the floor."

Ten minutes later, she walked in with an armful of newspapers.

For most people, the shift from living alone to living with someone is a dramatic change in lifestyle. For a deaf person, the change is even more dramatic—because a deaf person who lives alone is even more alone than is a hearing person who lives alone.

Living by myself in a rented room in a strange town, I had depended on my landlady to take or make telephone calls for me. Despite her gracious and unstinting help, such an arrangement was unavoidably inhibiting to people on the other end of the line.

It isn't easy for people to call up just to chew the fat and find out what's new when an intermediary is relaying the dialogue.

Phone calls to set up a get-together or to convey information were never a problem. But making small talk on the phone to keep in touch or to develop new friendships was awkward.

So marriage itself brought steady companionship into my life.

But beyond the factor of Barbara's presence, there was the factor of her hearing. Her ability to use the phone was my invaluable link to the world outside our home.

With Barbara in my life, I could not only reach over and touch her. I could also reach out and touch anyone over the phone.

An unfortunate by-product of marriage between two deaf people is that it perpetuates their isolation from the mainstream.

In the hearing world, social relationships tend to be built and maintained and expanded through telephone conversations.

The conversations themselves are social contacts through which people keep in touch and enjoy being with each other without actually being together. And the calls are a means for arranging get-togethers—either planned or spontaneous.

So, from a practical point of view, it makes sense for me, as a deaf person, to have a hearing spouse who can help our family build, maintain and expand relationships among hearing people without the inhibiting factor of deafness.

I am not belittling the friendships between deaf people and the ease with which they communicate within their own sphere. I am saying that there is a big world outside with all kinds of interesting people for those who wish to partake of more.

Nor am I saying I chose a life mate on the basis of Barbara's ability to make telephone calls. I can't say that I possessed great foresight about the telephone factor. Perhaps it was lurking not so deeply in my subconscious. But if it was, it wasn't the only factor, of course.

The main reason why I married Barbara was because, as an immature 22-year-old, I thought I was in love with her.

Today, as an immature 61-year-old, I still think I am.

There is most certainly a great deal more to Barbara than her ability to hear. She is very much a person in her own right, with her own life as a potter and a mother and a grandmother.

She is my best friend, although she does not share my obsession with computers.

And she is my worst (and therefore best) critic.

Still, the issue here is that she complements my person in many ways that only a hearing person can do...in practical ways that have had an undeniable impact on our lives.

It's a joy to chat with our daughters and grandchildren on the phone whenever the mood strikes. I get vicarious pleasure from watching Barbara's face light up as she listens to their voices.

Yes, we correspond by electronic mail and fax, but these can't compare with the immediacy and emotional impact of hearing each other's voices over the phone.

Today, I operate my marketing communications business from an office in my home. Sometimes only a phone call can take care of a situation with professional speed, efficiency and convenience—especially if it's a back-and-forth conversation.

I am also a computer consultant for Tel Aviv University. If the people there couldn't get real-time help to their problems quickly and efficiently by telephone, I wouldn't get the work.

Then there are are the phone conversations with banks or utility companies or governmental departments or doctors or lawyers or accountants or whatever.

It may not be fair, but it's an undeniable fact of life: the phone is so central to our society that those who cannot use it freely, efficiently and independently are definitely handicapped.

But what about the TDD (telecommunications device for the deaf), which allows deaf people to type messages to each other over telephone lines?

And what about TDD relay operators, who relay conversations between a deaf person with a TDD and a hearing person with a regular telephone?

Although the devices are quite useful, they are so painfully slow that using them has been compared to swimming in molasses. The relay operators can be okay for short, simple conversations—but extended or technical sessions are something else.

Tomorrow may well be a different story—for those who can wait for tomorrow. For example, it has been three decades since the introduction of the Picture Phone—a telephone with a television screen. At the time, I thought it was a godsend because I would be able to speechread the person at the other end of the line.

But I'm still waiting for the technology to become feasible.

Even the latest videophones are of no use to deaf people. Those that operate on regular phone lines have such poor images that there's no way they can be used for speechreading or signing. Those with usable video quality require special telephone lines that are available in only a few locations.

The evolving technology—what there is of it—is definitely better than nothing. But a hearing spouse is infinitely better.

When we go to a play or a movie or watch TV, Barbara helps me follow the dialogue (although I try to get the script from the stage manager, and many TV programs are closed captioned).

When we're traveling, she can hear announcements at airports and aboard aircraft. When we're abroad, it's easier for Barbara to understand people in hotels, restaurants, shops, banks and taxis than it is for me to speechread their heavily accented English.

When I was in small-claims court and the lawyer for the other guy was lying through his teeth to the judge, Barbara relayed his words to me in time for me to refute them. I won.

Individually, these benefits may not always be of earthshaking importance. But cumulatively, they dramatically improve the quality of my life.

Barbara's ability to hear has not only been essential in expanding and enriching our social and family relationships in the hearing world. Beyond that, it has facilitated our daily lives and my business activities.

For me—repeat, for *me*—to have married a deaf woman would have been to shoot myself in the foot.

When I said so on the electronic forum, I generated a flood of critical comments from people who thought I was putting down deaf women.

Obviously, they missed my point.

The flip side to the issue of deaf/hearing marriages is, naturally, the perspective of the hearing spouse.

Don't the benefits to me come at Barbara's expense?

Sometimes yes, sometimes no. Sometimes it's like being pregnant and eating for two; she's doing it anyway, and it's no big deal to do a little more. Such as when she's talking to our daughters and grandchildren on the telephone.

When she makes a phone call to a client or supplier, it's no different from what anyone would do to lend a hand (or an ear) in the family business.

As a matter of fact, it's even easier for Barbara—because she can make or take a call without getting up from her pottery wheel. Her studio, like my office, is in our home.

One thing that occasionally does get under her skin: sometimes she herself has to miss what's going on when she's explaining to me what's going on. She can't stop the play or the movie or the TV program while she fills me in (unless it's on the VCR), so she may not get some of the dialogue or twists in the plot.

I try to minimize the impact of my interruptions by waiting for a lull in the dialogue before I hit on her with a "Huh?" Still, she gets peeved once in a while—especially if we're watching a tightly knit detective story.

The advent of closed captioning on TV and videotapes has been a great boon to me—and a great relief to Barbara.

Just in case a deaf person may be tempted to marry a hearing person, Harlan Lane passes along a ridiculous warning in *When the Mind Hears,* his admittedly partisan chronicle of the deaf:

> Hearing persons willing to marry someone deaf are commonly inferior to their spouse morally, socially, or intellectually, or seek the alliance for reasons other than love.

When I showed this to Barbara, it made her day.

What I find notable is not only the idiocy of the statement (which Lane paraphrases from someone's speech).

Even more remarkable is that Deaf people who admire Lane don't seem to realize that it dumps on the deaf themselves, by characterizing them as undesirable spouses.

This passage has to be the ultimate put-down of the deaf, and Lane wrote nothing to dissociate himself from it.

But it did get me to thinking about Barbara's perspective.

Given the perceptions and misperceptions that hearing people have of deaf people, and the undeniable problems that many deaf people have, why did Barbara marry a deaf person when she could have married a nice Jewish boy with normal hearing?

So I asked her just now.

Her reply:

"I was only 18 years old. What did I know?"

12

Putting me on

My father's dedication to crossword puzzles, intense as it was, is exceeded by Barbara's. When she's working on the puzzle in the *New York Times Magazine* with a ball-point pen, she's in a seven-letter state derived from Sanskrit.

Close to midnight one Sunday soon after our marriage, Barbara was engrossed in that morning's *NYTM* crossword. I finished the book I was reading and stood up to go to bed. Barbara said she'd be there in a minute.

I went into our bedroom, stripped off my clothes, and stretched out on the bed. A few minutes went by as I lay there thinking about what would be happening as soon as Barbara joined me.

As my anticipation grew, so did my state of preparedness.

More minutes went by. No Barbara. The crossword must have been tougher than usual.

Finally, my impatience got the better of me. I got out of bed and strode purposefully into the living room, ready for action.

Unfortunately, I could not hear the two voices that would have warned me that Barbara was talking with our next-door neighbor, who had come over to borrow a bottle of cough syrup for her sick child.

Fortunately, the neighbor's back was toward me. Unfortunately, I spun around so fast in my haste to get out of there that my state of preparedness collided with the doorway. Doubled over in agony, I finally made it to the safety of the bedroom.

Deafness has calamitous moments, as I learned the hard way.

The months passed quickly. We wanted children, and pregnancy didn't mix with college, so Barbara opted out of going to Ohio State.

The following spring, Budd Gore told me he was going back to Chicago to be advertising manager of the *Daily News*. I saw no point in sticking around Cleveland, so I quit too. We loaded our furniture into a U-Haul and drove to Chicago. .

Budd had been my mentor at the *Sun-Times* and at Halle's, getting me into newspaper work and then into advertising. Now he would be selling advertising space. It was time for me to get out from under his wing and fly on my own.

So there we were—me without a job, and Barbara due to give birth in a few months. My parents let us stay in their house until we found our own place after I found a job.

I had decided that my future lay in advertising, so I made the rounds of the ad agencies and mailed out my resume.

But it was still the same old catch-22: they wanted writers with agency experience, and you couldn't get the experience without first breaking into an agency as a beginner. As the weeks went by and spring became summer, my spirits sank.

Early on, my father offered to buy me a hardware store. "All you have to do is stand behind the counter and take in the money." He meant well, I suppose, but I declined.

Then, during an interview with a creative director, he telephoned his counterpart at another agency across the river and asked if she would like to see me. She told him to send me over.

I walked across the LaSalle Street bridge to the Merchandise Mart for the impromptu interview and spent an hour with the creative director. A couple of days later she called me up and told me I had a copywriting job if I wanted it.

A week after that, Debby was born at the University of Chicago's Lying-In Hospital. Talk about timing.

As a neophyte, I was expected to keep my eyes open and my mouth shut while I learned what they don't teach you in school about advertising. It ranged from the sublime to the ridiculous.

In America's consumer-oriented economy, advertising is one of the most powerful forces in the marketplace. It informs people about what's available and helps them decide what to buy. It's a combination of teaching and selling—and I found that I hugely enjoyed being both a teacher and a salesman.

Writing a TV commercial for a Cleveland beer named P.O.C., I came up with an idea for an animated cartoon sequence in which the hops (the cone-shaped seeds added to the brewing process to impart flavor to the beer) had arms and legs, wore sunglasses, snapped their fingers, and talked hip.

I called them the hippity hops of P.O.C. Part of the jingle went:

The hippitier the hops,
the better the beer will be

This happened about 30 years before the California Raisin Board started running suspiciously similar commercials.

Ever since, I've regretted being unable to hear the chorus sing my masterpiece on television.

But my deafness had nothing to do with it. The storyboard was shot down at an agency review before it even reached the client.

Today, most agencies subscribe more or less to certain standards in advertising—partly because of the efforts of consumer watchdog groups and governmental regulators.

But a few decades ago, the field was more freewheeling. While the agencies didn't exactly sell snake oil, they did blow smoke at times.

One of our clients was a mattress company. As a traffic-building promotion for the furniture stores in the New York area, it ran a treasure hunt for a hidden $100,000 check. My job was to write the radio commercials containing the clues.

However, I didn't have the faintest idea where the check was hidden.

Rather than risk paying out $100,000, the client had bought an insurance policy for $5,000 to cover the possibility that someone would find the check.

The problem was that the insurance company insisted on hiding the check itself—and wouldn't tell either the client or the agency where it was.

All they would do was give us a list of places where the check was *not* hidden.

For example, I would be told that the check was *not* at Yankee Stadium. Then I would write the following so-called clue:

The Babe was 3 and Lou was 4 and Joe was number 5
But this is not the place to go to keep your hopes alive

The idiocy went on like this for two weeks.

Then, according to the rules of the promotion, the value of the check started dropping each day.

Finally, when the value was down to about $10,000 or so, the insurance company started providing us with clues to the check's location (but not the location itself).

Eventually, when the check was worth $5,000, somebody found it inside a hollow tree in a field somewhere out on Long Island.

The promotion may have complied with the letter of the law at that time, but the spirit was less than kosher.

I complained about it, but who listens to the new kid on the block?

The agency had two creative directors who competed fiercely against each other. Eventually, the one who had hired me left the agency and I came under the purview of the other.

One day, my new supervisor stopped by my office and told me that a friend of hers who owned an art studio needed some part-time copywriting, and would I be interested in moonlighting?

I would. Especially since we had an extra mouth to feed, now that our second daughter, Julie, had arrived.

The job was writing a 48-page catalogue for a trading stamp company. The space limitations were even tighter than those for department store ads, so the job was fairly mechanical: boiling down the information to about 20 words for each item.

It was easy, mindless work that I did at home during the evening and on weekends. Fortunately, it was the baseball season—so I positioned my typewriter and reference material in front of the TV and tuned in the Sox games.

The Sox won the pennant for the first time in 40 years (only to be blown away in the World Series by the then-Brooklyn Dodgers).

And the money from the catalogue job paid for a sleek four-month-old Oldsmobile to replace our five-year-old Plymouth.

Although the catalogue job was hardly in the forefront of creative advertising, it was an opportune initiation into freelancing. Soon I was moonlighting for a diverse group of clients—writing print and TV ads, documentary films, brochures and books.

The clients came to me by word of mouth. Some were small agencies that could not afford a full-time big-league writer. Some were large agencies that occasionally needed some outside help to handle an overload of work. And sometimes I worked directly with a company instead of through an advertising agency.

I enjoyed the variety and the independence of working at my own schedule, not to mention the money. Freelancers earned about twice as much per hour as did staff copywriters with comparable talent and experience.

Eventually, when I had been at the agency for four years, a senior writer came up to me with a message from the creative director.

"The Dragon Lady thinks that since your freelancing is going well, you might like to do it full-time. What do you think of quitting your job and putting all of your time into freelancing?"

It appealed to me, so I did.

It wasn't until later that I realized that for all practical purposes I had been fired, although quite subtly. And I eventually found out that the creative director simply wanted to get rid of the people who had been hired by her erstwhile rival—a common practice in the business world.

Still, it was a good time to make a move—and freelancing was a good direction in which to make it.

Much of my business came in by word of mouth. One client would tell another about me, and then I'd get a call asking me to come in and talk about an assignment.

On the first call from a new client, his secretary usually didn't know I was deaf—mainly because he didn't know, either.

So the call would go something like this:

"Hello?"

"Is Lew Golan in?"

"Yes, he is. Who's calling, please?"

"George Whyte of Red, Whyte and Blue Advertising."

"Okay, hold on and I'll get him."

Barbara comes over to my desk and picks up the extension.

"Yes?"

"Mr. Golan? Please hold for Mr. Whyte."

"Lew is here. Go ahead and put Mr. Whyte on."

"Please put Mr. Golan on. Then I'll switch him to Mr. Whyte."

"Lew is deaf. He cannot talk on the phone."

Suspiciously, the secretary asks, "Are you sure?"

"Yes."

"You're not putting me on?"

"No. And I'm not putting Lew on, either. I'm speaking for him."

The secretaries were playing the power game.

It's one-upmanship to have the other guy wait for you to get on the line.

So the secretaries sparred with each other on behalf of their bosses, each trying to get the other person on the line first.

Barbara always won.

Freelancing for an advertising agency in Israel, I was writing ads for one of the country's biggest food companies.

One day, Barbara received a phone call from the company's chairman of the board. He did not know me.

He had called the ad agency with an urgent request for a special project—a brochure on the foods of Israel, to be distributed to incoming passengers on El Al flights.

However, the agency people who worked on his account were at an international convention. So the agency secretary suggested that he call me directly.

"I'd like Mr. Golan to come up to Haifa and meet with me. My office is on the second floor of the main plant, and there is no passenger elevator. Will this be a problem?"

"Not at all. Why do you ask?"

"Well, the secretary at the advertising agency said that Mr. Golan is handicapped...."

Some deaf people say that they would rather be deaf, even if it were possible for them to somehow become hearing. They say—and many of them do believe—that it is better to be deaf.

This may sound like a sour-grapes coping tactic, and for many of them, that's exactly what it is—a way of accepting their deafness by denigrating hearing.

Most of the people who take this attitude were born deaf, and therefore cannot make a realistic comparison.

But some people who lost their hearing—and know what both hearing and deafness are like—also make the same claim.

Most hearing people are bewildered by this attitude. So am I.

I certainly accept that I am totally and permanently deaf. And I've been doing just fine without being able to hear.

But even after 55 years, I haven't lost my sense of proportion.

Given my druthers, I'd rather have normal hearing. I don't have to dump on hearing in order to show that I accept my deafness.

It's one thing to recognize that deafness has some indisputable benefits in certain isolated instances, and to wish you were deaf (or be glad that you're deaf) *at those times.*

I certainly do.

The buzzing of insects, for example, sometimes keeps Barbara awake on summer nights while I sleep soundly.

It's another thing to say, after considering all the pros and cons of deafness and hearing, that you'd prefer to be permanently deaf rather than have normal hearing.

I certainly don't.

I realize that whatever benefits there are in being deaf, they are far outweighed by the benefits of hearing.

The bottom line is that deafness is *not* the best of all possible worlds.

Still, although I would rather be able to hear, I'm not rending my clothes over being deaf or holding my breath while waiting for medical science or technology to restore my hearing.

And I certainly don't mind taking advantage of the major benefit of being deaf: freedom from noise pollution.

To a hearing person, a sound may be pleasurable or necessary (or both). If it's neither, it's noise. It all depends on the individual; noise is in the ear of the beholder.

The laughter of a child at play may be a pleasurable sound to his friends, a necessary reassurance to his mother in another room, a disturbing noise to his napping baby sister.

The honking of a horn may be a pleasurable stimulant to a joyriding punk, a necessary warning to a pedestrian crossing the street, an irritating noise to residents of the neighborhood.

An aria from Verdi may be a blissful relaxant to an aficionado, a necessary lesson to a music student, an incomprehensible noise to a heavy metal rocker.

Someone who is functionally deaf—with some residual hearing, but unable to distinguish the sounds of spoken words—can be bothered by loud noises. Certain sounds, such as the music from some instruments, can actually be painful to him.

Even those who cannot hear at all do not necessarily live in a peacefully silent world. A very common affliction is tinnitus. This is a buzzing, ringing or whistling sound that is generated internally.

Those who have it suffer the disadvantages of deafness without enjoying the advantages. They cannot hear pleasurable or necessary external sounds, yet they are compelled to hear internal noises.

Fortunately, my deafness is completely silent. No external or internal noises ever irritate me or distract me or disrupt my work.

Consequently, my environment is relatively pleasant and relaxed most of the time, wherever I am. Even when visual or emotional stimuli are creating tension or discomfort at a particular time or place, the lack of noise is a mitigating factor.

In practical terms, this means that I can work at my writing almost anywhere, oblivious to my surroundings.

During preparations for homecoming at the University of Illinois, half a dozen hammers were pounding on the framework of my fraternity's float; more hammers were attaching decorations to the house. The university's fight song blared from a loudspeaker. The pledges were chanting the war cry of the week: "Go, Illini...beat Iowa State!"

And in the middle of the commotion, I concentrated quite easily on writing a defense of my prediction that Dwight D. Eisenhower would win the Republican presidential nomination over Senator Robert Taft.

During the Scud attacks on Tel Aviv, I sat in our shelter and jotted notes as I conceptualized my next project—undisturbed by the thunderous roar of Patriot missiles being launched overhead, or the explosions of Scuds nearby, or the crying of babies upset at being taken from their beds at 2:30 in the morning.

I can close my eyes and take a 20-minute catnap just about anywhere, sitting up or lying down.

I can sleep peacefully through the night while Barbara is jolted awake by the crash of thunderclaps during a violent storm, or by the explosion of Katyushas a few meters away during a predawn terrorist attack in the Galilee.

At social gatherings where the din is overwhelming—such as at a large party where everyone is talking at the same time—I am spared the discomfort of listening to the racket.

Paradoxically, however, even though I can't hear it, the noise *does* bother me.

It has no effect on my speechreading. In noisy environments, in fact, I can often understand better than hearing people can.

But the noise makes it harder for others to understand what I am saying; it forces me to make a greater effort to speak clearly and at the correct volume.

That's why, at Lisa's wedding, I told the band leader to keep the volume down (instead of blasting it out as bands always do at weddings and bar mitzvahs). Everyone except Barbara thought I was cracking a joke.

But the fact is that a too-loud band not only bothers hearing people; it bothers me, too.

It's difficult to judge the volume of noise at social gatherings or in a public place, so the only way I know how loud to make my voice is through trial and error.

Rather than speak too loudly by accident, I try to err on the low side—then, if necessary, raise my voice until I get through to the other person.

Appearances often can be deceiving, especially in public places. There's a frozen yogurt store that looks like a noisy place. It has bright, high-key lighting, tiled floor and walls, is favored by teenagers, and usually has a crowd of customers. Whenever I go there, I automatically raise my voice—and Barbara has to tell me to turn down the volume because it's really very quiet.

Or we may go to a dimly lit restaurant with carpeting and drapes and a few scattered customers. It *looks* very quiet, so I try to speak softly—until Barbara tells me that hard rock is blasting from the speakers concealed in the ceiling overhead.

Sometimes I get so wrapped up that I simply forget where I am, and neglect to match my voice to the situation.

One time when I was a teenager, I was deep in conversation with a distant cousin I hadn't seen in a couple of years, and I let out a delighted laugh—only to have my mother hurry over and remind me that I was at my grandfather's funeral.

13

The nearest warm body

At the office one afternoon, I asked my secretary to call Barbara at home and tell her I would be a little late.

The phone was answered by Julie, then three years old.

"Hello, Julie," said my secretary. "I'm calling for your father."

"He isn't home."

It's really quite simple for people to make a call for me. Suppose, for example, I'm at a client's office and we finish up an hour sooner than expected. Rather than kill time, I want to move up my next appointment. So I ask the first client's secretary to call the second client. She dials the number.

"Hello. I'm calling for Lew Golan. Is it okay if he comes over at 1:30 instead of 2:30?" Pause. "No problem? Good." She raises her eyebrows at me to see if there's anything else. I shake my head. "Thank you. Good-bye."

The key to keeping my calls short and sweet is for the caller to remain anonymous and not get involved in the conversation. But some people add an unnecessary and detailed explanation of their own—especially if they are talkative by nature. They mean well, and I don't want to sound ungrateful, but....

During my years as a freelance writer and producer, working out of an office at home, Barbara has made most of my calls. Through repeated calls to the same people, Barbara has come to know them quite well—although she never meets most of them in person.

She also has made most of my non-business calls—such as when I talk to a friend about going to a ball game or solving a computer problem. Since my friends are her friends, too, she knows them and their spouses socially.

This means that when Barbara makes a call for me, she is usually calling someone who is at least an acquaintance and probably a friend of hers. Consequently, the call often turns out to be more *her* call than *my* call.

Barbara and the other person will start off exchanging the usual pleasantries, and ask what's new. Eventually, if they don't get side-tracked, they get around to the purpose of *my* call. Then, when my stuff is finished, they go back to *their* call.

Occasionally they go so far on a tangent that I have to remind Barbara that it's *my* call. And more than once they have been so wrapped up that they hung up without getting around to me.

When Barbara is on the phone for me, she listens and repeats the words at the same time, like a simultaneous interpreter at the United Nations. To avoid confusing the person at the other end, she does not use her voice when she repeats his words to me.

If we are talking about something in which she has little or no interest, such as computers, she often does not pay any attention to what she is hearing and repeating.

Which means that if I happen to miss a word and ask her to say it again, she may not be able to—because she can't remember what she said a moment ago.

This happens even if she is talking in Hebrew with the person at the other end and in English with me. She is not just repeating words mindlessly—she is translating from Hebrew to English one way, and from English to Hebrew the other way—yet for the life of her, she sometimes can't recall what she just said. She has to ask the other person to repeat it.

We were visiting a friend of ours who had come down with laryngitis and couldn't speak on the phone. While we were there, he asked Barbara to make a phone call for him.

But when Barbara started relaying to him the words spoken at the other end of the line, our friend couldn't understand a thing she was saying.

From force of habit, Barbara wasn't using her voice.

During the Big Blizzard in Chicago several years ago, it took me four hours to drive home. Halfway there, I pulled into a gas station to call Barbara and let her know where I was.

The owner gets Barbara on the phone and says:

"Hello. This is the Texaco station on Clark Street. There's a guy here who says he's deaf. Do you know him? Well, he says to tell you it will be another couple of hours before he gets there."

He hangs up. "Yeah, she says she knows you."

When I ask people to make a phone call, I know I'm imposing on them. Barbara doesn't have much of a choice; she married me for bad or for worse. But others have no such obligation.

Still, most people have been willing to lend me an ear when the need arises; I very rarely encounter resentment.

My ability to function with a high degree of independence in the hearing world is partly the result of my deliberate dependence on people in this one area.

Many deaf people refrain from asking someone to make a call for them; some are inhibited about imposing, and others want to remain as independent as possible.

I don't like asking people, either, but I see no point in handicapping myself further by passing up this essential facilitator of contemporary life. When I need to make a call, I just look around for the nearest phone and the nearest warm body and do what I have to do. It helps to have a thick skin.

One day I was sitting in the boarding area at O'Hare Airport, waiting for my flight to Paris.

To pass the time, I was thinking about the cost-control program I was developing for the marketing agency where I was executive vice president. At that moment, a programmer was writing the computer code according to my instructions.

Suddenly, I had an idea for a better way for the program to do a particular function. I had to reach the programmer immediately before he wasted time and money by going too far in the wrong direction.

There was a bank of pay phones on the wall. A few feet from me stood a group of young adults with ski equipment who were talking animatedly, laughing and shoving each other.

I stepped up to the nearest couple and said "Excuse me, can you make a phone call for me?"

The woman and the man standing next to her looked at me in surprise, burst out laughing, and turned their attention back to the group without saying anything to me.

You win some, you lose some. So I repeated my request to another woman in the group. She agreed instantly.

As we walked over to the phones, I asked her why the others had laughed.

It turned out they were on their way to the French Alps, and were trying to remember their high-school French.

The man had said in bad French, "The telephone in my hotel room is broken again." Then I had asked him to make a call.

They hadn't been making fun of me. They thought *I* had been making fun of *them*.

The woman spent 10 minutes on the phone as we gave the programmer my instructions and answered his questions. She was very nice about it, as most people are.

All I had to do was ask.

On the return trip, the plane to New York was late and I missed my connecting flight to Chicago. Barbara was supposed to pick me up. I had to let her know I would be on a later flight.

After I got off the plane at Kennedy, I walked over to the phones and looked around.

A young woman in jeans was sitting on the floor with her back against the wall. I squatted in front of her to bring my face level with hers. "Hello. Can you do me a favor, please? Will you phone my wife and tell her I missed my plane?"

"No problem."

Why don't I don't mention my deafness when I ask someone to make a call?

Because I don't want to sound as though I'm milking them for sympathy, like those people who go around airports and shopping malls handing out cards that say "I'm deaf, please buy my pencils."

I'm asking for a favor, which is something quite different.

Most people readily agree to call. Then, as part of telling them what I would like them to say on the phone, I may or may not explain that I'm deaf, depending on the circumstances. Some of the people may have already assumed that.

If people react to my first request with hesitation or a quizzical look, I explain right away that I'm deaf. In this context it's an answer to their unspoken question ("What's the matter, can't you do it yourself?") rather than an appeal for sympathy.

For whatever it's worth, that's my rationale. I don't mind asking for a favor, but I do mind giving the appearance of trying to play on people's emotions.

In case it isn't obvious, I am disgusted by the people who pass out those cards pleading for you to buy their pencils or whatever because they're deaf.

Given a choice, why do I choose to have a woman call for me rather than a man? Some people will say it's the sexist mentality of a male executive.

Not true. It's simply because women are usually easier for me to speechread. Their faces are much more expressive, and they tend to articulate more clearly than men do.

Today, many deaf people, both oral and signers, swear by the TDD (telecommunications device for the deaf), which looks like a laptop computer plus a telephone handset. It enables them to type messages to each other over the phone line.

And with the help of state relay centers, they can type a message to a TDD relay operator who reads it and relays it vocally to a hearing person on another line. The operator then listens to the spoken response and relays it to the deaf person on a TDD.

One enthusiast told me why he much prefers using a TDD to my system of grabbing the nearest warm body:

> I value my independence highly. Like most deaf people of our generation, I have wretched memories of depending on family and friends for phone communication.
>
> If my wife or son talks for me, the other person is inclined to take the easy way out and discuss with *them* what should be discussed with *me*.
>
> The issue is how the effort of adapting to my deafness should be shared by hearing people. I believe that hearing people should make reasonable accommodations [such as acquiring a TDD or calling through the relay center] to allow a deaf person to have more control over his own life.
>
> I find that professional and business people are becoming more comfortable in communicating via TDD and relay. My doctors, bank, clinics, lawyer and stockbroker all have machines. The state's relay service is free and efficient.
>
> I'm not dogmatic. I recognize that, notwithstanding technical advances, I'm communication impaired in the hearing world. So, at work or in family life, I'll relinquish the communication role if it is not important for me to be on top of the situation.

For example, we're now remodeling our kitchen, and my wife is handling the calls to the designers, sales people and contractor. On the other hand, when I refinanced my home earlier this year, I handled all the business with the lenders, title insurance company, appraiser and my lawyer via TDD or relay or in person.

Nobody values his independence more than I do, and I live a highly independent life.

But a TDD is an unavoidably slow method of communicating anything more than the simplest message.

And if you want to be able to call from anywhere, you must carry a TDD everywhere (although public TDDs are now appearing in airports and similar locations).

There's a trade-off between independence and efficiency.

I find that it is faster, more accurate and more efficient—and easier on the hearing person *at the other end*—for me to recruit the nearest warm body at my end.

Still, there's no question that using a TDD and a relay operator can be invaluable when there is no other way for a deaf person to make a call to a hearing person.

And many deaf people are simply determined to do it on their own, as did an irrepressible woman in Minneapolis who used a TDD and the relay service to raise money for her son's school during a phone-a-thon.

After using stockbrokers in downtown Chicago for several years, I switched to a broker closer to home in suburban Highland Park. After we filled in the forms, it occurred to me to tell him that Barbara would be giving him buy/sell orders over the phone.

"One more thing. I'm deaf."

He looked up.

"This means that other people will be calling you, giving you instructions from me. It will probably be my wife, but it might be my secretary or one of my children or a friend."

"How will I know they're really calling for you?"

"They'll give you my account number."

"Well, I don't feel comfortable about this."

"None of my other brokers ever had a problem with it."

"Okay, here's what we'll do. My middle name is Charles. When someone calls, have him say 'Charles' as the password."

So the first couple of times Barbara called the broker, she said "Hello, Charlie."

By the third call, however, he realized that the CIA stuff was overkill. Somewhat sheepishly, he told Barbara to forget about the password from then on.

But this does bring up a related point: when it comes to phone calls, I have no privacy, no secrets—even if I'm talking about something very confidential.

Since I buttonhole friends, coworkers and strangers on the street to make calls for me, it's like a perpetual wiretap; somebody is always listening in on the conversation.

One morning during the rush hour, I was rear-ended on Edens Expressway when the car behind me in stop-and-go traffic failed to stop. It cost me several hundred dollars worth of damage to the car, several thousand dollars worth of medical and therapy bills, and several years of back and neck pains.

After I filed a suit against the other driver, my lawyer took a sworn statement from her.

The best part was when she said that I had telephoned her and admitted that the accident was my fault.

My lawyer pressed her on that point.

"When did Mr. Golan say that?"

"The day after the accident, he called me up. He said that he was sorry, and that it was all his fault."

"Mr. Golan himself said that on the telephone?"

"Yes."

"Did you say anything to him?"

"Yes. I said he had to pay for the damage to my car."

"Did he answer you?"

"Yes. He said he would pay."

"Are you sure you were talking to Mr. Golan?"

"Yes."

A few days after that, the lawyer for the other driver's insurance company took a deposition from me.

When he found out that I was totally deaf and couldn't have conversed with his client over the phone—which meant that she had lied under oath—he didn't bat an eye.

But the insurance company settled out of court.

No, I hadn't called the other driver—but the fact is, I *could* have had a phone conversation such as she described. And I *could* have spoken directly to my broker on the phone.

Normally, I don't get on the phone myself. When someone calls for me, she functions as a two-way relay—repeating my words to the other person, and the other person's words to me.

But if the subject is complicated or technical, it's easier and faster to speak into the phone myself. Then I hand the phone back so she can listen to the response. In this set-up, she functions as a one-way relay—repeating the other person's words to me.

Carrying this a step further, I had two telephones on my desk when I ran the creative department at a marketing communications agency. I was on one phone while my secretary was on another extension on the opposite side of the desk.

I spoke into the phone, then held on while she listened to the words coming from the other end and mouthed them to me. When we used two phones this way, I did most or all of the talking from my end.

Actually, I had three phones in my office—the two on my desk plus one on the table by the sofa.

At first, a lot of people didn't believe that a *totally deaf* person had *three* telephones. So, for a while, my office was something of a tourist attraction.

All this means that even though the woman who had hit my car had lied when she said I had talked to her on the telephone, and my deafness made her statement appear to be self-evidently false, it wasn't necessarily so.

Although it was quite unbelievable that I would have said the things she claimed I had said, the call itself was not the physical impossibility that the lawyers assumed it was.

In the end, unfortunately, my own lawyer lied to me and ripped me off on the settlement—claiming I had misunderstood him.

On a drizzly May evening in 1967, in the middle of the Cold War, Barbara and I were sitting at a small table in a West Berlin night-club, trying to spot secret agents among the customers.

The club had an unusual feature: every table was connected to the other tables by telephones and pneumatic tubes, and each table had a number prominently displayed. Our table was 434.

It was a discreet high-tech pickup rendezvous. You noted a table number, picked up the phone, dialed the other table, and spoke anonymously with the object of your desires. Or you could send a note through the pneumatic tube system.

I've always been clean-shaven—except for a few months that year when I had a full reddish-black beard in the counterculture style to disguise the fact that I was a capitalist pig.

As we sat there taking in the ambiance, Barbara heard a thud in the pneumatic tube.

She opened the carrier and took out a slip of paper, then leaned over to the adjoining table and asked a man sitting there to translate the message from German.

It was for the man with the beard at table 434, from table 479, with a question that went right to the point:

Are you here alone?

Barbara dialed 479 on the phone. When a woman answered, Barbara said that her husband was unable to hear on the phone, but she would relay anything the woman might want to say.

The woman said that since we were together there was no point in pursuing the matter—but thanks anyway. The conversation went on for another minute, with no further reference to me.

James Bond never had such problems.

Driving back through East Germany, we came to a multi-stage checkpoint that barred our re-entry to West Germany. At the first stage, the East German soldiers searched our car thoroughly.

They found some books we had bought about the Berlin Wall, detailing the attempts of East Berliners to flee to the West.

The guards took the books and waved us on.

"Hey," I said. "Those are my books."

"No good. Lies. No wall."

"You kidding? We were there a few hours ago. We saw it."

"Lies. Go."

"I paid for them. Give them back or give me my money back."

The guard dumped the books in a trash can. "Go!"

It's hard to beat an argument like that, so we got back in the car as the guard picked up a telephone. I drove to the next stage, where more East German soldiers were checking passports.

A soldier looked at my beard, then at the picture of my clean-shaven face in my two-year-old passport issued for our previous trip to Europe. He shook his head. "Get out."

I got out of the car. He held the passport up to my face, then shook his head again.

He was standing in front of a guardhouse about the size of a toll-road collector's booth. It had no windows—just a slit at eye level about two inches high and eight inches wide.

The soldier stuck my passport through the slit. Moments later, a pair of hard blue eyes stared out through the opening.

Then the East German soldier turned his head and looked at me expectantly.

It dawned on me that whoever was inside the guardhouse was talking to me and waiting for an answer.

But I couldn't see his mouth.

"I can't hear you. I have to see your lips."

The blue eyes narrowed, then disappeared from the slit.

The door opened and an officer stepped out.

A Soviet officer.

"This is not your passport."

"That's what I looked like before I grew my beard."

"Then prove it. Shave it off."

Actually, I had been planning on taking it off as soon as we returned to the States. But my congenital stubbornness kicked in.

"You're kidding." I covered the bottom part of my face with my hand. "Look at my nose and eyes. Just like in the passport."

Behind our car, the traffic was backed up until it went out of sight around a bend in the road. But the Soviet officer acted as if he had all the time in the world. He shook his head.

"Besides, I didn't bring a razor with me."

The officer stared at me silently for a while. Then he handed back my passport and waved me on.

As visions of an expense-paid side trip to KGB headquarters faded from my mind, I drove quickly across the border into West Germany—with Barbara laughing all the way.

"What's so funny?"

"He was just teasing you."

"What makes you think so?"

"You were giving the guards a hard time about the books. So they probably phoned the passport checkpoint and fingered you for some hassling."

Naw. It couldn't have been that innocuous.

I'm still convinced that by bearding the Soviet officer, I came within a whisker of starting an international incident.

It could have been a very close shave.

14

Different from other fathers

When Debby was two years old, Barbara and I explained the facts of life to her.

"Daddy can't hear what you say. When you talk to him, he looks at your mouth. His eyes tell him what you are saying."

The next time Debby wanted to tell me a secret, she cupped her hands around her mouth and whispered into my left eye.

One day when I was working at home, the phone rang. Barbara was out.

Debby, then three years old, took the call.

"Who is it?" I asked her.

"I don't know."

"Is it a man or a woman?"

"A man."

"Ask him what his name is."

She spoke into the phone. "What's your name?"

She listened, then shook her head.

"I can't understand."

"Ask him to call back later."

"Call back later."

She listened, then held out the phone. "He wants to talk to you."

Obviously, it was someone who didn't know me. If someone called me and one of the kids answered, the caller would ask to speak to Barbara.

So it wasn't a friend, or family, or one of my clients.

"Tell him Mommy isn't home, and to call back later."

"My mommy isn't home. Call back."

She listened, then handed me the phone. "He doesn't want to talk to Mommy. He wants to talk to you."

Sheesh.

I took the phone.

"Hello. I'm Lew Golan. Sorry I can't talk on the phone with you, but I'm deaf. Please call back in a couple of hours, when my wife will be home. Thanks."

I gave the phone back to Debby. She listened.

"He hung up."

I wondered who it was.

Half an hour later, I remembered something: one of my clients had mentioned that a friend of his at another agency might need a freelance writer, so I had sent out a query.

Barbara called the fellow I had written to. Yes, he had received my letter. No, he hadn't called me. But he had given my letter to the creative director; maybe *he* had called me.

He transferred Barbara to the CD.

"Hello. I'm Barbara Golan, Lew Golan's wife. Did you happen to call him this morning?"

"Y-y-y-yes, I did. I was going to c-c-c-call you back."

"Sorry about my daughter taking the call. But as Lew told you, he's deaf."

"W-w-w-well, we ought to g-g-g-get along just fine t-t-t-together, then. I s-s-s-stammer."

The next morning I went downtown to pick up my first project from him.

Talk about a vicious circle.

Someone who stutters or stammers has a problem getting the words out. The listener can't help being aware of the problem. The speaker knows the other person is aware of the problem—and that puts pressure on the speaker, which intensifies the problem.

The more the speaker thinks about what the listener is thinking about his speech, the harder it is for him to speak.

So there I was, sitting across from the creative director with my eyes riveted to his face—staring at his mouth, focusing on his lips, concentrating on his struggle to enunciate each syllable.

And there he was, acutely aware that I was scrutinizing every movement his lips made.

I was, quite literally, his worst nightmare come true.

Fortunately, I understood him quite well.

And we were on the same wavelength. I usually knew what he meant before he finished saying it, so he didn't have to go into a lot of explanation.

So, despite the odd coupling (and the botched phone call), we hit it off from day one. He fed me a steady flow of work.

The agency wasn't an advertising agency. It turned out to be something I'd never heard of because it was one of the first of its kind: a sales promotion agency.

Structurally, a promotion agency is similar to an advertising agency. It has account executives who call on clients and bring in the business. It has copywriters and art directors and researchers and production managers to create and produce the work.

But it does *not* have a media department to buy time for TV and radio commercials or space for magazine and newspaper ads, since it doesn't normally do broadcast or print advertising.

Unlike advertising, which connects manufacturers directly with the consumers, sales promotion usually works step by step down the channel of distribution—pushing the product from the factory to the wholesaler to the retailer to the consumer.

Advertising is supposed to create an *image* for the product, to position it in the consumer's mind. Sales promotion is supposed to make something happen *now.*

Today, since marketing has become such a popular buzzword, sales promotion agencies tend to call themselves marketing services agencies or marketing communications agencies. This terminology reflects their greater involvement in the client's marketing function and their capabilities as full-service agencies.

An agency helps its client develop its marketing objectives and strategies. Then the agency creates the materials and activities that generate visibility and stimulate action by the sales force, the trade and the consumer—wrapped up in a coordinated program with a catchy theme.

For instance, I came up with a promotion that gave a double incentive for buying Kodak film: "Take 25 percent off...and take an extra roll free!" The theme: "Do a double take!"

This sketchy overview of sales promotion leaves out many other arrangements and elements. Chain stores, for example, have their own purchasing headquarters that buy the product directly from factory salesmen and distribute it to their stores.

And many companies such as airlines and hotels provide their customers with services, not products, so there is no product pipeline in the usual sense. But they can make good use of training and motivational programs (with seminars, videotapes, instructional manuals or whatever) to get their people to provide more efficient and courteous service.

For me, sales promotion has been a fascinating, demanding and rewarding field. At the highest level, it requires a broad range of expertise in addition to outstanding creative talent.

Creative people have to be at home with a gamut of objectives and strategies and tactics...a variety of channels of distribution and levels of trade...a kaleidoscope of end-user markets...and an array of communication vehicles. These include sales training, incentives, sales meetings, sales tools, trade incentive programs, traffic-building promotions, point-of-purchase displays, sweepstakes, games and contests, premiums, tie-ins between two companies, films, videos, brochures, manuals, multimedia presentations, coupons, sampling, co-op advertising and direct mail.

The top writers and art directors in promotion agencies are as talented, if not more so, than those in advertising agencies—and, from my experience in both types of agencies, I believe that they're more versatile and tend to be harder working.

And, unlike the account executives of 30 years ago who were basically salesmen, the client contact people in today's promotion agencies tend to have degrees in marketing.

Although the effects of sales promotion are seen and felt almost everywhere, the existence of these agencies is virtually unknown to the general public. People in the business are doomed to endless repetition of the following dialogue:

"What do you do?"

"I'm a writer in a marketing communications agency."

"What's that?"

"A sales promotion agency."

"What's that?"

"Something like an advertising agency."

"Ah, yes."

The purpose of writing is to communicate—but most business writing does not communicate well. At best, it is often unclear and ambiguous; at worst, it is misleading (unintentionally or not).

This applies not only to advertising and sales promotion. Reports, letters, memos, proposals and other written materials—especially instruction manuals—are also guilty of sloppy writing.

Sloppy writing isn't necessarily caused by a lack of facility with the language. More often it's the result of sloppy preparation and sloppy thinking. Too many people don't make an effort to get all the information they need and organize their thoughts *before* they start writing.

Good writing always reflects a clear understanding of what you are writing about, who you are writing to, and what points you want to make. Sloppy writing reflects the opposite.

In theory, an agency's account executives are supposed to bring back from the client all the necessary information. In practice, they often leave quite a bit to be desired.

In those early days of promotion agencies, as I mentioned, the account executives tended to be salesmen rather than the marketing specialists they are today. Their *modus operandi* was to get a go-ahead from the client, turn the project over to the creatives, and go looking for another assignment.

Once they got the order, all they wanted to do was hurry out of the client's office and get back to the agency.

When the client explained an assignment, they'd nod their heads confidently and say "No problem," even though they didn't really understand all the aspects.

Why?

First of all, they figured that asking questions would make them look dumb. This, by the way, is still one of the most widespread—and dumbest—attitudes in business.

It's incredible how much goes wrong simply because people are afraid to ask questions.

Second, they didn't realize how much background material it takes for a writer to really get a handle on all the aspects and nuances. They didn't—couldn't—look at an assignment through the eyes of a writer and go through the creative thought process in which one thing leads to another, one answer leads to another question.

Third, the client himself often didn't realize that the writer needs much more information than will actually appear in the finished product. This background helps give the writer a thorough under-standing of what he's writing about—which, in turn, helps him write more precisely and communicate better, even if he doesn't mention that particular bit of information.

But the client would regularly brush off probing questions with "I don't want you to mention that" or "Don't worry about that, it doesn't apply."

Sometimes the client honestly believed it wasn't necessary to provide that information. Sometimes he didn't know the answer and didn't want to admit it or go to the trouble of finding out.

Consequently, the account executives tended to avoid pumping the client for details. So I became an insufferable pest.

At first, the account executives tried to appease me by phoning the client with my questions. Sometimes this was enough.

Then I started going out to get the information firsthand from the advertising or sales promotion manager—sometimes with the account executive, more often by myself.

Finally, when I asked technical questions that the promotion managers couldn't answer, I started bugging the R&D engineers, laboratory technicians and production managers.

I loved it. Digging for information was exhilarating. I wanted to know everything—not just what and how, but why.

The information helped me write with clarity and precision. But even if I hadn't needed it for my work, I would have enjoyed the accumulation of all that nitty gritty for its own sake.

Before Japan Inc. took over the world, television sets were made in the United States. In addition to the promotions I developed for Zenith, Motorola and Admiral, I wrote sales training brochures that helped educate retail salesmen.

When Admiral started producing color TV sets, I went out to the factory with the account executive to get information. We talked with the promotion manager and some of the engineers. Then, sipping Pepsi from paper cups, we toured the plant.

In one area, perforated metal boxes were suspended from an overhead chain-link conveyer like gondolas from a ski lift. They moved slowly through an enormous oven that looked as if it had come from King Kong's kitchen, then rose up and away to some other part of the factory.

I turned to the plant manager, who was escorting us.

"What are those metal boxes?"

"Each one holds a picture tube."

"Why are the tubes inside the boxes?"

"For safety. The picture tubes are big vacuum tubes. When we bake the phosphors on the screen, a tube might implode. The box will keep the broken glass from flying all over the place."

I started to wonder how safe those picture tubes really were. After all, my family sat in front of one every day.

"Has a tube ever actually broken?"

The plant manager turned his head sharply to look quizzically at me. The account executive choked on his Pepsi.

How was I supposed to know that the spot where we were standing sounded like a Chinese New Year parade because of the intermittent barrage of ear-splitting implosions overhead?

The agency became my biggest freelance client. And soon after that, the creative director offered me a full-time writing job.

I was enjoying the independence of freelancing and was making more money than ever before. On the other hand, the proffered salary was as much as I was making freelancing, and I didn't know how long the flow of freelance work would keep up.

So, with three young daughters (Debby was 4, Julie was 2, and Laurie had just been born), I chickened out and opted for the presumed security of a job.

Some security. A year later, the agency was on the verge of bankruptcy.

With its assets attached by creditors, the agency had to let people go to keep from going belly up.

So the creative director took me out to lunch. As we were walking down Michigan Avenue, he fired me.

But this time my getting axed was no big deal; it was little more than a bookkeeping technicality.

I went back to my first love, freelancing, and the agency bought my work on a project basis. I picked up more clients, so the money came in faster than ever.

I enjoyed the working environment in my office at home in suburban Highland Park, where I could look up from my typewriter and out through the floor-to-ceiling window and across the backyard and into the woods beyond.

And it was nice not having to make the daily commute to and from downtown Chicago.

By nature I am competitive, and I set fairly high standards for myself. When it comes to evaluating my own performance, I am a nitpicker par excellence.

But I tried not to be as hard on our daughters as I was on myself. I pushed them, yes, but not in competition with each other or with other people—just in relation to their individual capabilities and interests.

What I expected was commitment and effort—a determination to do the best they could, whatever that might be.

So they grew up knowing that whatever they did was fine in their father's eyes—but, nevertheless, he was always going to ask why they hadn't done better.

If one came home with an A- on her paper, she knew I would ask why she hadn't earned an A; if another came home with a C+ on her test, she knew I would ask why she hadn't earned a B.

It wasn't as heavy as it sounds; my manner was playful and bantering, and it was something of a game. Still, they knew I was kidding on the square; always, there was that edge of "that's good, but let's try harder, let's see if we can do better."

They didn't become neurotic from the not-so-subtle pressure. With a mixture of exasperation and affection (mostly the former), they saw my push for excellence as a harmless idiosyncrasy, much as other children accepted their fathers' peculiarities and were none the worse for it.

And over the years, some of it seemed to have rubbed off on them. All four are motivated self-starters.

On the other hand, what did our daughters think about their father being deaf?

Recently, Julie told me that when I drove the car pool, she and her pre-teen friends ducked down in the back seat where I couldn't see them—then screamed and shouted dirty words at the top of their voices until they collapsed in giggles.

But the issue of our daughters' attitudes about my deafness never entered my mind—until we had the usual conference with Debby's third-grade teacher on Parents' Night.

The first 13 minutes of the 15-minute meeting revealed no real problems with schoolwork or relationships.

Then, looking apologetically in my direction, the teacher took a deep breath.

"In general, Debby is a happy and well-adjusted child. But you know how children have certain norms, and care deeply about meeting those norms. They don't want to be outsiders; they want to fit in with their peers, to be like them."

We nodded, wondering what was coming.

"Well, Mr. Golan, your daughter is bothered by the fact that you are different from the fathers of the other children. It isn't easy for her to cope with this difference. She wants very badly for her father to be like other fathers."

My heart sank as, for the first time, I thought about the impact of my deafness on our daughters.

"She is very concerned, Mr. Golan, because you don't go downtown every day like the other fathers do...."

15

Paddling a canoe upstream

When our daughters were growing up, they usually talked with Barbara rather than with me.

One reason, I suppose, is that children—especially girls—tend to talk with their mothers.

But in our case, there was another reason: as children habitually do, they brought up subjects abruptly out of the clear blue sky. Since I often didn't have the faintest idea what they were talking about, I had few if any clues to what they were saying.

By the time I figured out what the subject was, they were talking about something else or they had disappeared with the screen door banging behind them. If childhood is fleeting, children's words are even more so.

It wasn't a complete washout. There were a few things I could always get the first time around: "Where's Mommy?" or "I need some money for a notebook" were easy enough.

But the flow of words across the dinner table when Debby, Julie and Laurie were, say, 8, 6 and 4 (and Lisa was still a few years down the road) was more likely to go something like:

"We went in the submarine and looked through the periscope but couldn't see anything." *[Translation: her class went on a field trip to the Museum of Science and Industry, which has a World War II German sub parked outside.]*

"Annie's dog had puppies again, so her father is going to have her spayed." *[Translation: the dog, not Annie.]*

"I don't feel too good. Can I stay home from school tomorrow?" *[Translation: she didn't finish her homework.]*

"I don't like peas and carrots." *[Translation: she doesn't like peas and carrots.]*

Some of the table talk could be described as conversation—an exchange of thoughts on a topic. But much of it was a blur of non sequiturs and abrupt changes in subject.

If Barbara or the girls laughed, I'd ask "What's funny?" Or if an argument broke out, I'd ask "What's the problem?" Or if it looked like a discussion was under way, I'd ask "What's going on?"

If something particularly newsworthy came up, Barbara would repeat it for me. So I didn't miss anything very important—just the routine small talk by small fry.

None of this is meant to imply that I didn't have conversations with our daughters. I did, but nowhere near the extent to which Barbara did.

Did I feel left out?

A little bit, I suppose—but in balance, not really.

Just being with Barbara and our daughters, seeing them talking animatedly, made me feel content. My enjoyment may have been partly vicarious, but it was quite real.

The conversation flowing around me in the kitchen or at the dinner table or in the family room or on the patio was pleasurable, even when I couldn't understand all of it.

It was something like listening to *Aida* without knowing Italian or *Carmen* without knowing French. Yes, something was missing, but it was still very well worth the price of admission.

One way of looking at this is that it's a shame I wasn't more involved in the interchanges. Yes, on occasion I felt a twinge of regret.

But most of the time I couldn't help taking another perspective: that I was quite fortunate to be surrounded by a healthy, financially secure and reasonably happy family with no problems worse than an occasional touch of filial jealousy.

How could I complain? There was no way I could perceive the glass as half empty.

On the contrary, it runneth over.

Nevertheless, some people will pounce on this as an example of the supposed inadequacy of lipreading and the reason why all deaf people and their families should learn to sign.

If Barbara and I and the girls had all learned to sign, and if the conversations in our home had been conducted in sign, then, the argument goes, I would have understood more of the conversations that were taking place within my range of vision.

So why didn't we learn and use sign?

First of all, it never occurred to us.

Psychologically and culturally, I am a hearing person. My native language is spoken English.

While growing up, I communicated very easily and effectively with my parents and brothers and sister and friends and relatives through spoken English, so we had no need for sign language.

In school, sign language would have been useless—since my teachers and classmates didn't know it.

In my career, sign language would have been useless—because no one I worked with knew it.

With Barbara and our friends and relatives, sign language would be a meaningless redundancy—because we always communicate easily and effectively through spoken English.

So when our children were growing up, it was perfectly natural for spoken English to be the norm in our home.

Just as our home was a Jewish home, it was an oral home. Sign language was as foreign to us as a Christmas tree.

And just as I am not putting down other religions, neither am I putting down signers. I'm a Jew, not a Christian or a Moslem; I'm oral, not a signer. This is supposed to be a pluralistic society, with different strokes for different folks.

In one small area—following the jumble of words that tumbled from our daughters' mouths when they were young—signing might have helped somewhat.

But that benefit, while desirable, was not the most important thing in the world—and certainly not important enough to make signing the rule in our home. I had no intention of forcing my children to talk to each other and to Barbara in sign so that I wouldn't miss the big news about Nancy's puppy.

And there was no need for me to sign to them. Like everyone else, they understood my speech with no problems.

Aside from the logic (which I never even considered, anyway), there is the emotional aspect. Although I do not think about it much, I do take pride in the fact that I communicate orally. It's unquestionably an achievement to be able to communicate with hearing people on something close to their own terms.

Unfortunately, many proponents of signing don't see it that way. They claim that my non-signing shows that I am ashamed of my deafness, and that I am pretending to be a hearing person.

I'm not pretending. I *am* a hearing person, psychologically and culturally, even if I can't hear. And if I were ashamed of my deafness, would I be writing a book about it?

Oral communication is far from perfect.

But its occasional shortcomings in no way lessen the fact that it has been my passport to the cornucopia of opportunities in the hearing world—social, educational and professional.

The oral route is like paddling a canoe upstream. It's hard work just trying to keep from being swept away.

On the electronic forum, a student at a college for the deaf posted a message about the difficulty. Some excerpts:

> I've tried oralism, and it isn't as great as it seems. I got
> sick of pretending to understand...sick of laughing when I

saw others laugh even though I'd missed the joke...sick of struggling to follow lectures hour after hour...frustrated at the way I couldn't achieve my full potential, being stuck in a world where I couldn't understand enough.

I don't withdraw, I don't say "poor me," and I don't let the world go by. Although I do blame many people in the hearing world for not bothering to give me the chances I need to succeed, I also push myself to my limits and sometimes even past them.

Yet no matter how hard I push myself, there are some things I cannot do. Lipreading for effective communication is one of them. In cases like these, I feel I have a right to demand that the hearing people in my family and other close circles learn to sign.

I turned to my mother and sign language for deep conversations to contribute to my personal growth and make me happy.

Being denied signs caused me a lot of hassles that others around me didn't have.

I replied that I accepted the hassles as the price of making it in a hearing world. And I learned long ago that most people have problems of one kind or another; although my classmates did not have the problems I had, they had their own devils.

I told the student that I do not expect to get everything through the spoken word.

There are times when I cannot lipread a key word (usually the name of a person or a street), and I ask the speaker to spell it out (orally). If that doesn't work, I ask him to write it down.

This happens only occasionally within my family or circle of friends or business associates—that is, with people I'm in contact with more or less regularly—but it does happen. It's usually with a stranger whom I've never seen before and will never see again.

When it happens, I said, people use their forefingers to write invisibly on whatever surface is handy—which has included:

the rump of a traffic cop's horse
the back of someone at a party
a theater program
a computer screen
a glass wall at an airport
thin air

...as well as visibly in the dust on a car window, in the sand at the beach, in the grease on the floor of a garage. Not to mention the more mundane use of pencil and paper.

Then there was the art director who used to work for me. If I missed a key word, he would give me a visual clue. Regardless of the word, the clue was the same: he would point to his crotch. Believe it or not, there was usually some association that could be made with the word—even if at times it was tenuous.

No, I told the student, oral communication is not perfect; from time to time, I have to supplement it with whatever works. But the bottom line is that it allows me to function in the hearing world to a degree that signing would not.

Another deaf college student wrote:

Lew, I don't understand why you strongly support on oralism. I grew up with oralist and Signed English. I have never been able to feel like I am part of the hearing people.

I only understood about 20-40% of their conversations because they tends to turn their head away, cover their mouth, looking down, talk too fast, or say words that look alike. Don't that ever happens to you?

I understand your point about using oralism to get a good job and things like that, but what about your social life? Don't you ever feel left out of the conversation with Hearing people? I can't imagine living all my life being oralist because I have never felt fit in with them due to lackness of understanding them.

Later in my life, I met more and more Deaf people and started to use American Sign Language. I felt so good about myself after I started socializing with them. I rarely had a misunderstanding with them compare with hearing people.

I bet you had a short, surface conversation with hearies. I am sure that you might feel more comfortable with Deaf cuz you can share your experiences, frustration of deaf life. I am sure you rarely understood hearies 100% completely.

Maybe you should reconsider your past experiences with hearies. Have you feel fit in? Have you ever smoothly communicate with hearies without extended period of time and frustration?

Yes, I said, sometimes I feel left out of a conversation—usually when it's among more than four people. But if it's just me and one or two or three other people, it's no problem. Or if I'm in a roomful of people, it's easy enough to start or join a conversation with one or two others.

No, I said, I don't always understand 100 percent of what people say—but how about 95 percent with my friends and family? In conversations with one or two people, I get from 75 to 100 percent depending on how well I understand a particular person.

Most of what I miss comes at the beginning when a subject is being broached. Once I'm on track, I get virtually everything with some people, less with others.

If the subject is changed, I may get derailed. If an unfamiliar name comes up, I may have to have it spelled out. I can't tell the difference between "can" and "can't," between 15 and 50.

With some people, I told the student, I may miss one word every few minutes. With others, I'm constantly in deep trouble. I can barely understand a friend from England, and even my hearing wife has trouble with his accent.

I have all kinds of conversations—some short and superficial, some long and involved. It depends on the people, the subject and the circumstances.

I emphasized to the student that being oral is a tradeoff. No, it isn't perfect when it comes to socializing; there are times when I don't follow everything and when I feel left out. But speaking and speechreading allow me to converse with just about any English speaker anywhere in the world—which signing does not.

So oral skills are more useful to me than signing would be.

I told the student that three factors help me from being left out too much:

1. I'm not particularly reticent. I push. In a group conversation, I ask "What's going on?" "What's funny?" "What did he say?"

Yes, it takes an effort on my part to stay involved. As I said, it's like paddling upstream in a canoe.

2. *Some* of my friends are *sometimes* concerned about making sure I get something. If someone starts to tell a story, they interrupt and tell the speaker to face me.

Or they turn to me and make sure I understand that they're bringing up a new subject. Or they say "Did you get that?"

Some of my friends do this *some* of the time. It isn't a constant preoccupation with them, and I wouldn't want it to be.

3. My wife is hearing. If she's in the same group with me, I'll raise my eyebrows and she'll tell me what's going on.

As for fitting in: I usually have a feeling of belonging. But it has nothing to do with hearing and deafness; it's a matter of other factors that shape my identity.

Religiously, I'm a Reform Jew—at the opposite pole from ultra-Orthodox Jews here in Israel; we mix like oil and water.

Politically, I'm center-left—at odds with right-wingers on which road Israel should take toward peace.

Socioeconomically, I am professional, academic, western and middle-upperclass, and feel most comfortable with other people in the same categories.

I have four daughters and seven grandchildren, so I have the pleasure of being surrounded by a healthy, prospering family.

The list goes on and on. I have so many strong, well-defined identities that my deafness is a minor factor in who I am...and therefore unimportant in determining whether I fit in.

I told the student that I couldn't agree at all with his suggestion that I would feel more comfortable socializing with deaf people so that I could share experiences and frustrations of deaf life.

I have little, if anything, in common with them, since my deafness is of very little concern to me.

It's all a matter of perspective.

If you have nothing else to think about, I told him, then the frustrations of deaf life can loom huge in your mind like Godzilla, and you may well want to talk them over with somebody who has the same frustrations.

But I have neither the time nor the need to talk about such relatively picayune matters.

I would rather focus on getting my programs to coexist in my computer...or getting industry and nature to coexist in the environment...or getting Arabs and Israelis to coexist in the Middle East.

Now *those* are what I call frustrations. And *those* are what I would rather put my time and energy into—not bitching and moaning about being deaf.

16

Repairing the world

During the turbulent 1960s, I finally roused myself from a state of passive awareness and became actively involved on a number of fronts—civil rights, the anti-war movement, Judaism.

I had been a classic armchair liberal—sitting complacently in our big French country house on a private road on the North Shore, reading the proper magazines and books, saying the proper things, sometimes even donating to the proper causes.

Then came the bloody 1965 confrontation at the bridge in Selma, Alabama, where the sheriff's police broke up a march by civil rights demonstrators.

Literally overnight, the armchair became too uncomfortable to sit in any longer.

When Martin Luther King announced there would be another march the following week, I didn't think twice about what to do. I told Barbara I was driving down to help.

A day or two later, Barbara heard that some people from our synagogue were going to Selma on a bus chartered by the local umbrella organization of Reform Jewish congregations.

I called to put my name down for the bus. Since our daughters were too young to be left alone, Barbara stayed with them.

On the way to Alabama, a young man who had been injured at the bridge the previous week stood at the front of the bus and spoke into a microphone.

But instead of describing the passing sights, he gave us a short course in survival tactics.

As he demonstrated how to cross our arms over our heads to fend off clubs and how to use our handkerchiefs to block out tear gas, I started wondering what I had got myself into.

I hadn't given more than a passing thought to the possibility of being in any personal danger, despite the murders a year earlier of three civil rights workers in Mississippi.

We reached Selma that evening and spent the night dozing on wooden pews in a Baptist church in a black neighborhood.

I woke up around midnight and found that some of the others in my group were also awake.

I asked whether anybody was hungry. A few people said yes. I said I'd buy some food.

I went outside and walked past the darkened homes for several blocks until I saw a lighted area down the street.

I was in luck—it was an all-night diner. I walked in and asked the woman behind the counter if she had any sandwiches I could take out. She said she could make some chicken sandwiches.

Four or five local men were sitting or standing around, eating or smoking. They were looking curiously at me.

Everything seemed so normal that it took me a while to realize that something wasn't exactly right. Finally it hit me why the scene was familiar: the people in the diner were white.

Somehow, I had strayed from the black neighborhood.

I was on the wrong turf. And my voice doesn't have a trace of a drawl. They knew who I was and why I was there.

Fortunately, it didn't take long to make the sandwiches. The woman simply took a piece of fried chicken, bones and all, and put it between two slices of bread.

I took the sacks of food, paid her, and looked straight ahead as I walked out the door.

Returning in the direction of the church, I looked back every few steps. I couldn't see anything at all, but my hyperactive imagination kicked into overdrive.

I couldn't hear the roar of the engine, but I knew a battered pickup truck had to be speeding toward me with its lights off.

I couldn't hear the rapid pounding of boots on the sidewalk, but I knew that my pursuers had to be gaining on me.

I couldn't hear the twigs snapping in the shadows, but I knew that unseen thugs with dirty pillowcases over their heads had to be flanking me on either side.

I was sweating in the cool night air. The return trip was taking longer than it should have. Had I made a wrong turn?

The darkness finally ended when I stepped with relief into the lighted perimeter of the Baptist church...an appropriate site for my first immersion in the waters of social action.

The next morning we joined the river of marchers behind Martin Luther King. It flowed through the streets of Selma in the direction of Montgomery, the state capital.

Hundreds of rifle-toting National Guardsmen, called out by the federal government, were there to protect us. At the time, we didn't know that they had not been given ammunition.

Talking and singing and clapping our hands, we marched across the infamous bridge and down the highway and into the history books—where Martin Luther King receives all due credit, but nary a word appears about my chicken sandwiches.

On the chartered bus going back up north, someone from our synagogue, Congregation Solel, introduced me to the term "social action."

I thought it meant going to a lot of parties. But it turned out to mean active involvement in trying to improve our society.

Its roots lay in the concept of *tikkun ha'olam*—repairing the world—described in the Talmud.

Awakened by newspaper accounts of the incident at the bridge, I had become involved on the spur of the moment in a one-time action.

But Solel, like many Jewish and Gentile congregations, went much further; it was becoming increasingly involved in local and national issues on an organized and continuing basis.

Its social action committee informed members about the issues and tried to persuade as many as possible to get involved in one way or another: lobbying, petitioning, demonstrating, volunteering, fund raising, contributing, publicizing or whatever.

Since action was the name of the game, social action held an enormous appeal for me.

By the time the bus reached Highland Park, I had joined the committee.

Until then, my link to organizational Judaism had followed an all-too-common path.

For a decade after I left my parents' home, I did not belong to a synagogue.

Then, when Debby was five years old, we joined Solel so that she could go to religious school classes on weekends.

My parents were founding members. It was started in the late fifties by Jews who moved from Chicago to the suburbs.

We went to services on Rosh Hashanah and Yom Kippur, and occasionally on Friday evenings, and Barbara took adult education classes.

But I found it difficult to relate to the prayers—even though the Reform movement's prayer books took a contemporary approach, and Solel, being a new and innovative congregation, wrote some prayer books of its own.

I was proud to be Jewish, and I greatly enjoyed the sense of belonging to the Jewish community. Most of our closest friends were members of Solel. Either we had met them at Solel, or we had brought them into the congregation ourselves.

But sitting with the congregation during the services, I was often in a world of my own.

Not because I couldn't hear what was going on (I could follow most of it, since it was in the prayer book), but because I preferred to go my own way by ruminating on my own thoughts or reading a book from the synagogue library.

So, when I discovered early on that social action was a vital part of organizational Judaism, our membership in Solel took on a new and dynamic relevance. Barbara and I became deeply involved in the action.

When I became the editor of the congregation's newsletter, I turned it into an extension of the social action committee.

And when I was elected to the congregation's board of directors, my focus was always on getting people involved.

Repairing the world. It had a nice ring to it. And there were a lot of things that needed fixing.

The 1960s were the glory years of Jewish-black cooperation.

We pushed for civil rights not only down South, but also at home in Chicago and the suburbs.

We pushed for greater opportunities in employment, so blacks and other minorities could afford a better way of life...and for open housing on the North Shore, so they could live wherever they could afford to.

Unfortunately, what was once an unrivaled relationship between Jews and blacks has become unraveled since then.

Another issue in which we became involved was the Vietnam War. For the congregation, as for the country, it was a painful and divisive experience.

During the 1968 Democratic national convention in Chicago, our synagogue was a makeshift hostel for out-of-town anti-war demonstrators who slept on the floors of the classrooms.

The juxtaposition of television with real life created a surrealistic atmosphere.

One moment I was watching the electronic images of the rioting police charging through the demonstrators and clubbing them with nightsticks.

The next moment I was walking the halls of the synagogue as the demonstrators themselves came in with bleeding heads and bloody clothing.

And then came November 15, 1969. Along with 250,000 other Americans, Debby (then 13) and I and others from Solel marched up the mall to the Washington Monument in a massive protest against the war.

We gave high priority to supporting the Jewish state.

In 1967, after Israel ordered and paid for a dozen Mirage jets from France, the French refused to deliver the planes.

So, when the French prime minister came to Chicago, we joined thousands of Jews who surrounded the Palmer House and chanted "Shame on you, Pompidou!"

When Pompidou arrived in his soundproof limousine, he was unaware of what the crowd was shouting. He stepped out, smiling and waving—then glared when he finally heard the words.

If he had been a lipreader, he would have been better prepared for the reception before he emerged from his limousine.

We visited homes for the Jewish aged, bringing baskets of food and a few minutes of cheer. We lobbied for the release of Soviet Jews. We became involved in local environmental issues...in countering neo-Nazism...in fighting drug abuse.

Repairing the world.

It's a great concept, and I worship it.

When I was editor of the congregation's newsletter, I tried to make it as informal, uncliched and readable as possible.

I refused to let anyone gush in print. I rewrote almost all of the articles that were submitted to me, deleting endemic superlatives and endless thank-yous.

I never, ever used the titles "Mr." and "Mrs."—and, in particular, I never, ever referred to a woman by her husband's name. Barbara, for example, was Barbara Golan—not Mrs. Lew Golan.

I gave the greatest possible emphasis to whatever social action was coming up in the next week or two.

And I was always looking for a way to inject humor, usually in the headlines.

Like the time I wrote an article about the annual harvest festival of Succot, reminding the members and their children to come and help put up the large *succa* (a booth made of palm fronds and decorated with fruits) outside the synagogue.

The headline took its cue from "Rowan and Martin's Laugh-In," a popular TV show at the time. Each week on the show, a young Goldie Hawn announced "And now, folks, it's sock-it-to-me time!" before being drenched by a bucket of water.

The headline: *And now, folks, it's succa-to-me time.*

To get the next one, you have to know that there was a World War II movie, *Wing and a Prayer,* based on the autobiography of a Navy pilot. The title referred to a shot-up fighter plane barely making it back to its aircraft carrier, and the movie's theme song was *Coming in on a wing and a prayer.*

I wrote an article about an upcoming chicken dinner followed by Shabbat services.

The headline: *Come on in for a wing and a prayer.*

About the time I left the agency that introduced me to sales promotion, one of the salesmen also left. I went back to being a freelance writer, and he set up his own promotion agency.

For the next three years or so, his new agency was one of my busier accounts. Eventually, the agency grew to the point where he could make me an offer I couldn't refuse: to go on staff as creative director for a cut of the profits on top of a nice salary.

So I moved in.

One of my first projects was a promotion to get people to buy Admiral TV instead of Zenith. (We also did promotions to get them to buy Zenith instead of Admiral, but that's another story.)

This was in the middle 1960s, when television sets were being manufactured in America—and Japanese products had a reputation for very shoddy quality that matched their very low prices.

Admiral's marketing people were sitting in our conference room when I presented several ideas for them to choose from.

"The creative process is kind of weird," I said. "Sometimes you get a crazy idea that's not useable...but it can lead to another idea that's absolutely perfect. And that's what happened here.

"First, I'll show you an outlandish idea that came straight off the top of my head. It's okay to laugh at it."

I turned around the first concept board and tacked it on the wall:

Admiral TV
BANZAI SALE
American quality at Japanese prices!

The obligatory laugh went around the room.

"Now, I'll show you how this led to a truly believable message that hits the nail right on the head."

I flipped over the second concept board and held it up:

Admiral TV
BANZAI SALE
Japanese quality at American prices!

It took an entire roll of paper towels to soak up the spilled coffee.

Although we were caught up in the public turbulence of the Stormy Sixties, the sun shone on our private life.

We were all healthy, and my work was very satisfying and very rewarding.

When Barbara was pregnant with Laurie, we bought our first home—a small ranch in Highland Park on Chicago's north shore, with a down payment from my parents. I did some remodeling, refinanced the house, and repaid my parents within a year.

Five years later, we were able to buy a large 11-room country provincial home on a private street in Highland Park. When people asked me in awe how many bathrooms it had, I usually flushed when I admitted that there were five.

I wasn't completely satisfied with the house.

So I knocked down the wall between the den and the family room, knocked down the outside wall of the family room and added a 10-foot bay, and wound up with a 36-foot combination family room and office.

People couldn't understand how I could concentrate on writing with a mob of people doing their homework or playing games or yelling or reading or watching television or talking on the phone or playing the piano or making popcorn in the fireplace.

But the whole point was that I enjoyed being in the middle of the action and knowing what was going on. It relaxed me and actually helped me concentrate.

If I was in a room alone, unable to hear or see what was going on in the rest of the house, I would start wondering what was happening—and would get up and walk around to take a look.

So the combination office-family room helped me stay at my desk and at the typewriter.

At the other end of the house, I knocked down the outside kitchen wall and built a new wing with a large breakfast-family room and laundry room and the fifth bathroom.

I also knocked down the outside wall of the one-and-a-half car garage, put in a steel beam to hold up Debby's bedroom above it, and built out to make it a two-and-a-half car garage.

Upstairs, I expanded Julie's room and made it L-shaped by knocking out a bathroom and a hall closet, then building a new bathroom.

So Debby had the farthest and most private bedroom, Julie had the most unusual bedroom, and Laurie had the biggest bedroom—until Lisa came along and took a corner for her crib.

Barbara and I drew up the plans ourselves. I was my own contractor, and did much of the carpentry, wiring and plumbing myself; I hired a couple of moonlighting carpenters and worked with them on weekends.

I loved those hours of working with my hands after working with my head all week.

And what I really loved most of all was knocking down those walls.

I still have the sledgehammer, just in case.

The fence at the back of our lot separated our property from the clubhouse of a wealthy, old-line private country club. Eventually, I learned that the club did not accept Jews, blacks or women as members.

So there I was, going down to Selma to march with Martin Luther King for voting rights, and going into Chicago to work for equal employment opportunities, and demonstrating in downtown Highland Park for equal housing—while all along, literally in my own backyard, was a bastion of blatant racial, religious and sexual discrimination.

Yet I never did anything at all about it.

An anomaly? Not really.

Since country clubs are outside my realm of interests, I never paid any attention to the situation other than to deplore it.

I couldn't care less about golf or black-tie parties or the rest of the country-club scene, even though several of our friends and relatives belonged to clubs.

On my list of priorities, the things worth working for were voting rights, jobs and housing. I couldn't get worked up about restrictions on playing golf, any more than I could get upset about the luxury tax on pleasure boats.

It simply never occurred to me to do anything. I didn't even think about the apparent incongruity until just now, while writing about our home.

On the other hand, there was the time I spoke at the Rosh Hashanah (Jewish new year) services in our synagogue.

For many members, the High Holy Days are the only time they show up for services during the year—so Solel was packed with more than one thousand people.

The services included what was called a personal expression or a creative prayer or an original statement. Sometimes it was poetic, sometimes prayerful, sometimes political, sometimes pretentious—but always personal.

When I was called on to give a personal expression at the Rosh Hashanah services, I wanted to say something about more people getting more involved in more social action.

But the more I thought about it, the less comfortable I felt.

Even though I was far more involved than were most members of the congregation, I was nagged by the contrast between my own upscale, upbeat situation—safe and comfortable and well off—and that of people who were far less fortunate.

Was I involved in social action mainly to make myself feel better? Couldn't I have done a great deal more than I actually did?

Someone who is to give a personal expression is notified weeks in advance, and often spends quite a bit of time writing and polishing the words.

But I didn't even pick up a pencil. I couldn't figure out how to say what I wanted to say.

Finally, I was sitting there during the services and still hadn't written a word. It was time.

I walked up to the *bima*, the wheels turning in my head. I looked out at the sea of faces.

Some of the people were expecting to be moved by uplifting words of hope. Some of them were expecting to be bored silly by another pretentious speech. All of them were expecting to hear the usual five or ten minutes of whatever was on my mind.

I said: "My name is Lew Golan, and I am a hypocrite."

Then I walked back to my seat.

When our fourth daughter was born, we didn't get around to choosing her name for a few days. So we just called her by the name on her hospital ID bracelet—Baby Girl Golan, which we later shortened to Baby Golan. It stuck for a few years.

Since all of Lisa's sisters were in school, we bought her a West Highland terrier to play with. The girls decided that the appropriate name for Baby Golan's dog was Doggy Golan.

When Barbara was in the kitchen or laundry room, Lisa would be crawling around the breakfast-family room with the dog. It soon became their private preserve.

One morning, on her way out to go shopping, Barbara put Lisa on the floor by my desk and told me to keep an eye on her. Inevitably, Lisa got up and toddled out of the room toward her territory. The dog followed her.

When Barbara returned home and asked where Lisa was, I said that she was at the other end of the house with the dog.

Barbara went to look.

No Lisa. No dog.

Just then, the phone rang. Barbara picked it up.

"Hello. I've been trying to call you all morning. I live over on Rollingwood. There's a terrier here, and he's wearing a tag with your telephone number. Is he yours?"

"Yes, he is."

"Well, there's a little girl with him, about a year and a half old. Is she yours, too?"

"Probably."

My dependency on other people to make telephone calls means that my life is an open line.

Since there's always an intermediary, I have no privacy on the phone. On the rare occasions when a call must be confidential, Barbara makes it for me.

Actually, confidentiality isn't really the problem with my phone calls.

Rather, it's that some private moments cry out for a closeness that is impeded not only by the physical distance, but even more so by the lack of an aural link.

Like the time Barbara called me at the office and asked me to come home immediately.

She did not volunteer the reason.

I happened to be passing through the reception room at the time, so the receptionist took the call for me.

"What's wrong?"

The receptionist relayed the question to Barbara, then shook her head. "She just says come home now."

This wasn't like Barbara, who is very straightforward.

Was it one of the children?

"What happened?" I persisted.

The receptionist listened to Barbara, then looked at me.

"Your father died."

I was stunned. "My *father?* Do you mean my *mother?*"

My mother, who was visiting my sister in California, had cancer in remission.

There was nothing wrong with my 63-year-old father.

More words on the phone. "No, it's your father."

I drove home, confused and frustrated because I hadn't been able to talk directly with Barbara.

When I got there, Barbara told me that my father had been running for the train in downtown Highland Park, had collapsed in the station, and was dead by the time the paramedics arrived.

It had been so sudden and unexpected that no one was prepared for the news—and Barbara hadn't wanted to break it to me through a third person.

But she also knew that I would want to know immediately—so, with mixed feelings, she had given the receptionist the message to pass on to me.

It wasn't the best way to hear about my father's death.

At a time when Barbara wanted to be close to me—at least by voice, if not in person—she couldn't.

So we both bled a little.

Standing by the switchboard in the reception room, unable to hear Barbara's voice at a significant moment, I felt powerless in the face of my deafness.

It happens.

Fortunately, it's happened only a handful of times.

I can't complain.

17

Peter Piper picked a peck
of pickled herring

George Bernard Shaw, criticizing the English language's mess of inconsistencies in spelling, wrote that *ghoti* spelled "fish"—/f/ as in enough, /i/ as in women, and /sh/ as in motion.

Tell me about it.

As a voracious reader and full-time writer, I have a good-sized vocabulary. I can spell the words, and I know what they mean.

But most of these words don't come up in conversations. When people speak, they tend to use a relatively small pool of words. Most words, if used at all, tend to be used in writing.

As a result, there are many words in my reading and writing vocabulary which I have never spoken aloud, and which no one has ever spoken to me.

When I read or write one of these words, I give it a mental pronunciation that is usually correct.

Maybe I looked it up in the dictionary.

Or maybe I simply figured it out on my own by breaking it down into syllables, the way most people do when they come across a new word. Then I pronounce the syllables the way they are pronounced in similar words.

This usually works, but not always. The English language is so full of ambiguous spellings and inconsistencies that sometimes I get thrown off.

There are words that I mentally mispronounced for years while reading or writing them. Then I'd happen to speak one of them for the first time—only to get a blank look or a guffaw or a correction from the listener.

Similarly, I may see someone say a word for the first time—and may not know what he's saying, because his pronunciation is quite different from the way I imagined the word sounded.

In high school, for example, I knew that "meta*mor*phic" was accented on the third syllable, and so was "meta*mor*phism."

And I knew that "meta*bol*ic" was accented on the third syllable, which naturally led me to hear "meta*bol*ism" when I read the word in my biology textbook.

So when the teacher brought up the subject of "me*tab*olism," I didn't know what he was talking about at first.

Or take a word like "paradigm." When I looked it up years ago to get the meaning, I learned that the "g" was silent: *paradim.*

But I never bothered to look up the adjective "paradigmatic," so I read it mentally as *paradimatic*—since I didn't know that the "g" *is* pronounced.

As a kid, my mother sent me to the store to buy chives; no problem. Then I picked up the word "archives" and pronounced it incorrectly in my head for years.

I knew early on that an ar*ch* is a structural device, but it was another few years before I found out that the design of structures is pronounced ar*k*itecture. The logic of it escapes me.

Growing up Jewish, I never had an occasion to pronounce either "archbishop" or "archangel," but I assumed that the angels stuck pretty close to the bishops.

Then I looked over Barbara's shoulder at the *New York Times Magazine* crossword and saw that she needed a nine-letter word meaning spiritual being. I said "ar*ch*angel." She said "ar*k*angel."

Then there's "archenemy" and "archetype." Gimme a break.

Most words with the syllable "ger" seem to have a soft "g"—as in geranium, germ, germinal, and so on.

For decades, therefore, every time I read in the sports pages about a college football player being inducted into the Hall of Fame, I thought it happened at *rutjers*. But I never pronounced (or, actually, mispronounced) the word until a month ago; then Barbara told me there was a hard "g" in Rutgers.

And last month, when someone mentioned the Reuters news service to me, I didn't understand him—because in my mind, the first syllable was pronounced *rue*, not *roy*.

Many people resent being corrected when they mispronounce a word. They view it as a put-down of their intelligence or their education.

And many people refrain from correcting the pronunciation of others, feeling that it is rude to do so.

I understand how they feel, but I think they are wrong—no matter what Miss Manners says.

A deaf person needs this kind of feedback in order to minimize his mispronunciations.

Rather than being embarrassed or offended if someone corrects my pronunciation, I appreciate the help—because it prevents me from repeating the error.

To feel otherwise would not only reflect false pride and undue sensitivity; it would be counterproductive.

Actually, I pre-empt the issue when I know that I don't know how to pronounce a word, or when I'm not sure.

This usually happens when I want to use a word that's relatively new to me—perhaps a name or a word that's in the news.

Then, like any new immigrant just off the boat, I go through the "How you say it?" routine.

The first time I used "NASA," for example, I had to ask if it was pronounced as an acronym (*nahsah*) or as initials (*N-A-S-A*).

Still, mistakes happen. After a sixth-grade field trip, I told my parents that we had gone to the Chicago Hysterical Society.

My sister is a special education teacher in the California public school system.

Gail teaches speech to multiple-handicapped children, including the hearing impaired.

It may be hard to believe, but I never really thought about her motivation for entering the field.

I did note that there were points of similarity—like me, some of her students are deaf—but it wasn't until I was writing this book, after she had been teaching for 30 years, that I asked her if there had been a cause-and-effect relationship.

She replied that *of course* my being deaf had influenced her career decision. She had taken it for granted that I knew, even though she had never said so to me in so many words.

Like my mother, my sister *never, ever* misses a chance to prod me into enunciating my r's and l's more distinctly.

Although most people can understand my speech quite well, it sounds somehow *different.*

Someone with a trained ear will know I'm deaf.

But most people think I have a foreign accent. They can't quite place it, so they ask me where I'm from.

Within months after I became deaf, according to my medical records, there was a noticeable loss of timbre.

The quality of the human voice, like that of music, depends partly on a blend of overtones.

Without the aural feedback that lets hearing people monitor and adjust their voice quality, the voices of the postlingually deafened become degraded to a greater or lesser degree.

Speech therapy can reduce this degradation of quality (but not prevent or completely reverse it).

Although the *intelligibility* of speech is somewhat related to voice *quality*, it is basically a separate phenomenon.

You don't have to have a voice like Charlton Heston's or Colleen Dewhurst's to be perfectly understandable.

Intelligibility, too, tends to degrade without aural feedback—but compared with voice quality, it is easier to maintain or improve. Consequently, I have been able to retain most of the intelligibility in my voice.

When I was in elementary school, I went to a speech teacher for an hour or two each week. She would drill me on enunciating the consonants and vowels.

The short-term goal was to fine-tune my pronunciation.

The long-term goal was to instill a lifetime self-consciousness as a substitute for the aural feedback.

This is self-consciousness in a positive sense.

I monitor my speech not by hearing it, but by being aware of how I am physically forming the sounds.

When I was a teenager and people asked me how I did it, I demonstrated an analogy: I closed my eyes and held up one, two and three fingers in sequence.

I told them that I couldn't *see* what I was doing, but I *knew* how many fingers I was holding up. At the time, I didn't know the technical word for it: *kinesthesia*—the sensation of bodily position, presence or movement created by the stimulation of sensory nerve endings in muscles, tendons and joints.

That's how people have an innate sense of what their bodies are doing, even if they can't see or hear what's happening.

That's why you can tie your shoelaces or throw a ball with your eyes closed. And that's why I was able to play the drums in the school orchestra.

When I speak, my internal sensory feedback includes tactile monitoring. I can feel the muscles in my mouth and throat tensing and relaxing...the friction of air on my lips, tongue and palate...the explosion of air...the vibrations of my voice.

The level of my awareness—and the consequent precision of my speech—fluctuates depending on who I'm talking to.

With strangers, I make a greater effort to enunciate clearly. With family and friends, I ease off a little—shamelessly taking advantage of the fact that they can understand me even if I get sloppy.

But even at home, I don't let myself get much off course—mainly because my mother always refused to let me be lazy about my speech.

It made no difference to her whether I was a six-year-old kid or a college student or a family man or even a grandfather.

If one sloppy syllable came out of my mouth, my mother was on my case before you could say "Peter Piper picked a peck of pickled herring."

Today, more than 40 years after I left my mother's home and a decade after she died, I am still constitutionally unable to drop my clothes on the floor instead of in the hamper, or leave dirty dishes on the table, or get sloppy in my speech.

This awareness that my mother drilled into me has stuck in my mind ever since.

I would imagine that behind every reasonably successful oralist is a nagging mother. Or sister.

Necessity is another mother of articulation.

The more I deal with people outside my immediate circle of family, friends and coworkers, the more I have to enunciate as distinctly as possible.

This forces good speaking habits to become even more habitual. Although I am internally motivated, it helps to have an external goosing mechanism as well.

For example, I was a scoutmaster for a few years. This position required me to speak with the boys and their parents, in groups and individually, in a variety of environments.

I was involved because I enjoyed passing scout lore on to another generation of boys—not because I was consciously trying to hone my speaking skills. Nevertheless, it had the side effect of not letting me get too lazy in my speech.

Usage begets proficiency. And once you've got it, it really is a crucial issue of using it or losing it.

For someone who has been deaf for more than half a century, I have a voice that is quite passable. Most people can understand me, and the sound of my voice isn't particularly unpleasant.

But many other deaf people aren't as fortunate.

Their problem is compounded by hearing people who simply don't want to be bothered—who don't want to make an effort to understand the deaf person's speech, and who feel uncomfortable listening to a voice that doesn't sound "normal."

I know of someone who went into a computer store to buy some equipment. A salesman, hearing the fellow's voice, asked whether he was deaf. Getting an affirmative reply, the salesman said "Well, then, I can't help you," and walked away.

More typically, a salesman or counter clerk or waitress will wait on hearing people out of turn—ignoring a deaf person who came in first and leaving her for last, if at all.

When a deaf person stops a passer-by on the street and asks for directions, the other person—not understanding her question and put off by the sound of her voice—may simply give her a funny look and keep walking.

In social situations, a deaf voice may make hearing people feel uncomfortable or even embarrassed. So deaf people tend to be excluded from social groups.

And potential employers often reject applicants out of hand when they hear their voices.

There are two sides to this issue.

One is the need for deaf people to improve their speech as much as possible—which is what I emphasize in this book.

But the reality is that although they can reach a usable level of proficiency, most deaf people are not going to have perfectly clear, normal-sounding voices.

They are going to sound different, no matter what.

The other side of the issue, therefore, is the need for hearing people to accept this difference.

By withholding acceptance, they compound the disability of deafness—making it even harder for deaf people to reach their full potential in the hearing world.

Most people agree in principle with the need for acceptance— but when they come face to face with a person who doesn't speak all that well, their attitudes and actions often say otherwise.

This is not at all surprising, given the poor track record of human beings toward people with differences of whatever kind.

Those who are different from the norm in any way—physically, mentally, ethnically, racially, religiously—have always had to bear the added burden of rejection by the majority.

This is a strong reason for mainstreaming deaf children in school. That's where socialization skills are picked up...where people can learn to get along with each other.

It's essential for deaf children to learn to get along in the hearing world.

And it would make the world a better place if more hearing children learned to get along with deaf people.

Often, people don't use their voices when they speak to me. They simply mouth the words silently.

Sometimes they do it for the fun of it. Children discover the technique naturally, and are delighted.

First my daughters and then my grandchildren quickly found their silent mouthing to be a highly effective way of asking me for cookies right under their mothers' unsuspecting noses.

Sometimes people do it to say something to me from a distance. I may be at a crowded party, or at a meeting at which someone else is talking, and somebody on the other side of the table or the other side of the room may want to say something to me without interrupting the speaker.

Sometimes people do it to keep others from overhearing what they say to me; it's even more confidential than a whisper.

Sometimes people do it when they are making a phone call for me. They use their voices when speaking to the person at the other end of the line, but mouth the words silently when speaking to me. This keeps the other person from getting confused about who the go-between is talking to.

And sometimes they do it without any real reason. On occasion, I would be sitting in my office having a conversation with someone who wasn't using his voice—and people passing by, hearing only my voice, thought I was going off my rocker and was talking to myself.

Debby and Laurie are married to native-born Israelis whose first tongue is Hebrew but who speak English as well.

In their homes, the families speak Hebrew. When they come to our home, they speak English or Hebrew.

Our grandchildren's native tongue is Hebrew. But early on, they learn English because that's the language I use with them.

When Laurie's son Yonatan was four, she tested him to see how many English words he knew.

Since speaking to me is synonymous with speaking English, she asked him in Hebrew:

"How do you tell Saba Lew that you want a glass of water?"

First he waved his hand to get her attention.

Then he said *"Ani rotzeh kos mayim."*

Without using his voice.

18

Dvorak and me

It may be an exaggeration to say that war is too important to be left to the military.

Still, there is some truth to the comment.

The generals know how to fight, but they sometimes lack a comprehensive world view. Some of them do not see the broader geopolitical context in which wars are but one element.

There is a parallel between generals and educators. The ivory tower may be a cliche—but, as with the comment about war, there is some truth to it.

Like the military, the field of education sometimes tends to be an insular community that focuses inward on *what* it is doing—rather than outward on *why* it is doing it.

Deaf students, on the average, are several years behind hearing students academically—so some educators conclude that content should get more emphasis.

And some educators point to studies indicating that some deaf students who use sign language in the classroom are academically a year or so ahead of those who learn orally—so they conclude that sign language should be used to teach content, and that less emphasis should be put on speaking and speechreading.

They talk about the fact that there are only so many hours in a school day.

The more time a deaf student spends trying to learn how to speak and read lips, they say, the less time he has for learning history, math, science and other important subjects.

Within the context of the field of education, what could be more important to educators than content learning?

After all, isn't that why children are in school? And why should deaf children learn any less content than hearing children do?

Some educators take this reasoning to an extreme.

They push for the use of American Sign Language (which has no relationship to English, and no written form) as the language of instruction in the classroom.

And they also advocate that *speaking and speechreading not be used at all in the classroom* except perhaps during an occasional and optional class period for learning oral skills.

It's all perfectly logical for those who look at content learning as an end in itself, rather than as a means to an end.

But—*why* are we educating deaf children?

Logically, the goal should be to help them become self-sufficient adult members of society.

And how does a person become self-sufficient?

By getting a good job.

And how does he get a good job?

By convincing an employer to hire or promote him.

And what do employers say is the biggest obstacle to hiring or promoting a deaf person?

Do they say that deaf people don't know enough science? No.

That they don't know enough history? No.

That they don't know enough math? Sometimes.

According to those who make the decisions, the biggest obstacle to employment and promotion of the deaf is *communication*.

Employers complain that too often, their deaf employees cannot communicate adequately, if at all, on the job.

Fortunately, some educators *do* note what is happening in the real world. For example, Donald F. Moores, *Educating the Deaf:*

> Problems arise not because of the cognitive demands of a job but because of difficulties in communication, especially insufficient command of the English language....The major obstacle [deaf people] face on the job is difficulty of communication, which has restricted job mobility and advancement....The greatest problems noted by supervisors related to difficulties of communication....the deaf worker identified communication difficulties as the major on-the-job problem limiting the advancement of deaf individuals.

Christiansen & Barnartt in Paul C. Higgins & Jeffrey E. Nash, *Understanding Deafness Socially:*

> Amount of education is not as strong a predictor of the socioeconomic status of deaf workers as it is for hearing workers. Barnartt showed that, for hearing males, amount of education is one of the strongest predictors. For both deaf males and deaf females, on the other hand, it was one of the weakest of the statistically significant predictors.

Jerome D. Schein in Higgins & Nash:

> In their daily contacts with the general population—whether at work or in commerce—deaf people must depend upon [oral] skills with which they are uncomfortable and for which many have inadequate competence.

The journal *Training and Development* reported that recruiters ranked communication skills (interpersonal, oral presentation and written) as the most important factors in their hiring decisions.

For managerial positions, strong communication skills were deemed to be mandatory.

In regard to the entire workforce (not just to deaf people), the Center for Public Resources published a survey of companies, labor unions and school systems to see how well schools are meeting the needs of the workplace (*Basic Skills in the U.S. Work Force*). It reported:

The person who is deficient in the basic abilities (speaking, reading, listening, writing, and critical thinking) stands
less chance of advancement in the company; the handicap
may be for a lifetime.

The researchers were especially discouraged by the wide gap
between the perceptions of educators and the actual experience of
companies as to which skills are necessary in the workplace.

Non-oral deaf people tend to work in lower-paying, blue-collar
jobs that require little or no communication.

And most non-oral deaf professionals work in sheltered, signing
environments—in schools or organizations for the deaf.

Numerous studies show that deaf people are underemployed—
that they are qualified for better jobs than the ones they hold.

These facts, too, illustrate that the main problem is not that deaf
people don't have enough education for better jobs (although this
is often a problem as well).

The major problem is that many of them cannot communicate
well enough to get the better jobs.

But, say some educators, that's not our problem.

Our job, they say, is to teach as much content as possible so that
our deaf students will achieve higher scores.

The higher the scores, the better we teachers are doing our job.

What happens to the students after they leave school, they say,
is not our fault.

So they pass the buck to the Americans with Disabilities Act.

I have no doubt that some day the ADA will do good work in
helping some deaf people under some circumstances, just as the
Civil Rights Act of 1964 has definitely helped some blacks and other
minorities under some circumstances.

But three long decades after racism was supposed to have been
eliminated in the United States, racial discrimination is still very
much with us.

The ADA, like the Civil Rights Act, is a legal landmark and a step forward—but it's wishful thinking to expect it to come anywhere near ending discrimination based on disability.

The Civil Rights Act was not a panacea, and neither is the ADA.

The problem is not the ADA, but the unrealistic expectations of people who feel that the ADA will help all deaf people under all circumstances—and, thus, eliminate the need to learn and use speaking and speechreading. This viewpoint is represented by the claim of an ASL militant on the Internet:

> There is no reason why oral skills are necessary in to-day's world. Between written and electronic communication and the use of interpreters where required (particularly in large meetings), a Deaf person can advance as far as any hearing person in his career track. And if an employee is not promoted simply because he does not use oral com-munication, that's discrimination and that's illegal.

He and others who denigrate oral skills ignore a key point:

Under the ADA, it is legal to deny jobs and advancement to people who lack speaking and speechreading capabilities if:

1. the capabilities are related to essential functions of the job, or
2. the needed accommodations will cause undue hardship to the employer.

A great many jobs fall into these categories.

It is true that many jobs do not require oral communication. These include manual crafts and trades that have been traditional sources of work for the non-oral deaf. And in some white-collar jobs, most of the communication is in writing.

And if the oral requirements of a job are limited to an occasional meeting or training session, a part-time sign language interpreter can be brought in to help a non-oral deaf person participate.

Then there are workplaces in which communication that has traditionally been oral could be handled just as well (or perhaps even better) via high-tech solutions such as an electronic message system (e-mail) on computer terminals.

Yes—good will, human ingenuity and the ADA can help.

But in many jobs—usually the better jobs, and especially the management and executive jobs—the essential functions depend to a greater or lesser extent on oral communication.

It isn't a matter of illegal discrimination.

It's a matter of the requirements of the job.

It is a self-delusion to expect an advertising agency to hire non-oral men and women as account executives (let alone promote them to account supervisors or head of account services).

Or a food manufacturer to hire them to call on supermarket purchasing offices.

Or an insurance company to hire them for field investigations.

Although being able to *hear* is not an essential function of these jobs, being able to *communicate orally* is an essential function.

How can a garage, for example, promote a non-oral mechanic to service manager, when he must talk to the customers who bring in their cars and understand their descriptions of the problems?

If oral communication is essential to the performance of a job in an efficient, professional manner, that qualification is not removed by the ADA.

And even when there *is* discrimination, it will be difficult and time-consuming to establish precisely what acts are discriminatory, to define what constitutes undue hardship for an employer, and to enforce compliance with the law.

What people *should* do, for moral or legal reasons—and what they *do* do, for economic or other reasons—are often two very different things.

It bears repeating: not every deaf person can develop the level of oral skills required by these jobs—but many can.

Most prelingually deaf people may not be able to develop outstanding speaking capabilities. But they are capable of developing useful speaking capabilities.

And the postlingually deaf, by definition, already can speak.

Along the same lines, most deaf people may not become out-standing speechreaders—but they are capable of developing useful speechreading capabilities.

Some jobs require no oral skills at all, and some require an incredibly high level—but in between, there's a broad range of opportunities with a broad range of requirements.

A certain level of speechreading and speaking can help qualify a deaf person for a certain level of supervision over hearing people, or a certain level of responsibility in management.

Yet some educators or would-be educators, by denigrating and de-emphasizing oral skills, would deprive many deaf people of the opportunity to qualify for these jobs.

They can do serious harm to the future employability of the students with such a myopic never-mind-the-speech, content-is-all approach.

Possession of oral communication skills does not guarantee that a deaf person *will* get one of these jobs.

But a lack of oral skills guarantees that she will *not*.

ADA or no.

Many deaf college students believe they will have the luxury of holding out for jobs where their coworkers will be glad to learn sign language for their benefit, or where their employers will have to provide them with full-time interpreters.

Some coworkers may be willing to learn a few signs, but few if any would become fluent enough to carry on a business-related conversation. Learning sign, and especially ASL, takes a great deal of motivation and effort over an extended period of time.

Few people have enough time for their families, let alone time to spare for learning sign language—especially for the benefit of a coworker who *refuses* to speak or speechread.

There are many qualified, experienced *hearing* people looking for jobs or bucking for promotions. Non-speakers have to compete with them.

According to *Time*, a Labor Department study released in 1992 indicated that 30 percent of each class of U.S. college graduates between now and 2005 will be unemployed or underemployed.

It's tough for *anyone* to get *any* kind of job.

If two equally qualified people apply for a job or are in line for promotion—but one will cost the company extra for interpreters— why should the employer choose the non-speaker, when someone else can do the job just as well for less money? A company is in business to make a profit, and has an obligation to its shareholders to maximize its profits.

On one hand, many companies invest in worthwhile causes that don't necessarily improve their bottom lines. Some large, public-spirited companies have both the means and the desire to take on the additional expense of accommodations for non-speakers.

But the bluest of America's blue-chip companies are running into the red by billions of dollars and eliminating hundreds of thousands of jobs. A realistic view of the economy and the job market indicates that, given a choice between qualified applicants, an awful lot of companies will opt to minimize their expenses.

Thus, an educational policy that devaluates and de-emphasizes speaking and speechreading will effectively limit a deaf person's employability, as well as his ability to communicate with hearing people off the job as well.

It is a fallacy to believe that the ADA has made speaking and speechreading unimportant.

And it is irresponsible to minimize the amount of time devoted to teaching and using oral skills in the classroom.

When I took typing five decades ago, U-High gave students a choice of learning the standard QWERTY keyboard (named for the first six keys in the first row of letters) or the Dvorak keyboard.

Miss Merrick explained how the Dvorak's more efficient arrangement of keys permitted faster typing with fewer errors and less fatigue. So I opted for the Dvorak.

To do my homework, I bought a Royal portable typewriter with the Dvorak keyboard. I used it when I went on to the college at the University of Chicago and then to the school of journalism at the University of Illinois.

My friends and classmates were impressed when I typed faster and more accurately than they did.

But in the journ school, I discovered the other side of the coin.

For my first course in newspaper writing, the classroom had typewriters so the students could write their stories in class.

But all of the machines had QWERTY keyboards, so I couldn't use them.

So I shlepped my portable back and forth between my fraternity house and Greg Hall three days a week.

And I did the same thing when I took the course in advanced reporting.

And I did the same thing when I took the course in rewriting.

Finally, I graduated and went to work on the sports desk of the *Chicago Sun-Times.* Each of the copy editors around the rim of the desk had a typewriter for writing headlines and rewriting clumsy paragraphs.

Since I could not use the newspaper's QWERTY keyboards, I brought my Royal to work and left it there.

Then I went to Cleveland to work as a copywriter. Naturally, all of the typewriters in the ad department had QWERTY keyboards, and I couldn't use them.

So I left the Royal downtown for my work.

But now I wanted to start writing magazine articles and fiction at home. So I needed a typewriter at home as well.

At first, I lugged the Royal home two or three nights a week. Then, because of the hassle, I brought it home only on weekends.

Finally, one unbearably hot Friday afternoon during the dog days of August, I shlepped the portable home and peeled off my soaked shirt and sat down to think.

I was a writer.

No matter where I worked, I was going to have to use a typewriter.

And it was becoming quite clear that no matter what benefits the Dvorak keyboard had in terms of speed and accuracy and comfort level, the places where I worked simply did not have typewriters with the Dvorak keyboard.

Like it or not, QWERTY was universal in the workplace—even if it was slower and less accurate and more tiring than the Dvorak keyboard. That was a fact of life.

I had two alternatives.

I could shlep my portable around with me for the rest of my life, since I was helpless in the face of QWERTY.

Or I could learn the QWERTY keyboard and be able to use any typewriter in any job I had in any workplace. And I could leave my portable with the Dvorak keyboard at home, where it was just fine for my moonlighting.

It was an easy choice. I stopped at a bookstore and picked up a typing self-tutorial for the QWERTY keyboard.

Fortunately, it was quite easy to learn the QWERTY keyboard with a couple of weeks of practice. So there weren't any real problems associated with my belated awakening.

Unfortunately, it will take a lot longer than two weeks of practice for today's non-oral deaf graduates to catch up—when they try to find a job or get promoted, and discover a hard fact of life:

Signing—despite its indisputable benefits in permitting very fast, accurate and comfortable communication among signers—is no more usable in the hearing workplace than the Dvorak keyboard was for me.

19

Dr. Halfbaked goes to Israel

Out of the clear blue May 1970 sky, Barbara said:
"Let's move to Israel."
"Why?"
"Why not?"
Six weeks later, Barbara and I and our four daughters were going through immigration procedures at Ben-Gurion Airport.

When Barbara asked her fateful question, we had just returned a couple of weeks earlier from our first visit to the Jewish state.

Before that visit in April as a tourist, I had mentally pictured Israel as a place where half the people were kibbutzniks dancing the hora in the wheat fields, and the other half were ultra-Orthodox Jews dancing with the Torah in the yeshivas.

Not long after the turn of the twentieth century, that may have been an exaggerated but not-too-far-out-of-the-ballpark description of the pre-state Jewish community.

But in 1970, I discovered that the State of Israel included a great deal more than that. While the country still had an abundance of raw edges, it displayed a remarkable level of urban sophistication and technological development in many areas.

Its variegated social and geographical landscape was a potpourri of peoples, cultures and institutions, created by an influx of Jews from all over the world, intertwined with an archaeological testament to a Jewish history that went back thousands of years.

The idea of rebuilding the Jewish nation on its ancient site—land which had been seized by the Romans and successive invaders—had come to be known as Zionism.

In the late 1880s, the first wave of Zionist immigrants arrived from Europe to join the Jews who were already living there.

When the second wave started coming in the 1920s, during the British mandate over Palestine, the nation-building effort picked up steam on all fronts.

The pioneers turned the neglected wasteland into productive fields and verdant forests, built the new city of Tel Aviv on the sand dunes, and created the infrastructure for a future state.

Then Hitler's genocidal destruction of one-third of the world's Jewry during the Holocaust gave the final impetus to the birth of the State of Israel in 1948.

When we visited Israel, the state was 22 years old—no longer a newborn infant, but far from maturity.

The tiny state—smaller than New Jersey, with fewer people than the Chicago—was making extraordinarily good use of its human resources and innovative technology to compensate for the lack of natural resources.

It was surrounded by decidedly unfriendly neighboring nations with 300 times as much land and 200 times as many people, whose antipathy toward Jews predated the state itself.

Some people see the goal of Zionism to be the immigration of *all* Jews from *all* countries, but this is patently unrealistic. While Jews in many countries would be better off in Israel, this is not necessarily true of Jews in western countries such as the U.S.

While there are compelling practical reasons in other countries (e.g., overt antisemitic persecution or low standards of living) that push Jews toward a safer or more comfortable life in Israel, these factors are usually not applicable to American Jews. Especially not to American Jews who live very safely and very comfortably in upscale north shore communities.

Therefore, Americans who emigrate to Israel tend to do so for ideological reasons.

The thing is, however, Barbara and I were no more Zionist than were most American Jews. We had grown up knowing vaguely about the Jewish state and feeling proud of it in an abstract way.

In 1967, the Six Day War brought into sharper focus what was going on in that corner of the world. Israel became less of an abstraction, more the object of our concern and pride.

Three years later, when friends from our congregation suggested we share a car and guide on a tour of Israel, we readily agreed.

Israel's miniature size makes it quite easy to tour the country from end to end (260 miles at its longest point) and side to side (nine miles wide at its narrowest point, 70 miles at its widest).

It is only 40 miles from the Mediterranean Sea to Jerusalem in the Judean Hills, and another 20 miles down to the Jordan River.

Since touring was a matter of taking in the sights accompanied by a running commentary from our private guide, my inability to hear made little or no difference—for the most part.

On one notable occasion, however, my deafness did prevent me from fully experiencing the moment.

We were up north, staying overnight on a kibbutz. It was a pastoral setting in a lush green valley. Beyond the hills to the west was the sea; beyond the hills to the north was Lebanon.

After a long day of touring, we fell asleep quickly. As usual, I slept soundly.

On the way to the dining hall the next morning, Barbara told me that she had been woken by a noise in the middle of the night. She had looked out the window, seen nothing, and gone back to sleep.

At breakfast, we found out that katyusha rockets had been fired from across the border by terrorists.

One had exploded about 30 meters from the house where we were sleeping.

Fortunately, it caused no damage other than to the landscape. We stared at the raw pit gouged out of the earth.

Although the sight made a definite impact on me, my perception of this incident would have been somewhat enhanced if I had heard the explosion as well.

As I was saying: a couple of weeks after we returned from our trip as tourists, Barbara suggested that we move to Israel.

"Why?"

"Why not?"

We were very comfortable right where we were—among family and friends, in an affluent Jewish community, in one of America's finest school districts, amply compensated for doing the kind of work I enjoyed.

Those seemed like pretty good reasons why not.

"Let's try something different for a change," said Barbara. "We can rent out the house for two years and see what it's like."

Not exactly what you would call a strong Zionist motivation.

But it did get us moving.

Debby, 14, was inconsolable.

She had been looking forward to entering Highland Park High School in the fall, and now she was in tears about leaving her friends.

I drove her to a bluff overlooking Lake Michigan, and we sat there while I explained that we understood how she felt, but her mother and I had decided to do something—and that was that.

She finally calmed down by eliciting a promise that if we decided to move back to the States, she could stay in Israel if she wanted.

Julie, 12, was agreeable. Laurie, 10, was enthusiastic. Lisa, 2, didn't have much to say one way or the other.

We found a tenant for our house, and telephoned Israel to make arrangements to rent a furnished apartment there.

After a round of farewell parties, we stuffed our clothes into three suitcases and seven duffel bags the night before we left.

Then we flew off to do something different with our lives.

The Ministry of Absorption had a station at Ben-Gurion Airport to process new immigrants and provide them with documents.

As we gave the clerk the names of our children, she beamed. Daughter...daughter...daughter...daughter. When we finished feeding her names, she looked up expectantly.

"No boys?"

"No boys."

"Don't worry, you'll have more children—and they'll be boys."

The usual procedure for new immigrants from western countries was to live temporarily in a hostel-type absorption center at the Jewish Agency's expense for their first months in the country.

During this time they studied Hebrew in an intensive course called an *ulpan*—five or six hours a day, five days a week—and started becoming acculturated to the country. They also used this time to look for work and for permanent housing.

We, on the other hand, chose to skip the absorption center and plunge right in.

So we rented a four-bedroom apartment in a modern high-rise condo complex. It was built around an Olympic-size swimming pool and tennis courts near Tel Aviv University, about a mile from the Mediterranean Sea.

As Barbara says, we didn't go to Israel to be pioneers.

Like Highland Park, the area was an affluent neighborhood of businessmen, professionals, academics, government ministers and entertainers. The owners of the apartment were on a sabbatical at MIT, and had left behind all their furniture, dishes, books, record albums and toys—just as we had done in America.

Through a combination of *ulpanim* and tutors, the girls and Barbara soaked up Hebrew. Then, when school started the month after we arrived, the girls' immersion in the new language was almost total.

But on the first day of school, Debby came home in tears. She hadn't understood a word of what was being said in her classes—which included geometry, chemistry and Arabic.

She may as well have been deaf.

That evening, someone told us about the American School. It was mainly for the children of the diplomatic corps; the language of instruction was English.

If we enrolled Debby there, she would be able to follow everything in the classroom from the first day and would be happy with English-speaking friends.

We said thanks, but no, thanks.

As my parents had wanted for me, we wanted Debby to be mainstreamed despite the communication problem, not isolated in a sheltered environment.

The next day, we sat down with the headmaster of Debby's high school to see what could be done. He called in some students from her classes who lived in our neighborhood, and asked them to help her get along in and out of class.

He said that all he wanted Debby to do was sit in class and listen. Sooner or later, she would start understanding the language well enough to follow what was going on. He wouldn't expect much academically from her for a few months.

Within a day or two Debby was meeting people and having fun. And eventually she picked up the language, and she picked up an education, and she picked up her diploma four years later along with the rest of her class.

For Julie in seventh grade and Laurie in fifth grade, the situation was similar—but not quite as difficult and traumatic as it was for a freshman in high school.

Lisa went to a nursery down the block with other two-year-olds, and soon was chattering away in Hebrew without benefit of either *ulpan* or tutor.

In the meantime: from our first week in Israel, I was picking up paying work. All of it was in English.

First, I was introduced to somebody who introduced me to an architect who was developing a hotel and shopping center in the old city of Jaffa.

He needed a proposal aimed at American investors; I wrote it.

That led to other proposals, including one for a master plan for Ben-Gurion Airport, one for an air force base in Singapore, and one for an airport in Uganda at a place called Entebbe.

Second, I started writing scripts for the educational TV station. English is the country's second language. Most students took eight years of English—from fifth grade through twelfth—and, as part of the courses, watched my TV programs in their classrooms.

Third, I started freelancing for advertising agencies—writing ads to appear in the English-language *Jerusalem Post*, and brochures to promote Israeli products in Europe and the United States.

The agencies' clients included an airline, a bank, an oil company and an insurance company.

Fourth, I joined Tel Aviv University as an editor of academic papers to be published abroad in English-language journals.

Since my work—all in English—was keeping me busy day and night, I put little time into learning Hebrew. Barbara and the girls were far ahead of me from day one.

So there we were, not long after moving halfway around the world—comfortably settled in a nice home, immersed in a new culture, thriving in school, making new friends, and doing well professionally. We had landed on our feet and running.

But we didn't launch our new lives without help in greasing the skids, which made it less of a hassle.

In Highland Park, we left our power of attorney with some old friends. They collected the rent from our tenant...paid the mortgage on the house...paid bills that came after we left the country...bought a new furnace when the old one broke down in the middle of the winter...had the motor on my electric typewriter changed to 220 volts and air expressed it to me (this was in the pre-PC days of 1970)...shipped 20 heavy boxes of reference books...sent Barbara things she discovered she needed...cleared up a mistake on my American Express account...hounded my lawyer to speed up the personal injury suit from my traffic accident...had some diseased elm trees on our property cut down...sent me information for my income tax return...and arranged loans on my life insurance when we bought a home here.

They took quite a load off our hands and our minds.

In Tel Aviv, there was a family we had met a couple of times back in America. He had been director of the Jewish summer camp in Wisconsin which Debby had attended, and they had moved to Israel the year before we did. When we phoned Israel to arrange for an apartment, the call was to them.

They picked us up at the airport and got us settled in the rented apartment...fed us information on how to deal with the immigration bureaucracy...and introduced us to their friends, who became our friends. He was a director at the educational television station, and he introduced me to the producer of the English programs—who asked me to write a pilot, which led to contracts for several series for various grades.

So our running start was clearly facilitated by the presence and help of friends in Highland Park and Tel Aviv.

Unfortunately, my professional progress had an inverse effect on my learning Hebrew.

All of my work was in English, and all of the people I worked with—agency executives, university professors, TV producers— were fluent in English (and Hebrew and other languages).

Israelis, like Europeans, are multilingual.

There was no pressing need for me to learn Hebrew. And the more work I picked up, the less time was left for studying the language.

So I didn't have the time for a full-time *ulpan*, and anyway the classroom-type instruction wasn't for me.

Still, I made some more-or-less sincere attempts to break out of the monolingualism that curses Americans. I went to a tutor, and picked up some self-instruction books. I learned the alphabet and some of the grammar, and began building a vocabulary.

But I didn't stick to it or give it a high enough priority to get very far.

You learn a language by being exposed to it; the more you hear it, the more you learn. Since I couldn't hear Hebrew being spoken around me, I thought I had a good excuse for not picking it up.

But then I found out that there are deaf people here who are as multilingual as any other Israelis. So I can't use that as an excuse for my failure to become fluent in the language.

Barbara and our daughters, on the other hand, became perfectly bilingual; they speak fluent Hebrew without an accent.

Julie, in fact, is trilingual; she learned Japanese passably well when she was in Japan teaching conversational English to Japanese businessmen.

My connection with Tel Aviv University came through Barbara. She was studying at an *ulpan* with an American-born woman who was married to an Israeli-born professor of political science.

At their home, he showed me an article he had just written for an academic journal—an analysis of the previous year's national elections in Israel—and asked me what I thought of it.

I said that the substance was good, but that the writing could be improved. He asked whether I would be interested in editing it.

After I did the job, he spread the word about me at the faculty of social sciences, where most of the editing available had been of the spelling-and-punctuation type.

Mine, on the other hand, went very deep—rearranging sentences and paragraphs, deleting repetitious or irrelevant material, clarifying muddy points, and rewriting hopeless passages.

I soon received a telephone call from the head of the research committee at the faculty. Would I be interested in a part-time job on the faculty as an editor of academic papers in political science, economics, sociology, labor relations, statistics and so on?

I had office hours at the university twice a week for a couple of hours, so people could bring in their manuscripts and talk to me if they wanted. The actual editing I did at home, just like my other freelance work.

What I especially liked about the work was that it gave me a concise, authoritative and up-to-date education about Israel from various angles—historical, political, economic and sociological.

While editing a paper, I could learn more about the country in six hours than I would otherwise learn in months or years.

On top of that, some of the faculty members and their families became good friends of ours.

Writing the television programs was a great deal of fun. It also did a great deal for my ego, because it was an opportunity to do ground-breaking work in the public eye.

Until I came along, the programs for teaching English had been written by English teachers—not by professional writers—so they tended to be humorless and plodding, filled with head shots of a teacher talking to the camera.

I combined education with entertainment, making the programs fun to watch, but always making the point clearly and repeatedly. The fun never got in the way of the education; on the contrary, the fun was a tool that made the education more effective.

For format and style, I borrowed liberally from my American background—Mel Brooks, "Laugh-In," Sid Caesar, "Sesame Street," the Marx Brothers, "Superman," "Batman," Ernie Kovacs.

Since the purpose of each program was to complement what the students were learning that week from their classroom teachers, a linguistic consultant from the Ministry of Education gave us guidelines to work from.

Every Monday, I had a script conference with the linguist (born in Israel), the producer (England), the director (Israel), and the co-ordinator (America).

First, I presented the script I had written the previous week.

Then the linguist told us what she wanted the next program to accomplish. She might, for example, say that it should illustrate the difference between present simple and present progressive.

My response, of course, would be "Huh?"

I had no idea what she was talking about. I had learned English as a native tongue, simply by living in an English-speaking society. Israelis, on the other hand, learn English as a second language, which involves rules and terminology I had never heard of.

So she would tell me that in English, present simple is something like "I play the guitar," meaning that I am capable of playing the guitar; present progressive is "I am playing the guitar," meaning that I am actually doing it right now.

Hebrew, on the other hand, has only one verb form for both of these situations; the meaning is determined by the context.

Based on the linguist's definition of the program's objective, I would write a 20-minute script—usually a mixture of skits, songs and animation.

My favorite creation was Doctor Halfbaked—a classic screwball inventor who was, in fact, my alter ego.

I gave him a wild-eyed, wild-haired maniacal character copied by Christopher Lloyd two decades later in the *Back to the Future* films.

He had a great talent for coming up with ill-conceived ideas that were eminently sensible and yet eminently impractical, such as his Rube Goldberg-style pocket-sized popcorn machine.

First, with a cutaway diagram of the machine, he used present simple to show how the machine worked. Then he turned on the machine and used present progressive to describe how the machine was working.

The Sheriff of Hollywood Hills was a movie within a movie. Sheriff Goodman wore white clothes, had flashing white teeth, and was consistently bumbling and incompetent. Burton Badman wore black clothes, was suave and expert, and bested Sheriff Goodman at every turn. The schoolmarm was Miss Ding-Dong.

Here We Are was about a department store owned by a man and his five sons—with all six characters played by the same actor.

My first series went on the air in 1971.

Year after year, the programs were telecast to succeeding classes of students—a testament to either the high level of the programs or the low budget for new productions.

So most of the people who went to school in Israel during the next two decades or so have seen my programs—and, I hope, learned to speak better English.

I figured that it was a lot easier for me to teach the country to speak English than it was for me to learn to speak Hebrew.

Plan A was to try out the country for two years and see how it went. But from day one it went just fine.

The emotional high of being an Israeli, and of being part of history in the making, compensated for what we had given up in material benefits by leaving the States.

The life was interesting, stimulating, varied, challenging.

And simply living in Israel was one of the ultimate expressions of being Jewish.

After only two months, we decided there was no point in waiting out the full two years. So we switched to Plan B.

We bought our own apartment in the same complex, identical to the one we were renting, and had our furniture shipped over from the States.

It wasn't until we moved to Israel that my mother told me about a twist of fate in my father's life that I had never heard about—but which now became intriguingly relevant.

My father, born in Lithuania, had belonged to a youth group whose members were training to be farmers in Eretz Israel (the pre-state Jewish community in what was then Palestine).

But before the group carried out its plans, my father emigrated to the United States with his parents in 1919 when he was 16 years old.

Eventually, the Lithuanian group did emigrate and set up a farm.

Which means that if my father had gone with the group instead of going to the States, I would have been a native-born Israeli instead of a 37-year-old new immigrant.

Rudyard Kipling, referring to the omnipresent British empire of his day, wrote that it was impossible to go anywhere without hearing the melody of "God Save the Queen":

> *Take 'old o' the Wings o' the Mornin'*
> *An' flop round the earth till you're dead*
> *But you won't get away from the tune that they play*
> *To the blooming old rag overhead.*

But there's more to music than melody. There's also rhythm—just as Kipling's poetry itself is a beautiful example of rhythm.

Rhythm doesn't have to be heard. I can very easily imagine the throbbing rhythms of Kipling's verses as I roll them around in my head. And rhythm can be felt in the vibrations of music—especially the bass notes and the drums.

But what I particularly enjoy is *visual* rhythm. The sight of something moving rhythmically can be emotionally moving, much like the sound of music. And, like the British empire used to be, visual rhythm is all over the place.

First of all, there are the visual rhythms associated with music: the moving hands and arms of musicians and conductors, and the moving mouths and bodies of singers and dancers.

Many rock music videos are pure visual rhythm. And ethnic dances—especially fast or staccato dances like those of Brazilian or Russian or Spanish troupes—can be exhilarating.

Watching the simple, syncopated rhythm of reggae, the sharp accents of break dancing, or the joyous stomping of the hora may not be as richly rewarding as hearing the music as well.

But the visual pleasure is still quite substantial in its own right.

And it's easy for deaf people to dance when there's a steady beat that they can pick up from the other dancers.

Beyond the rhythm of music itself, there are many visual rhythms that can be almost hypnotizing in their attraction—

...the passing of people by a sidewalk cafe

...the flow of traffic in the street

...the ingenious movements of machinery in a factory.

Earlier, I mentioned the visual music of fire in a fireplace or campfire. A similar type of visual rhythm that I enjoy immensely is the movement of water—

...eddying around the fallen branches in streams

...splashing against rocks in whitewater rivers

...spilling in slow motion over majestic waterfalls

...undulating in whitecapped waves on windswept lakes,

...pounding in the surf along ocean shorelines.

Watching the fluid rhythms can be a spiritual experience.

Rosh Hashanah, the Jewish new year, fell on a warm, sunny September day our first year in Israel.

We decided to go down to the Mediterranean Sea, a mile from our home, and have a welcoming celebration of sorts.

Five of us sat on a bluff in the sand dunes overlooking the sea: Barbara, my younger brother Guy (visiting the country for a few months), two of our friends, and me.

Without thinking about it, we arranged ourselves like a scene in a Fellini film.

Several yards to my right, Barbara sat with our two friends.

Farther away to my left, Guy sat in cross-legged meditation.

For an hour and a half, our friends harmonized on a random selection of Hebrew songs. Barbara joined in from time to time.

Sometimes I watched the singers singing. Sometimes I watched my brother meditating.

But mostly I watched the rolling surf rushing up onto the beach, and then the ebb of the water back into the sea, and then another volley of crashing waves, and another long slide back into the sea, with the blue sky meeting the blue Mediterranean along a razor-sharp horizon in the background, and fluffy white clouds drifting by overhead, and the bright morning sun warming our backs.

And I mused about the year to come.

So it wasn't Handel's *Messiah*. No matter.

It was very nice.

When we moved to Israel in 1970, a State Department regulation (since changed) held that an American who applied for citizenship in another country lost his American citizenship.

However, the State of Israel makes it possible to acquire Israeli citizenship without applying for it. The state automatically grants Israeli citizenship to new immigrants.

This means that immigrants from the United States can hold dual citizenship, with both Israeli and American passports, without losing the benefits of their American citizenship. They can even vote in American elections.

So, after having the status of temporary residents for three years (the normal procedure for immigrants from western countries), we automatically became Israeli citizens in the summer of 1973.

To celebrate, we bought a larger apartment—a penthouse in a building to be constructed in the same complex—with completion scheduled for two years later.

A penthouse? Hey, you live only once.

We didn't know it at the time, but we wouldn't live there at all.

A month after we signed the contract, a thunderous blast shook the windows at 10 o'clock in the morning on the quietest day of the year in Israel.

It was a violent forerunner of events that would shake up our lives once again.

I easily felt the sonic boom, which had come from an Israeli jet fighter streaking by overhead.

But I couldn't hear the wailing of air raid sirens around the country four hours later, which signaled the attack of the Egyptian army across the Suez Canal and the Syrian army down from the Golan Heights.

It was Yom Kippur, 1973.

20

When the walls came tumbling down

Even before the sirens wailed on the first day of the Yom Kippur War, my next-door neighbor had already received a phone call to join his army unit. He, like most Israeli men up to the age of 55, was in the reserves.

He had fought in the 1948 War of Independence at the age of 17, in the 1956 Sinai campaign at 25, in the 1967 Six Day War at 36. Now he was in his fourth war at the age of 42.

I had lived through America's involvement in three wars. But I hadn't fought in World War II or Korea or Vietnam.

More to the point: the American soldiers had been fighting in Europe and the South Pacific and the Far East—a long, long way from home. Chicago had never been in any danger.

Here, the fighting was in the peripheries of Israel itself—only five or ten minutes' flying time from the heavily populated Tel Aviv metropolitan area along the coast.

In fact, an Egyptian missile was headed straight for Tel Aviv at the beginning of the war, but was shot down by an Israeli Phantom over the Mediterranean.

The news from the fronts was sketchy. Hundreds of Egyptian tanks and thousands of soldiers had crossed the Suez Canal. The

Syrians had advanced into the Golan Heights. We were fighting a holding action while reserves were being mobilized.

Nevertheless, we never felt any personal danger. There are some things you take on faith, and the IDF (Israel Defense Forces) is one of them. On the other hand, the United Nations is not.

During the Arab advance on the first two days, no one at the UN was interested in a cease-fire. The turnaround came on the third day, when we started pushing back the invading armies.

We crossed the Canal and surrounded the Egyptian army. Only when we were winning did the UN call for a cease-fire; such is the history of that ostensibly impartial body's attitude toward Israel.

By the second day of the war, virtually all of our friends had been called up. But I wasn't even in the reserves.

I had just become a citizen a few weeks before, so I hadn't had a chance to bluff my way through the army registration process as I had 22 years earlier in Chicago.

So I walked into the IDF induction center at Tel Hashomer, which borders Tel Aviv on the east, to try my luck. I stopped a passing lieutenant and asked him how I could get into the army.

"You want to get out of the army?"

"No, I want to get *into* the army."

He pointed down the hall. "Try room 133."

At the doorway to room 133, I looked at the nameplate before knocking and entering. It identified the occupant as a psychiatrist.

When I left his office 20 minutes later, I was still a civilian.

My age (40) was no problem at all. The fact that I had never spent a day in uniform (the Boy Scouts didn't count) was more of a problem.

But the crowning blow was the communication problem: I couldn't speak Hebrew to any worthwhile degree.

Still, the doctor did have a suggestion for me.

Most of the able-bodied men on the kibbutzim had been called up—and there weren't enough people left to do their work. I could substitute for one of the absent members.

One phone call later, I was driving northeast to be the interim carpenter at a border kibbutz by the Jordan River.

It was the fourth day of the war. Barbara stayed home with the girls—who had to go to school, war or no war.

Neve Eitan is a small kibbutz with about 65 families near Bet She'an, a town whose history goes back to Roman times. It's a few miles south of Lake Kinneret, an hour and a half from Tel Aviv, within sight of villages in the Jordanian hills across the river.

The kibbutz, just west of the Jordan River, was founded in 1938 by pioneers from Poland. It received an infusion of new blood in the 1950s from a group of young sabras (native-born Israelis). Later, several immigrants from America became members.

There was plenty for me to do—mostly fixing things. I enjoyed working with my hands, mainly because it gave me a break from working with the written word.

There wasn't much for me to do in Tel Aviv anyhow. The all-out mobilization had slowed down the country's economy. Many of the people I worked with at the television station and the university had been called up, and advertising was way down.

One of my first jobs on the kibbutz was to build up one side of a cotton wagon out in the fields, so that the cotton wouldn't spill out when it was dumped in from the other side.

Unfortunately, I had to do it while the cotton was harvested and loaded into the wagon right under my nose—so my hay fever had me sneezing my head off for the next two days.

I fixed locks, built partitions and shelves, rehung doors, mended fences, repaired furniture and did other odd jobs on the farm, in the homes, and in the communal buildings (dining hall, children's houses, laundry, school classrooms, and so on).

I spent most of my leisure time with the immigrants from the United States and Canada. I slept on a couch in the home of one. Two others were English teachers in the regional schools, so they knew of and worked with my television programs.

Another of the members was originally from Libertyville, not far from Highland Park.

The rural life was a whole new world for me. From time to time, I took a day off from carpentry to lend a hand in the fish ponds—getting up at 3 a.m. and standing in water up to my chest and dragging the nets.

Or I helped on the cattle ranch on the Golan Heights, rounding up strays that had wandered through holes ripped in the fences by battling tanks.

On Friday afternoon, before driving back to Tel Aviv, I promised to return for another week. The war was still going on.

During the second week, several people asked me whether I was interested in joining the kibbutz.

I said that it might be fine for me, but there was no way Barbara was going to live there. Everyone started work at 6 a.m. or earlier, and the kibbutz had few of the comforts of Highland Park or north Tel Aviv.

So, at the end of the second week, I said good-bye to everyone and promised to stay in touch.

That weekend, I couldn't stop talking about the kibbutz.

Barbara suggested that if I enjoyed it so much, why not go back up for a third week?

So I did. The fighting had stopped, but the reserves were still mobilized; the carpenter had not yet returned.

After a round of emotional farewells at the end of the third week, I relaxed over the weekend. Then, unaccountably, I found myself driving back up for a fourth week.

The fifth week, Barbara left the girls in Tel Aviv and came up with me. She worked in the baby house from 6 a.m. to 2 p.m. and loved every minute of it.

The sixth week, the girls came up with us.

A month later, during the Hanukkah break between semesters, we put our apartment up for sale and and moved to the kibbutz as candidates for membership.

Like our move to Israel, our move to the kibbutz started out as a passing thought that gradually turned into a "why not?" spur-of-the-moment action. Still, I don't know what gives people the idea that we are impulsive.

Although we sold the apartment we had been living in, we kept the penthouse that was under construction.

The original arrangement was that I would spend half my time doing carpentry and half doing my Tel Aviv work. However, it soon became apparent that I didn't have enough time to do both.

Regretfully, I gave up the carpentry. By that time, the regular carpenter had been demobilized.

Barbara's job was in the baby house. Later, when her babies moved to the toddlers' house, she went with them.

Barbara and I were given a three-room house—a living room, a bedroom and an office for me, plus a bathroom and a kitchenette. Since we had all three meals in the dining hall, the tiny kitchenette was basically for making coffee or baking a cake.

Lisa moved into the *gan* (kindergarten) with the other 4- and 5-year-olds. Julie and Laurie moved in with the 14- to 16-year-olds. That's where they kept their clothes and slept at night.

Julie and Laurie enrolled in the regional school for the kibbutzim in the area. Lisa's school was in a wing of the kindergarten.

Debby, however, was in the middle of her senior year and was preparing for her matriculation exams. Her teachers felt that if she changed schools, she would blow the whole year.

So she stayed in Tel Aviv with a friend of ours during the week, and came up to the kibbutz for weekends and holidays.

At 4 p.m., the children came to their parents' homes—then went to the dining hall with them at 7 p.m. for supper.

Predictably, our friends in Tel Aviv—especially the Israeli-born ones—thought the move was a halfbaked idea.

Since they couldn't understand why we moved from Highland Park to Israel, there was no way they could understand why we moved from Tel Aviv to a kibbutz.

It wasn't that we are socialists; far from it. We are firm believers in free enterprise and individualism, if not dog eat dog. Yet there were some things about kibbutz life that appealed to us.

For one thing, it was quite different from anything we had ever experienced. In some ways, the jump from Tel Aviv to the kibbutz was greater than the jump from Highland Park to Tel Aviv had been.

From my perspective, one of the biggest differences was that almost all of the contact between people on the kibbutz was face-to-face—which was a boon for me.

At that time, there were no telephones in the homes. Aside from a public pay phone, the only phones on the kibbutz were in the offices and farm buildings.

So people talked to each other in the dining hall, or on the sidewalks, or simply knocked on each other's doors when they wanted to say something or have a shmooze.

The absence of phones was the great equalizer. It was as easy for me to be in touch with people as it was for anyone else.

In the late afternoon and evening, people sat on their porches and on the communal lawns in front of their homes—talking with family or friends, or reading or snoozing or tossing a Frisbee or just looking out over the fields at the hills of Jordan.

The weather was usually pleasant most of the year, like in San Diego. In July and August, the mid-day sun could be blazing hot—but in the evening, the temperature became balmy.

In the winter, it rained a bit and sometimes was chilly—but not for long.

Like anywhere else, the members put in a full day in a job. But they had the option of changing their jobs every few years.

Someone might work in the fields, then the fish ponds, then for an organization linked to the kibbutz movement (an insurance company, an experimental farm, a marketing co-op, a fish-packing factory), then hold an administrative job on the kibbutz (such as farm manager or executive secretary), then with the milk cows, then run one of the pultrusion machines making fiberglass profiles in the factory on the kibbutz, and so on.

In theory, the managerial positions rotated among the members. In practice, however, some people were better managers and held managerial positions more frequently. Some people couldn't or wouldn't take the responsibility of management.

The women didn't have to cook (unless their jobs were in the kitchen); they didn't have to do laundry (unless their jobs were in the laundry); and they weren't tied down by their babies or toddlers (unless they worked in the baby or toddlers' houses).

And since they lived in one-bedroom homes without children, it took only a few minutes to clean house—usually with the help of their husbands.

So the women were free to do whatever kind of work they wanted, including all the traditional male occupations. They could work in the fields or the fishponds or the factory or whatever.

But in practice, women rarely worked in branches other than the cow barn or the chicken house, partly because the work was so physically strenuous.

Most of the women chose traditional female occupations as teachers or in the kitchen or the children's houses or in office jobs or as nurses or researchers. Like the men, they could change jobs every few years.

The kibbutz movement offered courses at an educational center where members could learn specialized skills such as carpentry and cooking, or how to manage a specific branch or the kibbutz as a whole.

In return, everyone received cradle-to-the-grave care; the kibbutz even had its own cemetery. The kibbutz provided each family with a home, meals, laundry, medical and dental care, child care and education—plus a monthly allowance with which to buy clothing, furniture and incidentals, and to pay for vacations.

Cars from the pool were available for personal trips.

All of my income from my work at the university and the ad agencies and the television went to the kibbutz.

The assets we had owned before we joined the kibbutz (the penthouse, our securities, our furniture) remained ours.

I asked Barbara: "Are we kibbutz people or penthouse people?"
She replied: "Both, I suppose."

One of the facts of life on a border kibbutz is that it's an inviting target for a terrorist attack.

And, in fact, there was an attack on our kibbutz a year before we joined. Fortunately, no one was hurt.

But other kibbutzim and towns near Israel's borders have not been so fortunate.

The indiscriminate terrorist killings of civilians in Israel, including children in their schoolrooms, have left a bloody record that spans several decades.

So all of the men on the kibbutz had their own automatic rifles— either the compact, lightweight Israeli-made Uzi or the big, heavy Soviet-made Kalachnikov.

The closest I had ever come to guns was when I had a Red Ryder BB rifle as kid. I did not care for guns at all.

But this was neither the place nor the time to be choosy.

So I accepted an Uzi and learned how to take it apart and clean it, and then how to shoot it.

On a neighboring kibbutz up the road, there was a patch of scrub land that was used for a practice firing range.

One morning, determined to improve my aim, I rode my bike to the range and spent five minutes alone shooting at a target.

Then I spent another half hour using my T-shirt to beat out the brush fires I had started.

That's how I found out that the red-tipped bullets were tracers.

The kibbutz buildings, not including the fields, were surrounded by a fence topped with barbed wire. A perimeter road ran around the kibbutz just inside the fence. An electric gate and guardhouse at the main entrance blocked the road.

Usually, we posted a guard at the gate only at night. However, depending on the state of alert (the border with Jordan ran along the river a couple of miles down the road), the guardhouse might be manned around the clock or not at all.

When the alert was high, a second guard patrolled the perimeter road in a jeep to check the other gates in the fence, which were chained at night.

As did all the men, I took a two-hour turn guarding the front gate during the night once every two or three weeks.

The gate was brightly lit by floodlights.

Beyond the pool of light, the fields faded off into pitch blackness on moonless nights.

Across the river, the lights of the Jordanian villages twinkled.

Above, the stars were clear and sharp.

Once in a while, if an army patrol along the river discovered tracks from a terrorist crossing, the night would be punctuated by flares as the soldiers searched for the gunmen before they could infiltrate a kibbutz.

And I would sit there in the guardhouse, my loaded Uzi at my elbow, staring out through the windows beyond the pool of light, seeing nothing because of the blackness, hearing nothing because of my deafness.

A mechanized division could have been roaring and clanking up the road toward me, and I wouldn't have known it.

Not to worry.

The IDF had aerial surveillance, and outposts and minefields and border patrols all along the Jordan River.

Small groups of terrorists could and did infiltrate into Israel—but there was no way a larger force, let alone mechanized, could even get ready to attack across the river without the IDF knowing and raising the alarm hours or days in advance.

Rather, we were on guard against raids by lone terrorists or small bands. Since they didn't announce their approach with noise, there wasn't anything for me to hear, anyway.

For some years, Barbara had been interested in making pottery. In America, she had potted regularly at art centers; in Tel Aviv, she had used a wheel in the studio of a friend.

Now she set up her own studio in one of the underground concrete bomb shelters that dotted the kibbutz.

During wartime, the children slept in the shelters; the rest of the time, the shelters were used as utility rooms.

She bought a second-hand kickwheel to use while she waited for an electric wheel to be shipped from the States.

Other people joined her after work and some evenings, and she started teaching the children how to work with clay.

Eventually the kibbutz allotted her a large room with real sunlight coming through the windows, and bought a kiln for her. The room doubled as an art studio and ceramics studio.

Normally, every physically capable member of the kibbutz put in a six-day week in some income-producing activity (either in one of the kibbutz branches, or outside the kibbutz as I did), or in a support service on the kibbutz.

Some kibbutzniks produced income as full-time artists, musicians or writers (just as I was a full-time writer, albeit not the literary type).

To some extent, the kibbutz movement supported the arts by subsidizing a few selected members who had demonstrable talent but were not producing enough income (if any) with their art.

Perhaps the art itself, such as poetry, was not lucrative.

Or perhaps the artist, such as a painter, had not yet broken into the market.

After an appraisal of the artist's talent, the members of a kibbutz might vote to give her a day or two a week to practice her art; the rest of the week she would work at her regular job.

That's what happened with Barbara.

At first, she was given one day a week to work in her pottery studio; later, it was extended to two days. The other four days she worked in the baby house.

Which means that six days a week she had her hands full of soft brown stuff.

Each kibbutz has a committee responsible for culture (*tarboot*). This is a rather all-encompassing term; the committee—or, more usually, the committee chairman—organizes various activities.

It's something like being the social director on a cruise ship, and it is in addition to his or her regular job.

Not long after we joined the kibbutz, I was put in charge of *tarboot*. The job involved arranging celebrations for each of the holidays...booking a stage play or singer or comedian...chartering buses for a trip to the Tel Aviv Museum of Art...getting movies once or twice a week and showing them outdoors...bringing in a popular professor or a member of the Knesset (parliament) to speak on a current topic...throwing parties on Friday nights...and more.

The outdoor movies were unforgettable. Actually, the movies themselves were forgettable—but the experience wasn't.

A white, billboard-size plywood screen faced a large grassy area. Everybody brought aluminum folding chairs or chaise longues, or spread blankets and pillows on the grass.

With a canopy of stars above and a backdrop of rustling palm trees, it was pretty close to nirvana.

All that was missing was coffee, tea and cookies.

So I posted a notice on the bulletin board in the dining hall announcing the next movie—and telling each person to bring his or her own cup. I didn't like paper cups, and I had no intention of washing a hundred or so cups after the movie.

That evening, I set up a table next to the movie projector and plugged a couple of hot-water urns into the extension cord.

Then I set out jars of instant coffee and tea bags and sweeteners and spoons, and three or four 25-pound boxes of cookies.

And that's the way the outdoor movie nights were for as long as I ran *tarboot*.

Instant nirvana. Just add hot water.

But that was two decades ago.

Today, unfortunately, the kibbutz has cable TV in the homes of all the members. So movies are no longer shown outdoors.

Alas.

The kibbutz put out a mimeographed newsletter every once in a while. So I wrote a series entitled *The Capitalist Kibbutz*, in which I proposed several innovations that I thought might improve the financial position of the kibbutz.

For example, one was to pay the members for productivity above the norm for people with their capabilities. The difficulty and disagreeability of each job would be factored into the formula.

Another was to convert the dining hall into a restaurant, with each member using his food budget to pay cash for each item taken at each meal. This would cut down on the amount of food taken but not eaten.

I was kidding on the square. But today, kibbutzim are actually experimenting with such non-socialist notions.

During the harvest festival of Succot, many Jews eat their meals in a *succa*—an outdoor palm-covered booth.

One of my *tarboot* responsibilities was to construct a huge *succa* for 400 people, attached to the front of the dining hall. So, a couple of days after Yom Kippur, I built several modular sections of open wooden framework for the walls and stacked them at the side of the dining hall, along with ladders, hammers and nails.

Then I took a van with a large roof-top rack and hauled in a dozen 30-foot aluminum irrigation pipes from the fields.

After dinner that night, the scene in front of the dining hall was like a barn raising in the Old West. Some of the men held the wall sections in position while others nailed them together.

When the wall framework was up, we laid the irrigation pipes on top to serve as rafters, then laid palm branches on top of the pipes. More palm branches were tied to the vertical framework to make the walls. In two hours, the structure was finished.

For the next couple of days, women and children decorated the *succa* with clusters of dates and other crops from the farm, along with paper decorations the children had made in school.

The Succot holiday lasts for eight days, starting with a festive dinner on the first night. For the second night, I booked a popular singer to give a performance in the dining hall.

After the celebration on the first night, a woman on my *tarboot* committee told me that the quality of the loudspeakers in the dining hall wasn't too good. She suggested that we move a couple of huge full-range speakers from the auditorium to the dining hall for the singer's performance the next day.

So I took the van and we went to the auditorium and picked up the speakers. By now, it was nearly midnight.

Since the speakers were so heavy, I brought the van close to the front door of the dining hall by driving for 50 feet inside the high-ceilinged *succa*.

When we were still about 35 feet from the door, the woman doubled over in the front seat—her face twisted in agony, her body flinching. She was apparently having some kind of attack.

Quickly, I drove the remaining distance to the door and killed the engine. The woman continued to shudder spasmodically.

Finally, she raised her head tentatively and looked around.

Then she pointed out the window in back of us.

I had forgotten about the rack that stuck up three feet from the top of the van. It had plowed straight through the roof of the *succa*, dragging down the structure behind us.

The aluminum pipes had been crashing against the top of the van and then bouncing on the stone plaza, one after another—sounding like the realization of Chicken Little's worst nightmares accompanied by the world's largest glockenspiel.

And I hadn't heard a thing, but just kept plowing merrily all the way up to the front door as the walls came tumbling down.

As I surveyed the wreckage—bent and dented irrigation pipes, broken palm branches, crushed dates, torn paper decorations—I felt an urgent need to be elsewhere. Anywhere else.

Finally, we decided to wake up the woman's husband, who had to get up at 3 a.m. anyhow to milk the cows.

Like thieves in the night, he and I surreptitiously dumped the fallen irrigation pipes behind the factory, piled the palm branches in a heap to one side, and swept up the rest of the debris.

When the members came in for breakfast and saw only half of the *succa* standing, they assumed that I had dismantled the other half on purpose.

The main topic of conversation that morning was the crazy way Americans observed Succot—putting up a *succa* and then taking down half of it the next day.

Then there was the time the kibbutz chartered some buses and took a five-day trip through the Sinai down to the Red Sea.

There were several mineral hot springs in the area—spas with supposed healing powers, where cure-seekers had been taking the waters for centuries—and we stopped at one to take a look.

Inevitably, someone pushed someone else into the water, and there was a chain reaction, and soon half of the people were splashing about.

Somebody blindsided me into the spa headfirst.

As my dripping head emerged from the steaming water, a look of amazement crossed my face. I raised my arms and shouted.

"A miracle!"

Heads turned in my direction.

"A miracle! I can hear! *I can hear!*"

Time passed quickly. In 1974, Debby started her army service (which is compulsory for all physically qualified 18-year-olds, male and female, except the ultra-Orthodox). She worked in the head-quarters of a huge ordnance base just outside Tel Aviv for a year, then at a small base near our kibbutz during her second year.

In 1975, after we had been on the kibbutz for two years, the penthouse in Tel Aviv was finished. Barbara said sell it, so we sold it and put the money in the bank.

In 1976, a month after Debby was discharged, Julie entered the army and was stationed in a tank unit on the Golan Heights.

Debby went to work in Tel Aviv as a translator. In 1977, she married an Israeli-born young man whom she had been dating for several years.

The wedding was held on the kibbutz, with the ceremony under a *chupah* on the lawn in front of our house. A buffet and dancing were in the dining hall.

Our friends came up from Tel Aviv, my mother and sister came from California, and Barbara's parents came from Chicago.

The next milestone in our lives was Michal. After four daughters, it was natural that our first grandchild would be a girl. We had been waiting long enough; I was already 44, and Barbara was 40.

In 1978, when Julie was discharged, it was Laurie's turn to go into the army. She was stationed at an outpost on a hilltop over-looking the Dead Sea.

Julie worked in the kibbutz milking barn for a year, then went to Hebrew University's school of agriculture to start working on her degree in horticulture.

Then came the fateful summer of 1978, after we had been in Israel for eight years (the last five on the kibbutz).

Barbara and I took 10-year-old Lisa on a trip back to the United States for our first visit in four years.

And our lives took another sharp turn.

21

Hitting an open switch

When we moved to Israel in 1970, we were prepared to take a big hit in our income. Compensation levels in the developing 22-year-old state were much lower than in America.

The potential disparity was increased by the fact that we had been doing unusually well in America. I didn't really expect to do unusually well in Israel, at least to begin with.

Talk about taking a hit. My annual income from working full-time at writing television scripts and editing academic papers and writing advertising was 20 percent of what I had been making in the States.

It was enough to live on in Tel Aviv, though, after we had bought a home and a car and furniture with money from our American assets.

Then, during the five years we were on the kibbutz, all of my income went straight into Neve Eitan's coffers.

None of this was particularly troubling, so long as we had one or two prime pieces of residential real estate free and clear. A fall-back like that is a comforting thought.

But when our tenant in Highland Park moved out, we sold the house.

And when we moved to the kibbutz, we sold our apartment in Tel Aviv. And when the penthouse was finished in 1975, we sold that, too—which meant that, for the first time, we owned no real estate anywhere.

But it didn't really hit me what had happened until we visited the States in the summer of 1978. Then I saw how the prices of real estate had skyrocketed.

In 1971, we had owned upscale homes in both Highland Park and Tel Aviv at the same time. In 1978, the money in the bank wouldn't have bought back *either* of them.

All of a sudden, I felt a lot less secure. A *lot* less.

So I called time out.

After agonizing for a couple of days, I told Barbara that I wanted to move back to the States and build up another nest egg.

"Okay," she said. "Let's give it a year or so over there."

A month later, Barbara, Lisa and I moved back to Highland Park. We left behind our three oldest daughters, our granddaughter, our friends on the kibbutz, our friends in Tel Aviv, and what had come to be our country.

It was a wrenching time, a real downer all around—completely unlike when we had left America eight years earlier.

Laurie, then 19 and in the Israeli army, said:

"I knew that someday I would have to grow up and leave home. But I never thought that my home would pick up and leave me."

The first problem to tackle was the language. Lisa had left the States at the age of two as a native English speaker. When she returned at the age of 10, she was more or less bilingual—more in Hebrew, less in English.

After three years of nursery school and five years of elementary school in Israel (and the concurrent eight years of playing with her friends), she could speak, read and write Hebrew fluently.

Since we spoke English at home, her spoken English was okay—not perfect, but pretty good.

But her level of reading and writing in English (which we had taught her on and off through children's books and letters to and from her grandparents) was substantially lower than that of other fifth graders in Highland Park.

So when we returned to the States, we enrolled Lisa in a Jewish day school in a neighboring suburb. Much of the instruction was conducted in Hebrew, which she could follow as well or better than anyone else. She took remedial English reading and writing courses to help her catch up—which she did fairly quickly.

We chose the school as a halfway house to ease her way back into the English-speaking world—much as my parents had decided on Parker to ease my way back into the hearing world.

We picked up where we had left off with our friends and my work. Within a couple of weeks, it seemed as though we had never been gone. Since we were returning to Israel the following fall, we rented a house in Highland Park for a year.

I freelanced for a number of advertising and marketing agencies, and found some new clients.

Charging top rates and regularly working as many as 80 hours a week or more, I started filling up the reservoir at a nice clip.

With everything running right on schedule like the 8:06 from Highland Park to downtown Chicago, it was inevitable that I'd hit an unexpected open switch and wind up on a new track.

I was freelancing for the agency in which I had been creative director before moving to Israel—the one where I had come up with the Banzai Sale. Now it was well on its way toward becoming the largest marketing services agency in the country.

The owner and I went back a long way together. A couple of decades earlier, we had first joined forces at the promotion agency where he was a salesman and I was a copywriter.

So when I came back to the States and walked into his agency's Michigan Avenue offices—straight off the kibbutz in my beat-up sandals, without jacket, tie or socks—he let out a whoop and grabbed me in a bear hug and danced me up and down in a circle. Then we went out to lunch at a plush rooftop restaurant where the headwaiter's nose went north at the sight of my bare feet.

As the months went by, I was in the agency two or three times a week to pick up and drop off assignments from the creative department.

Every once in a while I'd bump into the owner, and we'd chat for a few minutes.

And sometimes he'd start doodling on a pad of ruled yellow paper, drawing an organization chart of the agency with boxes and lines of authority.

First he split the creative department in half. Over one half, he wrote the name of the current creative director; over the other half, he penciled in my name. And then he scribbled some numbers about salary and bonus and profit sharing and car and expense account and life insurance and health insurance.

I'd shake my head. "Thanks, but we're going back in the fall."

And then some other time we'd be talking, and the yellow pad would show my name over the entire creative department instead of only half, and the numbers would be bigger, and I'd smile but shake my head again.

The agency was dominated by the account executives, led by the owner himself. There were no creative people among the vice presidents or on the management committee. The creatives worked under the supervision of the account people.

As the summer wore on, another version of the organizational chart appeared on the yellow pad.

Now the box over the creative department had been moved up to parity with the head of account services at the vice-presidential level, just below the owner himself, and the numbers had taken a big jump.

"And you'll have a free hand to do whatever you want in order to get the creative department into shape. Hiring, firing, salaries, promotions, total reorganization, whatever. But don't take it unless you can stay for at least three years."

I was sorely tempted.

As I writer, I worked alone with my thoughts most of the time. My contacts with people, such as clients and art directors, had been peripheral to writing.

I had never managed anyone in my life.

Now I was being offered a chance to do something radically different: to develop and manage scores of writers and art directors and others.

I would be finding talented people, training them, motivating them, guiding their creative efforts.

I would be building a top-flight organization—and making it function efficiently and profitably.

And after three years, my family would be in much better shape financially.

I turned it down.

"Think it over, anyway."

With our timing for returning to Israel dictated by the cycle of Lisa's school year, we had to make a go/no-go decision.

At a provisional farewell party, our friends gave me a nonstop razzing.

Were we leaving? Then go already.

Were we staying? Then why were they wasting their time at a farewell party?

They presented me with a T-shirt imprinted with an exhortation, in somewhat earthier language, to get my excrement together.

Finally, my ego won the tug of war.

A new challenge was like a stone on the sidewalk.

I just couldn't resist taking a kick at it.

I joined the agency as vice president, director of creative services, and member of the management committee.

And later, when a new top management level was created, I was promoted to senior vice president and member of the executive committee.

Overnight, the volume of my communication with people took a quantum jump.

Conversations and meetings filled most of each day.

My office door was always open.

I made it clear that anyone was welcome to barge in at any time if no one else was with me—regardless of what I was doing.

I didn't want any barriers to communication, be they physical, procedural or psychological.

The only limitation I set was that if someone had a problem or a gripe, I wanted her to take it up with the head of her creative group first.

If that didn't work out, she was free to dump it on me. I wanted to reinforce the authority of the group heads.

If I wasn't in my office, I was wandering in and out of the offices of my writers and art directors and keyliners to see what was going on with their projects.

I had never heard of MBWA, but that's the technique I was using: management by walking around.

Or sometimes I was over with the account executives, pressing the flesh and opening up lines of communication.

Or I was in the controller's office, going over figures and learning the financial side of the business.

At any given moment, quite a few people could be away from their desks. So we had a PA system for paging people.

Occasionally, a voice would come out of the speakers:

"If anybody sees Lew, please call extension 321."

Whoever I was talking to would pick up a phone and take the call for me.

Soon, the request was shortened for convenience:

"Lew, please call extension 321."

And nobody thought twice about the fact that a deaf person was being paged.

My usual method of working before I moved into management had been to get information, think things through inside my head, come to a decision, and then go ahead and do whatever I had decided to do.

So when I made changes in the structure and operation of the creative department, I worked out the details and then wrote memos explaining what people should do and why.

Eventually, three or four group heads banded together and marched into my office to tell me that it was a hell of a way to run a railroad. They had no objections at all to what I was trying to accomplish—just to my style.

It seems that when I announced something new or different, the staff would question the group heads—who would have to confess that this was the first they had heard of it, too, and that they were just as much in the dark as anyone else.

It didn't make them look good in the eyes of their people.

The group heads wanted more access to what was going on in my head, and a chance to add some input of their own.

So I started a Wednesday lunch in the conference room for the group creative directors and associate creative directors and the head of production.

I sent out for food that could be eaten in 15 minutes or so— pizza, Chinese, ribs, deli trays.

Since I couldn't understand what people said when they had food in their mouths, the conversation was limited to small talk until everyone was finished eating. Then we spent the next hour and a half talking business.

Before the first meeting, I wasn't sure how much I would be able to follow with a dozen people around a 16-foot oval table. So I brought my secretary along to fill me in if I got lost.

It was an unnecessary precaution; the first meeting was her last.

Since I was running the meeting, it was my agenda. I started each subject, laying out the groundwork. This meant that, for the most part, I knew what people were talking about—and for me, that's the key factor in speechreading.

As we got farther into a discussion and the speakers brought up new information or new opinions or related issues, I sometimes might start missing a bit.

By the reactions of the other people, I could usually tell whether it was pertinent. If I thought it was relevant, I let it continue and asked whoever was sitting next to me what the point was.

If I considered it to be off the track, I interrupted and asked what what this had to do with the subject. If it was beside the point, I usually cut it off.

As a result, the meetings tended to say on track and to the point, and I missed nothing of any importance.

When my agenda had been covered, other people could bring up new business: problems, information, suggestions, whatever.

Once every month or six weeks, for a change of pace, I held the Wednesday meeting outside the office.

It might be in an authentic Mexican restaurant in the Pilsen neighborhood...or under a sprawling oak tree in the atrium garden of an old Italian restaurant...or sitting on the breakwater by Navy Pier, eating fish and chips from a nearby kiosk.

These weren't as businesslike as the in-house meetings, but we did get some work done.

Once every few months, there was a management committee meeting of the agency's 25 or 30 top and middle level managers. It was somewhat more difficult to follow these discussions.

There were more people, and many were sitting some distance from me. Since I didn't chair the meetings (the owner did), I didn't start off each subject and people didn't respond directly to me.

On the other hand, there were some helpful aspects. The owner, whom I could speechread quite easily, did most of the talking.

Sometimes there was a printed agenda; if not, whoever sat next to me filled me in on what each new subject was if I missed it at the beginning.

Some speakers tended to repeat what previous speakers had said, so I didn't have to get every word that every person said.

If I missed something, somebody would fill me in—if not right away, then after the meeting or the following morning.

What I had to get, I got in one way or another.

Every once in a while, the top five people in the agency would get together for an executive committee meeting. These meetings were relatively easy for me to follow and to participate in.

Everyone sat within a few feet of me. It was no problem to interrupt and ask someone to repeat a word. From time to time I'd reach over and read the owner's notes as a double-check.

I expected the writers and art directors—especially the group heads—to combine creativity with a business orientation.

Awards for creativity were nice, but profits for our clients were even nicer.

The agency's business was to help our clients get more people to buy more of their products; that was the measure of our success.

I pushed for clarity of communication. This meant a clear and persuasive message expressed with clearly understandable words and graphics.

If an offbeat approach was able to get the point across quickly and effectively, fine; otherwise, forget it. I would not sacrifice clear communication for the sake of doing something different.

Today, too many misconceived promotions are being executed (=implemented) instead of executed (=killed) simply because the agency and the client think that being different is a *raison d'etre*.

For too many agency people, being different is an ego trip. For them, the measure of success is how innovative they are.

I am all for innovation—so long as the audience gets a clear message and responds to it.

For what shall it profit a company if it gains a whole world of difference, but loses its sale?

I inherited a mixed bag of people in the creative department. Some of the writers and art directors were excellent; some were okay; and some simply couldn't hack it.

The structure of the department, what there was of it, needed a complete overhaul. The agency had been growing rapidly, and people had been added randomly.

Rather than being a cohesive group, the creative department was a collection of various writers and art directors who were adjuncts to various account service groups; most of them worked on only one account.

Since the fastest way to go stale is to keep banging your head against the same wall every day, I wanted each person to have an opportunity to work on a mixture of accounts. Such variety and cross-fertilization can help refresh the mind, avoid creative blocks and trigger new ideas.

So I started from scratch and set up new creative groups. Then I assigned accounts to the groups, spreading the goodies around. Some accounts were so big I split them up and gave each group a piece of the action.

I got no joy from firing people or encouraging them to seek jobs elsewhere, but that was part of the cost of raising standards and improving the output. I could help someone who had potential gain the necessary experience and perspective—but if he didn't have the talent and desire, there was usually no alternative.

The group heads weren't immune to the overhaul. I demoted some who were long on creative talent but came up short on leadership, and let others go.

I did some highly selective hiring so that we wound up with fewer but better people. Those who had the needed combination of creativity, business sense and leadership were my group creative directors and associate creative directors.

I set up no other levels besides the GCDs and ACDs, no layers of supervision, no obstacles to efficient operation; I simply found the best people I could and gave them free rein within my general guidelines.

I stayed away from the title inflation and proliferation that are endemic to marketing and advertising agencies. When people did well, I didn't pay them off with titles; I rewarded them with more money.

Depending on the circumstances, I might give someone two or even three raises in one year. In addition, the year-end bonuses were another opportunity for me to give high-performing GCDs and ACDs a pat on the bank account.

I reviewed everyone's salary at least once a year, so there was no need for anyone to ask me for a raise.

But one day, a week before I went on vacation to visit our daughters in Israel, one of my managers came into my office.

"Can we talk about my raise?"

I looked in my file. "Your review isn't scheduled for another three months. Why now?"

"You're going to Israel next week, aren't you?"

"Yeah."

"Well, a bomb might drop on your head. I'd feel better if I got my raise before you go."

I was touched by his concern. So I gave him the raise.

Since I had committed myself to staying with the agency for three years, we bought a house on a private street in Highland Park. We turned a large wing into a studio for Barbara.

After that first transitional year in a Jewish day school, Lisa's English reading and writing had improved to the point where she would have no problems in Highland Park's public school system. She entered junior high school and joined a gymnastics club.

We called our daughters in Israel every couple of weeks. As Barbara spoke with them and repeated their words to me, I watched the play of emotions on her face and vicariously shared the moment. Twice a year, we flew to Israel to spend a few weeks with them.

Laurie finished her army service, joined a kibbutz by the Dead Sea, and married a member of the kibbutz. A chartered bus brought our friends from Tel Aviv down for the ceremony and celebration around the kibbutz swimming pool.

After Julie received her degree in horticulture from the Hebrew University of Jerusalem, she worked her way through the Far East for a couple of years—teaching English to Japanese businessmen, shearing sheep in New Zealand, and so on.

Debby had our second grandchild. After four daughters and a granddaughter, we finally had our first grandson—Ben.

And then came the phone call from Julie.

Debby's 28-year-old husband, Avi, had collapsed with a burst aneurysm in his brain and was in a coma.

Barbara flew to Israel.

Two weeks later, Barbara called me at the office. Avi had died without regaining consciousness.

The funeral was the following day.

I took the next plane to Israel.

Again, as when my father had died, the words came through my secretary instead of directly from Barbara's lips.

Again, there was one of those rare moments when I felt a sense of frustration, when the barrier created by my deafness intruded into my consciousness.

Again, there was the realization that no matter how much I did with my life, no matter how many ways I was able to overcome the problems of deafness, there would always be times when there was no satisfactory substitute for hearing to bridge the distance.

22

Naked on the Michigan Avenue bridge

I must have been doing something right in running my end of the agency, because the results were good.

The creative quality improved. Productivity and profitability went up. *Esprit de corps* flourished.

Those who survived the house-cleaning and those I hired knew they were among the best in the business.

Recognizing the improvements, the owner put more departments under my wing. In addition to the creative department and the art production department I started with, I took over responsibility for the print production and premium purchasing departments.

Here, too, I cleaned house.

My bailiwick covered everything except the account executives and the bookkeeping people, who reported to the owner.

As our reputation as a top shop grew, it became increasingly easier to recruit top creative people. I didn't have to go looking for them—they came to us.

I placed a high value on integrity. The owner had built a good reputation on the basis of mutual trust between the agency and its clients, and between the agency and its suppliers.

I wanted our people to keep it that way.

On one occasion, we submitted an idea for a back-to-school promotion with backpacks custom-made in the client's color. One of our people in the premium department obtained bids from some backpack suppliers.

The client liked the idea, and was expected to approve it at any moment. The supplier who had submitted the winning bid was put on standby, ready to go.

But in the end, the client decided not to do the promotion.

A few days later, the supplier (whom I had never met) came in to see me. He said he had already cut the cloth.

Now he was stuck with thousands of dollars worth of custom-cut material, and he wanted us to pay for it.

"Do you have a purchase order from us?"

"No. But your buyer told me over the phone to go ahead. I knew you needed them fast, so I didn't wait for a P.O."

I called our buyer into my office and asked her what happened.

She said she had told the supplier to get ready to move, but had not told him to actually go ahead and cut.

So I told the supplier that we appreciated his initiative in trying to save time for us, but we could not take the responsibility for his loss because we had not given him the go-ahead.

He argued, but I was firm. Finally, he gave up and left.

A minute later, as our buyer left my office, she said I had done a good job.

No big deal, I said—the facts spoke for themselves.

But her parting words to me rubbed me the wrong way.

I called her back into my office.

"What did you tell the supplier on the phone?"

"Like I said, that the chances looked good and he should get ready to make the backpacks."

"Did you tell him it was a go?"

"Well, not exactly."

"You did or you didn't?"

"Uh, well, maybe it came out sounding that way—but look, it's no problem, we don't have to pay. You talked him out of it."

Sheesh.

I phoned the supplier and told him to send us the bill. And the buyer was gone from the agency not long after.

We spent millions of dollars each year on outside suppliers for illustrations, photography, typesetting, printing, videos and other creative and production services.

I wanted our people to buy smart—to spend the client's money as carefully as if it were our own. This did not mean sacrificing quality. It meant choosing the right quality for each project, and getting the best price for that quality.

When I came across some production bids on a film we were going to do, the prices seemed out of line in relation to the script we had written and the purpose of the film.

It was a low-budget training film to be seen by a few hundred people—not a top-of-the-line network TV commercial to be seen by millions.

Seeking an independent opinion, I asked my younger brother, Guy—himself a film director. He gave us a line-by-line explanation and evaluation of the suppliers' bids—types and amounts of rented equipment, amount of footage to be shot, types and numbers of crew people, prop building, days of shooting, days of editing, costs for locations, transportation, food, etc.

Guy pointed out, item by item, what reasonable costs would be, and ways of doing the production in order to hold down costs.

The total was 35 to 60 percent lower than the bids. Armed with this information, our writer was able to negotiate a better deal.

I didn't have much face-to-face contact with the agency's clients, other than to show the flag and press the flesh once in a while. Normally, I left the day-to-day client contact in the hands of the group heads.

But if I became personally involved in working on a project, I would also handle client contact for the creative end.

This happened when we received a trial assignment from the producers of the Muppets television series.

Since this would determine whether we picked up the company as a steady client, the owner and I flew to New York ourselves to get the assignment. An account executive accompanied us.

The marketing VP spent a couple of hours explaining what he wanted and giving us the background. I followed his New York accent as best as I could, interrupting occasionally for clarification.

When the client was finished, I said that I had missed some things and that the assignment wasn't clear in my mind.

The owner held up his notes. "I have it all here. No problem."

I scanned his notes, but there were still some things that didn't make sense to me. So I went ahead with my questions.

Back in Chicago, the owner and I disagreed on what the client wanted. The AE backed up the owner's interpretation.

Finally, at my insistence, the owner picked up the phone and called the client.

After he hung up the phone, he glared at me.

"Dammit, Lew, aren't you *ever* wrong?"

The point of the incident—and many more like it—is that having perfect hearing doesn't guarantee perfect understanding.

And lack of hearing doesn't necessarily mean lack of understanding—if you make an extra effort to get it straight.

But no, I wasn't always right. I could also be embarrassingly wrong. When I made a mistake, it was usually a beaut.

Most of the writers and art directors were unknowns to me when I first joined the agency. So, in order to help me evaluate their creative and leadership qualities, I asked several people for their opinions of each creative person.

I didn't give much weight to any one opinion, but I figured that a consensus ought to mean something. I used the consensus for background information, but I let my gut feeling be the deciding factor; sometimes I went against the consensus.

The book on one young writer was that she was talented and talked a good game, but that she wasn't as good as she thought she was. A number of people warned me not to be taken in.

Around the same time, I hired a senior writer with a great deal of experience. In addition to having a good feel for marketing, she had an aura of maturity.

The next time I needed a new associate creative director, I had to decide whom to promote.

I admired the creativity, spunk and potential of the younger one. But the maturity of the senior writer contrasted quite obviously with the other's somewhat raw edges.

With the account executives' caveats about the younger writer in the back of my mind, I gave the promotion to the senior writer.

It wasn't exactly a disaster, but it was nothing to write home about. The new ACD couldn't get along with the group creative director or with the writers in her group.

It was a perfect example of the Peter Principle: she went from being a competent writer to being an incompetent group leader.

So I soon took the stripes away from her and gave them to the younger woman—who took off like a rocket and never stopped.

I blundered again when the creative department's parity with account executives was formalized by the promotion of the group creative directors to vice presidents.

The head of account services and I (as head of creative services) were already the agency's two senior vice presidents.

The owner asked me to pick two creatives to be vice presidents. I had three groups—two headed by men, one by the rocket.

"Three," I said.

"Two."

"All three deserve it."

Eventually, he agreed to three.

He announced the appointments at the annual office party in a Loop restaurant.

As the assemblage broke up and moved from the dining room to the disco, I figured I'd initiate the new VPs with a little razzing.

So I took the microphone, called each one up in turn, and gave an off-color explanation of why he or she had been chosen.

Fortunately, the bar was open again and the music had started and everybody was talking to each other and few people were paying attention to my utterly tasteless comments.

In retrospect, it's the only time I've wished that people could *not* understand what I was saying.

Shouting is in the arsenals of many managers, but not in mine. I simply don't shout at people who work for me.

I don't know whether it has anything to do with my being deaf, but it isn't part of my style. I don't think it does any good.

And, of course, it doesn't do anybody any good to shout at me. But one of my group creative directors became so incensed at a decision I had made that he couldn't restrain himself.

He rose and carefully closed my office door (which was virtually never closed). Then he started shouting.

He was well aware that I couldn't hear him, of course, but that didn't stop him.

It did, however, get a rise out of me.

So I started shouting back at him.

I don't know who was more surprised—him or me.

We went on like that for half a minute. I didn't change my decision, but he seemed to feel better about getting it off his chest.

Nevertheless, he never tried it again.

In on-the-job performance, I really couldn't see that it made any difference whether someone was a man or a woman.

In some ways, some writers or art directors or group leaders were better than others, yes, but not because of their sex.

There was a fairly general agreement that a person's sex was immaterial to creative ability. But not everybody saw women as being as strong as men in leadership ability.

Some of the veteran males on the account service side had trouble perceiving the reality:

In supervising the creative efforts of writers and art directors, in estimating budgets and controlling expenses, in selling our work to clients, in making new-business presentations—a woman could be as good as or better than a man.

Regularly, someone would voice a knee-jerk disparagement to me about some woman I had put in a leadership position.

Just as regularly, I would respond that the complainer had shit for brains, and I would recount the achievements of the person in question. Week in and week out, I chipped away at the perceptual barrier.

In the end, it wasn't so much what I did as it was what the women themselves did. Their leadership performance became too obviously outstanding to ignore.

I simply bought time for them, keeping the wolves at bay until they could prove themselves.

However, there was a big difference between the perception that women were weaker leaders than men, on one hand, and the perception that the creative people were less business-oriented than the account executives.

When I joined the agency, there was some truth to the second perception: some creatives *did* lack business sense.

For example, when I asked one of the writers for the marketing rationale behind something he had written, he told me proudly: "I don't know. I'm a creative writer, not a marketing person."

When he couldn't change his perspective, I had to let him go.

Inevitably, the perception of creatives as marketing lightweights tarred everyone with the same brush—the innocent along with the guilty.

A number of people outside the department tended to see only the weaknesses of some, not the strengths of others.

I not only had to change the perception that creatives *per se* were dilettantes in business. I also had to change the reality that, in the beginning, some of them actually were.

The Michigan Avenue bridge over the Chicago River is an easily identifiable landmark. I used a picture of it for a speech I gave on creativity during a marketing seminar for one of our clients, AT&T.

I said that coming up with a creative idea is often a matter of recognizing relationships between two subjects.

I retold the legend of Archimedes discovering the principle of specific gravity. When he submerged himself at a public bath, a certain amount of water was displaced and overflowed.

He was able to make the connection between the overflowing bath and the scientific measurement of solids.

When the idea hit him, he jumped out of the bath and ran naked down the streets of ancient Greece, shouting "Eureka!"

Similarly, something may come together in the minds of our creative people at any moment—even while, like Archimedes, they're taking a bath.

To illustrate that moment in my speech, I wanted to show a slide of one of our writers or art directors running naked across the Michigan Avenue bridge, brandishing a sheaf of papers.

But the creatives adamantly refused to pose for the picture— even though I compromised and said that the model could wear a towel.

Which is why, on a chilly October morning several years ago, you could have seen me running across the Michigan Avenue bridge wearing only a bath towel and goose bumps. Chicagoans being what they are, nobody gave me a second look.

The seeds of my infatuation with computers were planted when I helped develop a computerized job control system for the agency.

This was in the pre-PC days, and I didn't know anything about the mainframe computers used by the service bureaus. All I knew was what kind of information I wanted the computer to provide; the programmers took it from there.

We also set up a word processing pool with dedicated word processors. Then we gave word processors to the writers to replace their typewriters. When I went to a training course, it was the first time my fingers had touched an electronic keyboard.

The physical part of the writing business is mostly editing and rewriting, and the word processor made these functions infinitely easier and faster than with a typewriter.

I was awed by the capabilities of computers.

And hooked.

The owner had the northeast corner office. I had the southwest corner office. We couldn't have been farther apart.

On one hand, we were a mutual admiration society. I felt that he was the best salesman in the business.

He was aggressive, tenacious, visionary, articulate, street-smart, hard-working, critical, impatient, dedicated to his clients. He built his agency from scratch to No. 1.

He thought highly of me as well; that's why he brought me in to run the creative department.

He knew my creative track record firsthand, since a great deal of my work over the years had been for his agency. He knew my personality—the no-bullshit, irreverent way I was with creatives, with account executives, with clients, and with him. And we shared many of the same personal traits.

The one unknown had been my managerial ability, since I had never managed before.

He took a risk on that.

Within months it was no longer an unknown, but had become part of my track record. He kept putting more departments under my responsibility.

When he promoted me to senior vice president and member of the executive committee, his memo said that my contribution to the management of the agency had been productive and dramatic, and that the most important of my contributions had been the growth of the people I worked with.

The memo closed with a line that pinpointed one of the main reasons behind my accomplishments:

Thank you, Lew, for being Lew.

He hired me because of the way I was.
I was successful because of the way I was.
He promoted me because of the way I was.
And, in the end, he fired me because of the way I was.
I recognized no sacred cows—not even him.

As he had promised, he gave me free rein. Early on, as I was feeling my way around, I sometimes bounced my thoughts off him. But I soon started keeping my own counsel.

It was faster and more efficient for me to run things without interference—making all the decisions myself and expediting their implementation.

It was good for the company's bottom line to get things done as quickly and smoothly as possible. And it was good for my ego.

One of my self-appointed functions was to serve as a buffer between the owner and the creatives. In much the same way as many hearing people perceive deaf people, he often looked on creatives as being somehow naive and childlike, not capable of functioning properly without being told what to do.

Once, in a misguided attempt to build a bridge or two, I invited him to a Wednesday meeting. Even before the corned beef sandwiches were gone, however, he launched into a rambling monologue about how bad everything and everyone was.

I was as embarrassed for him as I had been for myself when I razzed our new vice presidents at their initiation.

We both aimed impossibly high; we both wanted people to do better, regardless of how well they were already doing.

But whereas my style was to recognize something as good (if it *was* good) and then push for even greater excellence, his style was to dump on people for what he felt were their shortcomings.

Although he was smart enough not to try to tell me what to do, he did try to convince me to make certain moves. But my intuitive philosophy of organization differed from his—such as my goal of lean-and-mean versus his view that bigger is better.

So, for various reasons, we had some legendary arguments.

I was fully aware that it was *his* company, not mine (which is why I refer to him here as the owner). Obviously, discretion on my part would have been the better part of valor.

But, since discretion has never been my long suit, I had no compunction at all about disregarding his suggestions.

Once, in frustration, he bellowed: "You really *are* deaf!"

Actually, we were both deaf to each other. During my fourth year at the agency, when everything was going swimmingly in the creative department, our relationship was sinking like a stone.

He felt that the problem was my ego.

That was part of it, yes—but he never understood that I didn't operate the way I did simply to feed my ego.

I operated the way I did because I felt it would produce the best results for the company—and when it *did* do great things for the company, *that* fed my ego.

But he couldn't deal with it, and communication between the two of us became minimal and unsatisfactory. Which is ironic, since the whole thrust of this book is about the importance of being able to communicate in the real world.

Finally, an advisor told him to either talk with me or fire me.

He found it easier to fire me.

The timing wasn't particularly good: my fiftieth birthday. Our daughters had flown in from Israel to help me celebrate.

We threw a big bash anyway. And my friends responded to my unemployed status in characteristic fashion. One of the more thoughtful gifts was a tin cup and a sign to hang on my neck.

Since my performance had never been in question, I probably could have sued. But that, too, is not my style.

"Look," I said to the owner, "so it didn't work out. So it goes. That doesn't mean we have to hate each other. Let's stay friends. I'll break in the new guy for you."

"Hey, I like that. Okay."

Barbara wanted to wait until Lisa finished high school before we returned to Israel. So I went back to freelancing—not only writing, but also consulting and producing.

The owner and I refurbished our friendship, and his agency was, as in the past, my biggest client. With my usual luck, I managed to take home more as a freelancer than I had made at the agency.

I spent some time showing my successor the ropes.

He was given a narrower scope of responsibility than I had held, and he wound up two levels below the owner (instead of directly below, as I had been).

But people tell me that he was quite successful in getting along with the owner.

Obviously, that's one thing I can't claim credit for teaching him.

A few years later, the owner wrote a book about the business. It used the "Do a double take" package I had created for Kodak film as an example of a successful promotion.

And the chapter on creativity lifted big chunks verbatim (but without attribution) from my speech at the marketing seminar for AT&T, including the parallel of Archimedes in the public baths.

Indirectly, I suppose, he was giving me credit for having known what I was doing and what I was talking about.

23

Turning a deaf ear

Every morning in urban areas all around the world, millions upon millions of people get into their cars and drive to work.

And every afternoon and evening, they get back into their cars and drive home or wherever.

Rush-hour driving is all too often a frustrating hassle, with slow-moving traffic and interminable jams and frequent accidents.

And the added complications of snowstorms or floods can make grown men and women weep with exasperation and anger.

And when the traffic isn't bad, the monotony of the daily round trip, back and forth, day after day, week after week, month after month, year after year, can become a tedious bore.

And through it all, each driver is a prisoner in his own car. He is forced to sit there, gripping the wheel and staring through the windshield.

How do you spell relief for those commuters who, for whatever reason, choose to drive or have no convenient alternative?

R-a-d-i-o.

No wonder drivetime radio is so popular.

It has a captive audience that's dying for a diversion from the headaches of the highway.

And the drivers are getting all the diversion they want:

All kinds of music. Local and national and international news. Humor. Gossip. Sports. Talk shows. Game shows. Soap operas. Weather reports. Traffic reports.

You name it, they get it.

Unless they're deaf.

After having used a word processor at the office, I found an electric typewriter to be unbearably klutzy. So when I went back to freelancing in 1983, I bought my first personal computer.

For a year, I used it for nothing except writing. I had no idea whatsoever of its communication capabilities.

Then I read a newspaper article about a fellow who had started an electronic bulletin board system on his computer. People used their computers to call into his computer's BBS, where they posted and read messages to each other.

I bought a modem, which enables a computer to communicate with other computers via telephone lines, and discovered a fantastic new world of electronic communication.

For me, as for millions of other people, it is a tremendous benefit to be able to exchange all kinds of information with all kinds of people and resources all over the world in seconds.

And since the process is visual, with everything displayed on the screen, hearing doesn't count. Which makes computers especially great for deaf people.

So, for a variety of reasons, I became involved in computers.

As a writer, I could manipulate words faster and more easily without the hassle of endless retyping.

As a manager, I could quickly and accurately get the numbers I needed to find out where we'd been, where we were, and where we'd be under various circumstances.

As an information junkie, I had a world of knowledge from people and from databases at my fingertips—for my work, for my computermania, and for my insatiable curiosity.

And as a deaf person, I had a new mode of communication in which hearing was irrelevant.

One of my freelance writing clients was a promotion agency with no computers, no job control system, and a handwritten mess that was supposed to be a bookkeeping system.

A programmer was trying to put together some programs for them. But he didn't understand their business, and they had no understanding of computers.

Since I understood both, the owner asked me to analyze their operation and develop a small-scale version of the system I had been using where I had been head of creative services.

After I finished writing up the system, I warned him that the system itself was only part of the solution; somebody in the agency had to be responsible for making it function all the way down the line. If people didn't use the system properly, it wouldn't work.

He agreed. And since he knew that neither he nor anyone else in the agency was capable of taking over that responsibility, he asked me to join the agency as executive vice president.

So I did.

What I had seen of their bookkeeping from the outside, as a consultant, was a mess. What I saw from the inside was a disaster.

The problem was that the owner never wanted to hear bad news (especially not on Fridays, so as not to spoil his weekend).

The bookkeeper, to keep him happy, had a very simple system for making the books look good: she threw away many invoices from suppliers without recording or paying them.

So the agency's balance sheet looked nice, but it was as kosher as a platter of pork chops.

At first, I didn't know that I wasn't playing with a full deck. All I knew was that there was a mess to straighten out.

I fired the CPA and the programmer, brought in my own CPA to clean up, and hired a new programmer to develop my system.

Over a period of several months, the missing cards turned up—along with several jokers. Supplier after supplier called me and asked why their invoices hadn't been paid; when I checked the books, I found that they hadn't been entered.

Even the bookkeeper didn't know what invoices she had thrown away or what the total was. So, week after week and month after month, another unknown payable would float to the surface and throw off the balance sheet.

Early on, the bookkeeper caught on that I wasn't happy with the situation; before I could fire her, she quit. The CPA found me a real pro to replace her.

Since the owner held all the stock, there were no other stockholders to worry about. But the bank that handled our financing was another matter.

I told the owner to tell the bank that the balance sheet was, to put it charitably, inaccurate. If he didn't, I would. So he did.

Somewhere between half a million and a million dollars worth of discarded invoices eventually showed up. The agency had been virtually bankrupt, but the owner hadn't known it.

Before I came in, he may have suspected that things weren't what they appeared to be on the books—but he had made it plain to the bookkeeper that he didn't want to hear about it.

I did a fast tap dance—cutting the owner's salary in half, trimming expenses, persuading our clients to pay us faster, borrowing money from the bank, asking suppliers to trust me for another two or three weeks.

Despite the evidence, the owner did not respond to the seriousness of the situation. When he went on vacation, he called the bookkeeper from the airport and told her to send a check for $6,000 to an art gallery for a painting he had just bought.

She asked me what to do. I told her not to send it.

The owner ranted on the phone, but it got him nowhere.

While he was gone, another $100,000 worth of ignored invoices materialized. I lost my cool and told the bookkeeper to pay them immediately, even though there wasn't enough money in the bank. Then I went to the bank and asked the chairman for an overdraft for a few weeks; unfortunately, he refused.

So I sold $60,000 worth of my own securities and put the money in the agency's bank account to cover the checks.

I still can't believe I did that, especially since I knew firsthand how precarious the agency's financial situation was.

Months later, when things turned around, I took back the money with interest. So it worked out okay.

It was an insane thing to do, but it was fairly typical of my seat-of-the-pants *modus operandi*.

Not everything worked out the way I expected.

Most of our clients were located out of town, so the telephone bills were astronomical.

So I shifted to a cheaper long-distance carrier. But since I couldn't hear on the phone, I didn't know the new carrier's lines were terrible—and nobody thought of telling me.

Our people were climbing the walls because their conversations with clients and suppliers were often unintelligible.

Finally, somebody made the connection between the new long-distance service and the line noise, and we switched back.

Eventually I finished organizing and computerizing the agency. By the end of the fiscal year, the financial statements were reliably accurate and the agency was solidly in the black.

After I sent the new statements to the chairman of the bank, he replied, in part:

> It is obvious that the company has made great strides in the past year, and we are pleased to note the outstanding results that you have achieved in a short period of time.
>
> It has been fun to get to know and work with you.

Fun. That's an important part of my payoff. Satisfaction and money are the meat and potatoes, but fun is the gravy.

With the agency in shape and accurate numbers in hand, the owner was able to negotiate a sell-out to a larger company.

The new owners brought in their own people to replace me, so I freelanced during the months before our long-planned return to Israel.

As soon as I left the agency, the new owners threw out my job-cost system and installed their own.

Theirs was less sophisticated, less informative and less useful to the creative, production and account service people—but it was easier for their accountants to deal with.

Another agency I was freelancing for heard about my job cost system and asked me to computerize their shop.

To hold down the outlay, I suggested that they buy the almost-new computers from the agency that had discarded my system.

Newer, more powerful and more expensive computers were available. But for the small number of employees and clients there, my system provided a more cost-effective way to have precisely what the agency needed.

The senior owner plunged into the computerization process with gusto. It came about at his initiative, and he was enthusiastically involved from day one.

He quickly grasped what the system could do for him and his company, and he kept asking for more add-ons that gave him more information and functions.

But the junior owner, like a great many people, was intimidated by computers. After I installed the equipment, I tried repeatedly to walk him through the procedures—but he always had one excuse or another, and wouldn't listen to my exhortations.

He had books and magazines piled atop his computer—which was all-too-visible evidence that he wasn't using the system for any function other than as a bookshelf.

His obvious reluctance was matched by the agency's controller, who stubbornly dug in her heels and lagged far behind the others in learning how to use the system. I told the owners I didn't think she was going to work out, but they turned a deaf ear and said not to worry about it.

I held group and individual training sessions for the employees, explaining in detail how to use the system to do their work faster and more accurately. By the time I moved back to Israel, the system was running smoothly.

But the junior owner still hadn't started using it. And in order to keep the system up-to-date and generate financial reports, a fellow who had been working for me on the project had to step in and do the things the controller was failing to do.

Not long after I left, the controller was finally replaced. The owners had closed their ears to my warnings, but they couldn't close their eyes to the damage she was doing.

A few years later, I crossed paths with the junior owner—and found out he was holding a grudge against me.

Having finally stuck his toe into the computing waters, he now considered himself to be an expert—and believed that I had stuck his company with obsolescent equipment and a defective, untested, unworkable system which he said they had to replace.

But the system had been tested at the previous agency, and it had been working just fine when I left. In fact, the owners had taken me out for a farewell lunch at which the senior partner had expressed great satisfaction with the system.

So I did some investigating. It turned out that they were still using the same system—but the gung-ho partner was requesting and getting additional functions from the programmer.

Each time the system was enhanced, there was the chance of bugs creeping in—so there was a constant process of change, shakedown and debugging.

There had been nothing wrong with the system I had sold them.

As for the equipment being obsolescent—it is well known that almost everything in the computer field is well on its way to being obsolete before it even hits the market.

No matter what you buy today, something better and cheaper will come along within weeks, if not sooner.

I am now on my sixth personal computer in 11 years. Some people like hot new sports cars; I like hot new computers. My old computers are functioning just fine for my daughters.

I had told the agency up front that the computer equipment I recommended for them was all they really needed.

They could spend more and get more than they needed, but it wouldn't be cost effective.

But the second owner hadn't been listening.

If I was nuts enough to put $60,000 of my own money into a company I didn't own, it shouldn't be surprising that I took other risks as well. But my way of doing business was based on trust. Usually, it worked out just fine.

A neighbor of ours owned a software company, and a business magazine had given him a marketer-of-the-year award.

But when I started producing magazine ads and spec sheets for the company, a supplier of mine warned me that my neighbor's reputation wasn't so hot. He had gone through a succession of ad agencies and wasn't too good at paying his bills.

But that wasn't unusual during the go-go days in the computer field when everyone and his wife was starting up a new business on a shoestring. Besides, the fellow lived directly across the street from us and was a member of our congregation.

So I turned a deaf ear to the admonition. I did the work to their satisfaction, and got paid to my satisfaction.

The only problem was that the person in charge of advertising and promotion was qualified for the position only by dint of her being the wife of the owner.

Operating as a one-man agency, I handled the projects from start to finish. I conceived the ideas, wrote the copy, did rough layouts, and handled the contact with the client. Since this was in the days before desktop publishing eliminated my need for them, I bought the services of an art director, a typesetter and a keyliner, as well as those of a photographer and a printer.

Finally, with a big trade show coming up at McCormick Place, the client needed a large, full-color catalogue.

This involved a hefty outlay for my suppliers. So I asked the owner for a partial payment up front to cover those expenses.

He said not to worry about it—he would pay them directly. This was a fairly common practice, so I said okay. My only condition was that he pay us on delivery of the catalogues; he agreed.

I finished the catalogues the day before the show started. The owner was at McCormick Place; the ad manager/wife said she didn't have the authority to write a check for that much money.

The smart thing to do, of course, was to hold onto the catalogues until the suppliers and I were paid. But that wasn't my style.

I gave her the catalogues. And I paid the suppliers with about $25,000 of my own money, so they wouldn't have to wait.

After the trade show, I gave the client my invoice and told him I had paid the suppliers.

He asked why I had done so, after he had said he would pay them directly.

I said that I had hired them, and I had a relationship with them, and I had no intention of making them wait for their money until he got around to paying them.

Then it turned out that, uh, he was a little short of money at the moment, but he was negotiating a line of credit, and....

Right.

After paying a little bit of my bill and stalling me for months, the company went belly up. I was never reimbursed for the $25,000 I had given my suppliers, let alone paid for my own work.

And the owner was adamant that it was all *my* fault I lost the money—because he had *told* me not to pay my suppliers.

Lisa was the gymnastics team's captain and MVP at Highland Park High School. In her senior year, she tore a ligament and had surgery to repair her knee. During her rehab therapy, she became interested in sports medicine and decided to become an athletic trainer.

So, after graduation in 1986, she enrolled at Indiana University.

We drove her down to Bloomington. As going-away gifts (*we* were going away), we gave her our practically new one-year-old car and my practically obsolete one-year-old computer.

Eight years earlier, we had left Debby, Julie and Laurie in Israel when we moved back to the States for what was supposed to be a one-year sojourn with Lisa.

Now we were leaving Lisa in the States and moving back to Israel permanently (or, at least, what passes for permanently in our family).

By necessity, our daughters had learned to be independent at an early age. We weren't exactly overprotective parents.

We sold our home in Highland Park.

Once again, in what was becoming a familiar routine on both sides of the world, our friends gave us a farewell party.

Then, with Lisa settled in college for the next four years and our furniture and computer equipment on a container ship somewhere in the Atlantic, we flew back to Israel to rejoin our three other daughters and our grandchildren.

On an earlier trip, we had seen a penthouse for sale in a new area near Tel Aviv University. Later, when the owners came down in price far enough, we told Debby to close the deal for us.

So, when Barbara and I cleared customs at Ben-Gurion and stepped out into a balmy Mediterranean evening, we were all set to segue smoothly back into being Israelis again.

24

You *can* go home again

I am sitting at my computer late in the evening, staring at the screen and sweating out the words. Barbara is in the kitchen, out of sight, making a huge bowl of popcorn.

As the kernels explode like strings of firecrackers, I try to ignore the distraction.

No, I can't hear the increasingly rapid tattoo. Nevertheless, the unseen, unheard activity in the kitchen forces me to visualize a quivering, rising mass of fluffy white popcorn relentlessly pushing up the lid and spilling out onto the stove.

That's at least one way the sense of smell can compensate for the absence of hearing.

In 1978, when we moved back to the States after eight years in Israel, we easily picked up where we had left off.

Now, moving back to Israel in 1986 after eight years in America, it likewise seemed like we had never left.

I soon renewed my contacts at Tel Aviv University and resumed editing and rewriting academic papers. And, capitalizing on my increasing expertise in personal computers, I became a part-time guru in word processing at the university.

I rebuilt my marketing communications business through phone calls, letters, personal contacts and word of mouth.

I am again writing and producing ads, brochures, catalogues and proposals for companies in such fields as plastics, electronics, food, shipping, petrochemicals, insurance, computer peripherals, finance, and so on.

And I am editing and publishing academic reports and journals.

The big difference in my work is that now I am using desktop publishing (DTP) equipment and software.

This enables me to do almost everything myself—saving time, money, and the hassle of trying to get other people to do exactly what I want them to do.

It reflects the adage that if you want it done right, do it yourself. It gives me continuous control over the process.

In addition to handling client contact and doing the concept and copy and rough layout—which I had always done—I now do the finished layout and typesetting and graphics and page make-up electronically on my computer.

All that I have to buy from others is the photography, if any (although I sometimes do that myself, too), and the printing.

Anyone who has the money to buy the hardware and software can get into desktop publishing. And that's the problem.

Much of what is being turned out today is atrocious, because people may have the physical equipment but not the necessary combination of skills.

The key word is *combination.*

No single skill makes a person capable of doing professional-quality desktop publishing.

Just as different skills are required to create and produce something by traditional methods, many of the same skills are required for desktop publishing.

DTP *enables* a single person to do all those things, but does not *qualify* him to do them competently.

The required capabilities include a facility for ideas and words, on one hand, and for graphic arts (including design, typography and production) on the other.

But even in the non-DTP world, few people can work both sides of the street well.

In addition, desktop publishing calls for a comfortable familiarity with computer equipment and software.

Once again, good fortune shined on my life. My decades of experience as a writer, editor, creative director and head of creative and production in advertising, marketing, journalism and academia, plus my obsession with computers, make me one of those who have the requisite combination.

So I have been able to make good use of DTP in my marketing communications business.

DTP has been not only a moneymaker for me; it has also enabled me to volunteer my services in the name of social action—*tikkun ha'olam* (repairing the world).

I edit and produce newsletters and brochures at no charge to help support causes I believe in, such as the Civil Rights and Peace Movement of Israel.

The CRM, known by the Hebrew acronym Ratz (rhymes with lots), is a left-wing political party. Most of its members broke away from the Labor Party, seeking a more activist approach. It really gets into the nitty gritty of societal and national issues.

For me, action is the name of the game.

So, in editing the party's English-language newsletter distributed in the United States and other countries, I focused on the specific actions taken by the CRM in the Knesset (parliament), in the courts and in the streets.

The CRM has been at the forefront of the struggle for religious pluralism.

The Orthodox and ultra-Orthodox account for only about one-third of the Jewish population—but, since the small parties can swing the balance between the two major parties (Labor and Likud) in Israel's electoral system, their political clout has given them a virtual monopoly on religious affairs.

In Israel, only Orthodox and ultra-Orthodox rabbis are permitted to conduct weddings, funerals and conversions. Civil marriages and divorces are not permitted.

The Orthodox and ultra-Orthodox also managed to shut down essential public activities on the Sabbath and holidays, including transportation and cultural, sports and leisure activities.

And, in return for their votes, the Orthodox and ultra-Orthodox have been getting large sums of public money for their educational and religious institutions. As part of the deal, ultra-Orthodox men and women are exempted from army service (a situation which galls most Israelis).

It is political extortion, pure and simple.

The CRM has been fighting this situation with legislation, legal actions and demonstrations. Recent reforms in the electoral system are helping. And in Israel's 1992 national election, the political power of the Orthodox and ultra-Orthodox parties was cut back substantially.

One of the CRM's original causes was and is women's rights. It is working for legal equality in marriage and divorce; for equality in employment opportunities and compensation; and for freedom from sexual harassment and stereotyping.

And, above all, there is the issue of peace with the Arabs. The CRM has long favored a more flexible approach, a readiness to compromise with the Palestinians and other Arabs in the area.

In the 1992 election in which Labor returned to power under Yitzhak Rabin, the CRM ran on a combined list (Meretz) with two other left-wing and center-left parties.

Meretz helped form the government coalition as Labor's major partner and strongest supporter of the peace process. Two CRM leaders, Yossi Sarid and Shulamit Aloni, became ministers in the government.

Inside or outside the government, the party is committed to pressing for faster progress in civil rights and regional peace.

When the people at the instructional television center heard that I was back in Israel, a director called and asked whether I was interested in writing a new series of English programs.

So I went in and met with the director and a producer.

Unlike in the earlier years, there was no linguist from the Ministry of Education to provide direction and guidelines. Now, the ministry was leaving it up to the television people to do whatever they wanted. We had a free rein.

We talked about the new series for a couple of hours. Then I went home and wrote a script for the first program.

At our next conference, the director liked the script; the producer didn't. The producer suggested I try such-and-such a tack.

Next conference: the producer liked my revised script; the director didn't. The director suggested I try such-and-such a tack.

Next conference: neither the director nor the producer liked the re-revised script. The director suggested I go this way; the producer suggested I go that way.

I called time out.

They had been talking to me for weeks—but, apparently, neither had been listening to what the other was saying to me.

There was obviously no clear agreement between them on what they wanted from me.

So I suggested that they discuss it between themselves until they knew what they wanted, and then get back to me.

Fine, they said.

A few weeks later, the director called me and said they were all set with the final word.

We made a date for the following week.

The day before the conference, the director called me again and canceled the meeting. They weren't ready for me, but they'd get back to me real soon and set up another meeting.

I never heard from them. A year or so later, I heard that nothing had been done and they had been taken off the project.

It isn't easy to communicate, even for people who can hear.

One weekend, Barbara and I went down to the Dead Sea with a group of friends for a walking tour through a nature preserve.

Overnight accommodations were in cabins that slept six people in double-decker bunks. We took four cabins—two for the men, two for the women.

The next morning, the women unanimously awarded Barbara the prize for being the loudest snorer.

For four decades I've been sleeping with her—yet I never knew she snored.

That's one way that having a deaf spouse can help make a marriage work.

From the terrace of our penthouse, you can look west and see the Mediterranean Sea about a mile away.

Then you can look east and see the hills of the West Bank, about 20 miles away.

Israel is a tiny country.

You can see clear across it with the naked eye.

And it has only five and a half million citizens: 81 percent are Jewish, 14.2 percent are Muslim, 3 percent are Christian, and 1.7 percent are Druse. Most of the non-Jewish citizens are Arabs.

The Jews are split ethnically (European/American origin versus Asian/African origin, which often means haves versus have-nots)...religiously (Reform and Conservative versus Orthodox and ultra-Orthodox)...and politically (hawks versus doves).

It is rare for a nationwide consensus to emerge on any issue.

But on one subject there is no disagreement: all Israeli Jews share an intense desire to survive as a people and as a nation.

No one has forgotten the Holocaust in which Hitler destroyed one-third of the world's Jews.

The disagreement is on how to ensure Israel's survival without compromising her democratic, humanitarian values.

In Arabic, there are two different words for peace—with two different meanings.

One is the absence of open warfare, such as the peace during the Cold War between the United States and the former Soviet Union. This is what many Arabs have had in mind when speaking of making peace with Israel.

The other word means a full peace as English speakers know it, such as the United States has long had with Canada—friendship, open borders, commerce, tourism, and so on. This is what Israelis would like to have with their Arab neighbors.

An end to war would certainly be welcome, of course, but our aspirations are much higher.

We want real peace with our neighbors.

For many Israelis, the peace with Egypt has been something of a disappointment—little more than an official cease-fire.

A major problem in the region is that Islam makes no provision for religious coexistence. It sees all non-Muslims (including Jews) as infidels.

Extremist Arab fundamentalists such as Hamas and the Islamic Jihad want to destroy Israel.

That they cannot do so doesn't alter the fact that they want to, and this mindset colors the situation.

Right-wingers think we can achieve peace while holding on to all of the West Bank.

Left-wingers feel we should give up at least those parts of the West Bank that are heavily populated by Arabs.

Standing on our terrace and looking clear across the country, it's easy to see why the right-wingers want to hold onto the West Bank as a buffer.

But I have no desire to rule over the Arabs in the territories, nor to transfer them elsewhere against their will.

Right-wingers believe strongly that only maximum security will bring peace.

Left-wingers believe just as strongly that only taking a risk will bring peace. The alternative, they say, is more war and a loss of the Jews' humanitarian values.

In 1967, Israel captured the West Bank in a defensive war against Jordan, which (1) attacked us, and (2) never held legal possession of the West Bank in the first place.

What the world's self-appointed experts usually forget or ignore is that the Arab-Israeli conflict predates 1967. In fact, it predates the establishment of the state in 1948.

Yet people tell Israel to "give it back," as though this all that's needed to end the conflict.

American Indians have a greater legal claim to tribal lands in the United States than Arabs have to the West Bank.

The same goes for Mexico's right to Texas and California.

Would the American government or people even think about giving these lands back to the Indians or to Mexico?

The double standard is alive and well.

Still, the Israeli left believes that giving (not giving back, but giving) much of the West Bank territory to the Palestinians *under circumstances which ensure Israel's security* is one of the key elements in forging a lasting peace with them.

It will take a series of steps by both sides to build confidence and trust—such as self-rule, trade, the sharing of water and other resources, arms control, and so on.

The same holds true for Syria and the Golan Heights. Israelis are understandably leery about relinquishing the natural barrier of a mountain range for the dubious security of a piece of paper.

Until there is confidence and trust, there won't be peace.

While we were living temporarily in the States, our tribe in Israel increased.

Laurie and her husband had a son, Sagi. Debby found herself a new mate.

After we returned, Laurie had another son, Yonatan. And then Debby had a son, Dor, and a daughter, Noam, to go with her daughter and son by her first husband.

So we had six delightful, exuberant grandchildren who divided their Friday evenings between Savta Barbara's spaghetti and Saba Lew's computer. (Saba Lew. Sounds like that old Ricky Riccardo song, "Babalu.")

Debby sold her apartment and bought a house in suburban Ra'anana. Laurie left her kibbutz and bought a home in suburban Herzliya. Julie decided to settle down and bought an apartment near Tel Aviv University.

The sledgehammer took a fearful beating as I knocked down walls all over the place.

Lisa came to Israel during her winter breaks from Indiana, and Barbara and I went to the States each summer. In between, we spoke to Lisa on the phone twice a month or so.

Which means that we were in touch with our youngest daughter at least as much as are the parents of most students who go away to college.

Everything was going well with our family.

The greatest scare I got was when Lisa and I took a rappelling lesson at a desert survival school run by Laurie's kibbutz.

I wanted to back out, but I was embarrassed to quit in front of Lisa.

So there I was, dangling halfway down a cliff overlooking the Dead Sea, held by a rope tied to a harness around my body.

I couldn't imagine a more dangerous situation.

That was before we sealed ourselves up in our rooms, donned gas masks, and watched CNN's footage of Scud missiles streaking through the sky above Tel Aviv and exploding near our homes.

25

When the Scuds came crashing in

Friday, January 11, 1991: Barbara goes to the bookstore to buy a copy of *Chemical Warfare: A Family Defense Manual.*

The clerk asks Barbara whether she wants it gift wrapped.

The army phoned Laurie's husband, Avi, and told him to stand by for reserve duty next week—a month earlier than usual.

The January 15 deadline for Iraq to get out of Kuwait triggered a last-minute rush for masking tape and plastic sheeting to seal windows and doors against a chemical attack.

The government has handed out four kinds of CW (chemical warfare) protective devices: adult-size and junior-size gas masks, a clear plastic hood (like firefighters wear) with a battery-operated filtration system for small children, and a clear plastic tent (the size of a playpen) for infants. Each kit includes a hypodermic syringe filled with an antidote for nerve gas.

The order goes out for classroom windows to be sealed.

The huge central hospital where Julie works in the genetics lab is holding a practice emergency exercise tomorrow.

Our building is constructed of pre-cast reinforced concrete; the exterior walls are about 16 inches thick, and the roof/ceilings are about 20 inches thick. In the basement is a shelter with walls and ceiling about 24 or 30 inches thick. The shelter has several rooms, running water, electricity, a toilet, sink, ventilation system, a couple of huge water storage vats.

But: the consequences of a chemical warhead can be far more serious than those of a conventional warhead. And chemicals tend to sink downward. And most shelters (including ours) do not have filters against CW, and are difficult or impossible to seal.

So the government announces that people should *not* go down to the shelters if there is an attack; instead, they should stay in their homes—the higher, the better.

Tuesday, January 15: The radio says the IDF (Israel Defense Forces) expects Iraq to attack Israel within the next 24 hours.

There's a sense of unreality.

Here we are in our duplex penthouse, warm and clean and well-fed, with modern appliances in the kitchen and laundry room and an office full of sophisticated computer equipment and eleven telephones on two lines.

Yet we just finished putting together a cache of basic supplies for survival: water, candles, matches, canned foods, portable radio, flashlights, scissors, towels, toilet paper, buckets, talcum powder, bleach, burn ointment.

And gas masks.

While Barbara takes the gas masks out of the closet, it occurs to her that we will need paper and pencils, too.

Because when she's wearing a gas mask, I won't be able to read her lips. She'll have to write down everything.

Thursday, January 17: 3 a.m. Debby calls. The Americans have launched their attack against Iraq. We call Julie and Laurie.

I break the seal on the carton and unpack my gas mask. Since this is just a dry run, I attach a training cap to the mask inlet instead of a filter canister. I put on the mask and tighten the straps.

I put my open palm against the hole in the training cap and take a deep breath. The mask is sucked inward by the vacuum, proving that it is properly airtight.

I remove my palm. The small hole in the cap is supposed to reproduce the airflow I would get through a filter. I try to breathe normally, but I can't. I am suffocating. I exhale, and the moisture from my breath fogs the eyepieces.

I can't breathe. I can't see. And I can't hear.

I grab the mask and jerk it off, forgetting to loosen the straps first. I breathe in deeply and wipe the sweat off my face.

We take our gas masks upstairs to the den and turn on the television. The first reports about the allied attacks are encouraging. But what about the Scuds earmarked for Israel?

We wait.

I try on my gas mask again. This time it doesn't seem so hard to breathe. Especially if I sit quietly and take shallower breaths. And the eyepieces clear up when I inhale.

Now I can breathe and see. Two out of three isn't bad.

We sit up until dawn watching the TV news and waiting for the sirens to wail. At 6 a.m., I fall asleep on the couch.

I wake at 9 a.m. Barbara has stayed up to watch the news on ITV and CNN. She has jotted notes on scraps of paper.

I sit down at my computer and call into the mainframe at Tel Aviv University to check for e-mail. But today, of all days, the IBM is down. Since the university is closed, the computer center is also closed—so no technicians are around to get it back up.

Barbara calls Debby and Laurie. Their rooms are taped, their gas masks are ready, and they have all the supplies they need.

There's no answer at Julie's. She left for work in the medical center across the street from the Ministry of Defense.

I decide to go to Julie's newly purchased apartment to scrape and patch the walls. I put my gas mask and atropine syringe in my knapsack and pedal my bike the eight blocks to Julie's.

It is a beautiful day—warm and cloudless. There are almost no cars on the street, almost no people on the sidewalks. I ride by the rows of closed stores in the shopping center (only the supermarket is open), the closed university.

I work on the apartment all day. At 8:30, I ride back home in the dark. I see few cars, even fewer people on the sidewalks.

Barbara has spent the day in her ceramics studio upstairs, turning out pots and taking notes on the news. She hands me her notes, smudged with clay. She has talked to our friends on the phone. Everyone is fine.

Our bedroom and adjoining bathroom form the sealed room. The two bedroom windows and the single bathroom window are taped and covered with plastic sheeting. The shower stall is filled with our cache of emergency supplies; we use another bathroom for showers and baths. So, if anything happens during the night, we don't have to go anywhere. We're already there.

Around midnight, we go to sleep.

With our clothes on, just in case.

Friday, January 18: 2 a.m. The blast of an exploding Scud missile wakes Barbara. She turns on her bedside light and the radio. Then she wakes me up.

"It's an attack. Put on your gas mask."

Our reactions: exasperation, annoyance, a momentary twinge or two of fear. But at least the waiting is over. I roll out of bed. We slip on our masks and tighten the straps.

Barbara goes into the bathroom and pours some bleach into a bucket of water. She soaks a towel and sticks it under the bedroom door. The fumes from the bleach sting our nostrils.

We sit on the bed. Barbara listens to the radio and writes down what the announcer is saying.

But we hadn't thought about the fact that I can't wear my glasses inside a gas mask. To my eyes, sans bifocals, her writing is blurred and unreadable. I tell Barbara to print in large letters.

The radio announces that Scuds have hit Tel Aviv. There is no mention of where, or how much damage, or casualties.

We sit on the bed as the radio switches to music. We wait.

Half an hour later, the radio says to take off our gas masks. Barbara calls Debby, Julie and Laurie. Everyone is fine.

Minutes later, the radio says we can leave the sealed room.

We go upstairs to the den and turn on the television. We learn that there has been some damage, a few light injuries. But no one was killed, and there were no chemical warheads.

At dawn, we hear that a house six blocks from us had been hit by a Scud.

The mayor of Tel Aviv says there's nothing to worry about. Even though a Scud can reach the city in five minutes, it will take at least an hour and a half for it to find a parking place.

I put my gas mask in my knapsack and ride over to Julie's apartment. I knock on the neighbor's door and tell her I'm working alone. I spend the day scraping the ceilings, then start to leave.

At that moment, the neighbor rushes into the room.

"The siren. Put your gas mask on." Then she hurries back into her apartment.

I go into Julie's bedroom, put on my gas mask, and press a wet towel under the door. I sit down on her futon and wait.

And then it hits me what a stupid thing I've done. I'm alone and can't hear anything. How will I know what's happening?

The bedroom door opens. The neighbor's husband is standing there in his gas mask. He gestures for me to follow him. The same thought must have hit them, too.

We hustle next door and squeeze into the children's bedroom. The room is no more than 7 by 10 feet, with a crib and a child's bed, plus a dresser and a cabinet. There are now four adults and two children in the room—the neighbor, her husband, a friend, a four-year-old boy, a two-month-old baby, and me.

The adults are wearing regular gas masks. The boy is wearing the firefighter-type hood. The baby is lying in a plastic tent.

The neighbor's husband closes the door and sticks tape around the edges. Watching him, I realize we had forgotten to tape our bedroom door during the Scud attack the previous night.

The neighbor writes on a pad of paper with a felt pen: "Do you want us to tell Barbara you're with us?"

I nod and write down our phone number.

So there I am, sitting and thinking that these two young people have a baby and a small child to worry about during a missile attack, and a sealed room that was already uncomfortably crowded without me...yet they took the trouble to think about me being alone in Julie's apartment, and to untape their door and come and get me and share what little room they had, and to think that Barbara would be concerned about whether I was okay and that I would be concerned about whether Barbara was okay.

A few minutes later, the radio announces that we can leave the sealed room but should stay home. I thank the neighbors and ride my bike home down the deserted streets.

A police van with three men in chemical-protective clothing pulls up. A cop leans out and says "You're supposed to be home." I nod. "That's where I'm going." The van drives off.

Saturday, January 19: 7:15 a.m. An explosion wakes Barbara. She turns on the radio and wakes me up. We put on our gas masks. This time, before putting the wet towel under the door, I seal the door with tape.

The force of the blast has set off automobile alarms in the parking lot behind our building. They wail, unheeded.

After about half an hour, we get the all-clear signal. We go upstairs, open the sliding doors, and step out onto the terrace.

In a building across the street, a man is standing on his balcony and looking toward a section of the city that is blocked from our view. "Hey," Barbara calls. "You see anything?"

The man shakes his head. "There were some army helicopters around there before, but they're gone."

There's a small airport on the sea near us, like Meigs Field in Chicago. It's used by Arkia (the inland airline), private planes, and the IDF. Most of the traffic consists of IDF helicopters.

Whenever the army goes into a high state of alert, the traffic steps up. Barbara can tell the level of tension in the situation simply from the change in the frequency of the choppers.

We walk around our terrace, looking at the trees and plants growing in tubs around the perimeter. Our largest tree has been knocked over by the explosion and is leaning drunkenly at a 45-degree angle. I manhandle the tree back into position.

With the schools closed and the children home all day every day, parents are climbing the walls.

Our grandchildren seem to be taking things pretty well. Debby's 13-year-old daughter, Michal, gets a little bit nervous during the attacks. Her 9-year-old son, Ben, is bored by the waiting and looks forward to the excitement of the alerts.

Her 3-year-old son, Dor, didn't want to put on his firefighter-type hood—but then, seeing other children wear it on television, he accepted it; now he doesn't want to take it off. Her baby girl, Noam, cries a bit in her tent.

Laurie's sons, Sagi and Yonatan, are 7 and 4. Both of them feel comfortable with their CW equipment—Sagi's junior-size mask and Yonatan's firefighter-type hood.

The VCRs in both households get heavy use.

Lisa finally gets through after trying to reach us by phone for the past two days; the lines from the U.S. have been jammed. A few hours after that, my sister calls from Los Angeles.

Sunday, January 20: I ride my bike to Julie's and ring the bell next door. No answer. I ring at another door. No answer. A third door. No answer. Everybody seems to have left town.

I work on the walls, looking out the window every 15 minutes or so. If I see someone strolling by, I know there's no alert.

In the late afternoon, Julie comes in. I haven't seen her since before the war started. She showers, packs some clean clothes, and goes back to the hospital. At sunset, I pedal back home.

I call into the university's IBM. It's up!

I download my e-mail, including messages from our daughter and friends in America. I feel much better now that I'm back in electronic contact with the outside world.

The hospital found out that Julie is a photographer. It assigned her to take pictures of unidentified casualties among the severely wounded or dead victims, to aid in identifying them.

It's hard to be a moderate Israeli these days, willing to negotiate with the Arabs on the basis of mutual trust.

What is an Israeli supposed to think when Arafat and Jordan's King Hussein rush to give their support to Saddam? When crowds of Palestinians exhort Saddam to launch his missiles at Israel, and cheer and dance to celebrate the destruction?

What do you respond when right-wing Israelis say "I told you that you can't trust them"?

Monday, January 21: Stores, businesses and factories are opening their doors. It's time to get on with it.

But with the schools and nurseries closed, what is a working mother supposed to do with her children?

Alon goes back to work. But Debby stays home with her kids. Avi goes back to work. Laurie goes to work, too—but she takes her children with her, and stays for only a few hours.

Tuesday, January 22: We are in the living room, after dinner, when Barbara cocks her ear. "The siren. Let's go."

We go to the bedroom, put on our gas masks, and start taping the door closed. Barbara looks up at the ceiling, listening.

Moments later, she writes: "Two explosions."

Pointing at the radio, she writes: "Gas mask instructions in all languages." The alerts are being given in Hebrew, English, Russian, Arabic, Yiddish and Amharic (the language of Ethiopians).

"The Patriots sound just like planes," says Barbara. "They went right over us."

I turn on the portable TV. It shows the now-familiar instructional film on gas masks and window taping, with Russian captions. In a corner of the screen, a woman is repeating the instructions in Israeli sign language.

An announcer appears, speaking in Hebrew. Next to him are captions in Hebrew, English, Arabic, Russian. The English caption says "All Clear." We take off our gas masks. I start to take the tape off the door, but Barbara holds up her hand. "Not yet."

I point to the screen. "But it says all clear."

"The all-clear is for the rest of the country. The announcer says that people in Tel Aviv should stay in their sealed rooms."

We hear that the Patriots stopped one Scud missile, but another missile fell somewhere in the area.

We go upstairs and turn on the television. Eventually, the news comes on with the ubiquitous CNN footage.

We are shocked by the amount of damage that has been done to several residential buildings, and by the announced casualty toll of 76 wounded. We hear that most of the casualties were taken to Ichilov Hospital. That's where Julie is working.

It is close to midnight by the time we turn off the television and go back downstairs. Barbara, hearing some sounds in the outside hallway, opens the front door.

Our neighbors are entering the elevator, suitcases in hand.

Wednesday, January 23: Three of the victims of last night's attack are dead. They were 88, 76 and 70 years old. They died from heart failure or suffocation in their gas masks.

Julie calls. When the victims of the attack were brought to the hospital, she took pictures of the dead people.

Laurie calls. They have decided to go into their concrete shelter on the ground floor rather than the sealed room.

Barbara and I talk about whether the two of us should go to our sealed room or down to the shelter.

If there's a chemical attack, we're better off in the sealed room.

But—our corner bedroom has two exterior walls that face east toward Iraq. The walls are reinforced concrete, but each wall has a window that could be blown inward by a blast. And many (if not most) of last night's injuries were caused by flying glass.

The underground shelter will give us good protection against an explosion. But gas, if any, will collect down there.

Since the siren gives us only a few seconds' warning (if that), we won't have time to get down to the shelter before a missile hits. Which means we'd have to sleep in the shelter (as some people in the building are doing) in order to be there in time.

And right then, before we can decide, the siren wails. I go to the coat hook by the front door and get my knapsack, which holds my gas mask. Barbara goes into our bedroom, where she keeps a carry-on bag with her gas mask and our documents.

Then I go down the hallway toward our bedroom, carrying my knapsack, at the same time that Barbara comes out of the bedroom with her bag. We meet in the middle of the hallway.

"Hey—where are you going?" I ask.

"Where are *you* going?" she asks.

At the end of the radio traffic report, the host signs off with a hopeful message: "Have a boring day."

Thursday, January 24: The Patriot batteries on the beaches are clearly visible from the coastal road. One installation is about a mile from us and half a mile from Julie's home.

With my indelible World War II orientation, I think of an air raid as a time when people sit in shelters and wait—sometimes for hours—for bombs to fall. In those days, the all-clear signal meant that no more bombs were expected.

It took me a while to catch on to the fact that taking shelter from a missile attack here has a radically different pattern from what went on during the blitz of London.

There's little or no warning. After you've been in your sealed room or shelter for five minutes or so, you know that no more missiles are coming. But the all-clear doesn't sound for half an hour or more after that, yet you continue to sit and wait.

What makes this sitting and waiting different from London is that you're not waiting for the explosion of another stick of bombs or another V-2 rocket.

The attack is over. You're waiting for Haga (the civil defense people) to check for chemicals where the missiles hit.

Whatever happens, happens quickly. It's over almost before it begins.

Friday, January 25: With people tending to stay home at night, there has been less face-to-face socializing after dark. Instead, we keep in touch more by phone.

A friend calls and invites us over for a get-together tomorrow—pancakes at high noon. He tells Barbara that the sound of the siren—an irritating, screeching wail—is driving him nuts. It doesn't help that he is a psychiatrist.

In the middle of the day, I cover my keyboard and go over to Julie's apartment to do some more work on the walls. In the late afternoon, Julie comes home after 24 hours at the hospital, sinks into her futon, and is asleep in seconds.

At 6 p.m., just after dark has fallen, I am atop the stepladder with a scraper in my hand when I feel a tugging on my pants leg. I look down and see Julie.

"It's the siren," she says.

We go into her bedroom and put on our gas masks. I tape the door shut.

She sits on the futon and calls Barbara. I sit on the floor with my back against the closet.

A thundering roar shakes the room.

I can't hear it, but I certainly feel it in every bone. Julie ducks and puts her hands over her ears.

Julie makes an arcing overhead gesture, like a basketball player making a hook shot, indicating that Patriots have been fired.

In quick succession, two tremendous explosions jolt us—sonic booms from the Patriots climbing skyward directly over us.

I feel the explosions with my body, and the pressure hits my eardrums. Julie covers her ears.

Julie again makes the arcing gesture. Two more explosions.

Again, the arcing gesture. Two more explosions.

Julie makes an explosive gesture with two hands, then waves one hand to indicate that the explosion was farther away. I don't feel anything.

We sit and wait. Julie gestures like a conductor to indicate music on the radio.

Then we get the okay to take off our gas masks.

Julie has to go back to the hospital, so she takes a shower. I scrape the wall until she's ready to leave.

We lock up. She gets on her bike and rides to the hospital. I get on my bike and ride home.

Later, we learn that one person had been killed and 69 injured in a nearby suburb, and several hundred homes had been damaged or destroyed.

The doorbell rings. It's a neighbor from the floor below.

She says that the building committee is setting up shelters in the lobbies on alternate floors. The lobbies are in the core of the building, with no external walls and no windows.

If there's an alert, everybody is within one floor of a shelter.

At 3 a.m., the phone rings. It's Lisa, calling from Highland Park. The computer at Northwestern is down, so she can't get through on the Internet. Television coverage of the Scud attack is terrifying. People are calling her and asking her if we are okay.

Yes, we're okay, says Barbara. We're all just fine.

Saturday, January 26: Before and after the establishment of the state of Israel, the border kibbutzim and Jerusalem were the trip wires in the Arab-Israeli conflict.

For decades, the safest place to be was in Tel Aviv, in the center of the coastal area. When people living near the border sought relief from the tension, they went to Tel Aviv for a visit.

Overnight, the Scuds have completely reversed the situation. Now people are going from Tel Aviv to kibbutzim (on the border and elsewhere in the country) and to other cities away from the coast: Jerusalem, Eilat, Beersheva.

Today, a family on our former kibbutz calls and invites us to stay in their house. We say thanks, but no thanks.

At noon, we drive to Herzliya Pituach for pancakes. It's the first time the group has been together since the war started.

I discover that I have been spared the worst of it. The worst of it, our friends say, is what assaults their ears.

The screeching, wailing sirens in the middle of the night. The earthshaking roar of the Patriots blasting off. The sonic booms that rattle the glass in the windows. The explosions when the climbing Patriots meet the falling Scuds.

None of us has suffered any physical harm or property damage. But the sounds, the God-awful sounds, can be unnerving to many people and terrifying to some. Especially the children.

After the pancakes, we visit our children and grandchildren. We pace ourselves so that we get back home just before dark.

Barbara and I decide that from now on, we will go down to the lobby on the floor below. I take a folding lawn chair from the terrace and put it by the front door with my knapsack and the radio. The knapsack holds my gas mask, felt-tip pens and paper. Barbara puts a blanket and her gas mask by the front door.

Just after the evening newscast is over, the siren sounds.

The lobby is 20 feet long and 10 feet wide. There are a dozen people—seven adults and five children—on mattresses, on chairs, on the floor, standing. Plus a dog and two cages of parakeets.

By now, Barbara can tell by the sounds what is happening.

The roar of the Patriots blasting off from the beach behind us.

The sonic booms as they break the sound barrier above us.

The explosions, farther away, as they hit the Scuds—or as the Scuds hit their targets.

And then the waiting: conventional or chemical warheads?

After 20 minutes: okay to take off the masks. Another 20 minutes and we can go back up to our apartment.

We turn on the TV and see what we heard above us moments ago: Patriots screaming across the sky toward incoming Scuds.

And people all over the world are seeing it, too.

There's no time lag. It's the Instant War.

Sunday, January 27: We finally get some good news: the Super Bowl will be shown live on Israel TV at 1 a.m.

Barbara says that she keeps writing the same words and phrases to tell me what the radio is saying during an alert. So I take a thick felt-tip pen and print in big letters on a piece of cardboard:

    Patriot | Scud | Plane   *Sonic boom | Explosion*
    Near | Far   *North | Central | South*
    Clear | Hit   *Music | Foreign*

All Barbara has to do is point to the appropriate words.

As it gets dark, I wait for the alert. I hope it will be over before the Super Bowl starts.

When the night passes quietly, I am pleasantly surprised.

The only bomb is thrown by the Buffalo quarterback.

Tuesday, January 29: Today there's an announcement of a newly invented siren for the deaf. It plugs into the earphone jack of a radio. When the siren sounds on the radio, it flashes a light. Also, there's a wrist beeper that vibrates when the siren goes off.

Thursday, January 31: It is just after dark. I am working alone in Julie's apartment. I shoot a sideways glance at the portable TV, expecting to see yet another newscast about the war.

The slide is on: *ALERT.*

I pick up the TV and carry it into the back bedroom, put on my gas mask, and tape the door shut. I plug in the TV and turn it on. For 10 minutes or so I watch old footage of singers—just like the rain-delay fillers during the telecasts of local baseball games.

The announcer comes on with maps of Jerusalem and the central belt outside Tel Aviv. I think he's saying that people in these areas should stay put, and the rest of the country can go.

But on every alert so far, Tel Aviv has been the last area to be released. So he might be saying the opposite: that people in these areas have the all-clear, and those in Tel Aviv should stay put.

I think about the Ethiopian immigrants, early in the war, who heard the alert and went to their sealed room. The all-clear was not announced in their language, so they didn't know it was okay to come out. So they stayed in the sealed room for eight hours....

Five minutes later, the bedroom door opens. It's a friend who lives around the corner.

Barbara, watching TV at home, had noticed the visual ambiguity. So she called the friend and told her to go get me.

"Just like the Ethiopians," the friend says.

"Not really. I was just waiting for the end of this song."

Saturday, February 2: An attack comes in the early evening, just as I am walking in the front door. Residents of our building have been coming back from the outlying areas, so the shelter in the lobby of the floor below us is becoming more crowded. During tonight's alert, 30 people fill every square foot of space. They can't move without stepping gingerly over or around others.

It is somewhat surrealistic to see the younger children—three and four years old—wearing gas masks. They squirm and fidget and pull off their masks every few minutes.

The missile lands on the West Bank, so the all-clear is announced a few minutes later. We disperse back to our apartments.

2:30 a.m.: Barbara shakes me awake. Another alert. We grab our gas masks, stumble down to the floor below, and shoehorn ourselves into the throng.

Barbara listens to the radio, then writes: *1 Scud.*

A few minutes later, she starts writing again. The first word flows from her felt-tip pen: *nerve.*

The thought stuns me. My God—they're using nerve gas!

She writes four more words: *in middle of night.*

It takes my sleep-numbed mind another couple of seconds to figure out what her shorthand means: *Saddam has a lot of nerve waking us up at 2:30 a.m.*

Saturday, February 9: The siren starts wailing a few hours before dawn. On the way down the stairs, Barbara hears the roar of Patriots blasting off from the beach-front batteries.

We're in and out in half an hour. We're used to the routine.

But for others less fortunate, the attacks have been devastating.

The latest missile demolishes 10 apartments, guts another 50, and damages 500 or more. Incredibly, only 26 people are injured today—none seriously.

Many of the residents are aged. It is heartbreaking to see them sifting through the rubble in search of their few possessions.

A few hours after the attack, we make the rounds to see the grandchildren.

They have been fighting cabin fever. They are anxious to go to school, go to movies, go to parties.

The town of Ra'anana has trucked snow from Mount Hermon for the children. Most of the children in the town have never seen snow. They make snowmen and have snowball fights.

We go to a daylight get-together of our circle.

Monday, February 11: At 1:30 a.m., the sirens wail again. This time the Scud hits a wealthy suburb. Seven people are hurt; 30 houses and 190 apartments are damaged.

Tuesday, February 12: All of our grandchildren are finally back in school or nursery school or the baby's day-care center. They take their gas masks with them. Debby has to shlep the baby's crib-size folding tent back and forth each day.

Saturday, February 16: Since everybody wants to be home before dark, our daughters and grandchildren have not been coming over for Shabbat dinner on Friday evenings, as they did two or three times a month before the war. So we have fallen into a routine of visiting them twice a week, on Saturday mornings and Tuesday or Wednesday afternoons.

Tonight, at the end of a quiet weekend, the sirens wail. We squeeze into the mass of men, women, teenagers, children and babies in the lobby, and don our gas masks.

For a change, there is no roar of Patriots blasting off.

No explosions.

Nothing but music on the radio. Maybe it's a false alarm.

Then the radio says one Scud fell somewhere in the Negev, and another in the sea.

It's a welcome respite for Tel Aviv.

Monday, February 18: My brother calls. He says the Chicago Symphony Orchestra is sending a letter of solidarity to the Israel Philharmonic Orchestra.

I wonder if there are any strings attached.

Tuesday, February 19: Another Scud attack.

Putting on our gas masks and going into the sealed room is getting to be like taking out the garbage.

We hear the siren, heave a sigh, and go do what has to be done. For us, it has become little more than a chore. Sitting there, we feel little or no sense of personal danger.

Saturday, February 23: Today is our turn to host the Saturday kaffeeklatsch. It is a beautiful day—70s and sunny. The city is quiet for Shabbat. The sky is blue and cloudless. To the west, the sea is a gently rocking blue-green. To the east, the hills of the West Bank shimmer in the haze.

Davka, it makes me think of the death and destruction raining down on Iraq and Kuwait a few hundred miles away.

Our friends arrive, drop their gas masks in the front hall, and climb the spiral staircase to the upper level and the terrace. Soon there are 20 gas masks at the foot of the stairs.

Laurie is here with her boys, too. Avi is on reserve duty down south. I swing the boys in circles for a while, as much for the exercise as for the opportunity to stop talking about the war.

As the day passes, the 7 p.m. deadline set by Bush's ultimatum looms. By 6 p.m., everyone has left to get home before dark.

I am working at the computer when Barbara goes upstairs to watch the news. Five minutes later, she comes back down.

"Alert."

It's garbage time again.

Sunday, February 24: We wake up and learn that the ground war started a few hours earlier—3 a.m. our time.

Nobody knows what's going on, or where. The news blackout continues throughout the morning and into the afternoon.

The worse the war goes for Saddam, the more likely he is to lash out at Israel. This adds an undercurrent of caution to our joy when we finally hear of the allies' achievements.

Monday, February 25: At 3:30 a.m., Barbara shakes me awake. As we grope for our gas masks and stumble downstairs, I am not too irritated. The way the war is going, this may well be the last Scud attack. The missile falls harmlessly in a bare section of the Negev.

At 5:30 a.m., Barbara shakes me awake again. This time, I do get irritated. The second Scud also falls in the Negev.

The civil defense ban against large gatherings at any time—and any gathering at night—remains in effect. Mann Auditorium stays closed. The Israel Philharmonic gives duplicate concerts to small groups at noon and 3 p.m.

Zubin Mehta, who detoured to Israel when the war broke out, is conducting a series of concerts this week. Barbara goes to an IPO concert in the renovated Noga Auditorium in Jaffa.

A Scud hits the American barracks in Saudi Arabia, killing dozens of soldiers. It's a reminder of how lucky we have been in Israel. There has been a great deal of property damage here, but the casualties have been miraculously low.

Thursday, February 28: The war ended (more or less) at 7 a.m. It's anticlimactic, like the end of a lopsided football game.

The army spokesman announces the end of the emergency. We are to store our gas masks and open our sealed rooms.

It's a kind of catharsis, like throwing away your crutches after a broken leg has healed.

I pull the tape off the windows and fold up the plastic and pull up the shutters. Yes, it makes a difference to see sunlight flooding into our bedroom for the first time in seven weeks.

Restrictions on public gatherings are canceled. The streets of Tel Aviv are filled with people. Restaurants, movie theaters, stores and cafes are open after dark. The mood is upbeat.

The children are out in their Purim costumes.

Haman has been foiled again.

Epilogue: For seven weeks, Israel focused on the threat of death and destruction. The numbers:

39 Scuds were launched at us

1 person was killed

12 people died from heart attacks or suffocated in gas masks

200 people were wounded

4,095 buildings were damaged or destroyed

1,644 families were evacuated

Fortunately, our family is fine.

And we're happy to break out of the holding pattern and get moving again.

Onward.

* * *

The foregoing excerpts are from my running account of the Gulf War which I sent periodically by e-mail to our family and friends in the States. It was written from our perspective at the time.

Now we know that Bush was not the savior of Israel that he made himself out to be. Had we known, the radio stations would not have been playing "Sugar Bush, We Love You So."

Now we know that the Patriot missiles were nowhere near as successful as Schwartzkopf and the rest of the military claimed. They had little, if any, effectiveness against the Scuds.

Now we know that none of the mobile Scud launchers was definitely destroyed by the Allies during the war.

Now we know that it wasn't Israel's restraint that kept us from retaliating against Iraq and fighting our own war, but Bush's threats and his withholding of essential battlefield information.

Now we know that the allies' great "victory" over Iraq was anything but that...and that Iraq remains a deadly threat to Israel and the world.

Nevertheless:

Onward.

26

Biting the tongue that feeds them

An elderly woman on a bus in Tel Aviv was speaking to her young grandson in Yiddish.

The boy was answering her in Hebrew.

"Speak Yiddish, not Hebrew!" the woman kept commanding.

Another passenger on the bus interjected: "Lady, why do you insist that he speak Yiddish instead of Hebrew?"

The old woman replied: "So he'll remember that he's Jewish."

Somewhere between 5 and 10 percent of deaf people identify themselves as Deaf (capital D). The core of this identity is American Sign Language.

What I say here about Deaf people applies only to them, not to most deaf people. And what I say about Deaf extremists applies only to the extremists, not to most capital-D Deaf people.

The Deaf claim that ASL is the language of the deaf.

It isn't.

ASL is the language of the Deaf, not the language of the deaf, since fewer than 10 percent of deaf people know ASL.

Having their own language, distinct from English, gives the Deaf a sense of pride and kinship.

And ASL lets them communicate among themselves with perfect understanding, in family and social settings and in classrooms where the teachers and students use ASL.

This easy, comfortable communication generates a camaraderie and a sense of belonging among the Deaf.

They say they do not have such feelings in the hearing world—which, deliberately or inadvertently, tends to exclude them.

As a mechanism for coping with deafness, therefore, ASL plays a dominant and effective role within a precisely defined sphere: the Deaf community itself.

Thus, ASL is a valuable asset—as far as it goes.

But outside the Deaf community, American Sign Language is no more usable in schools and workplaces and on the street than are other foreign languages.

Language capability reflects intelligence. Consequently, people tend to judge a person's intelligence by how articulate he is.

Someone who does not speak well—or at all—is often perceived as mentally retarded.

This perception is wrong and unfair. Although spoken language is the norm, it is not the only form of language.

The fact that ASL is a rich and expressive language is a major reason why the Deaf are intensely proud of ASL. It helps disprove the falsehood about their intelligence.

But even if the public realizes that ASL is a legitimate language, and accurately perceives signers to be as intelligent as anyone else, this does not change an obvious fact: *people who do not know ASL cannot understand what signers are saying in ASL.*

The *legitimacy* of ASL as a language and the *utility* of ASL in the hearing world are two separate issues. Japanese is a legitimate language, too, but its usefulness in America is severely limited.

Like many ethnic groups, the Deaf community is protective of its language. The strong sense of group identity which ASL gives the Deaf can be very beneficial and even indispensable.

So the Deaf find it impossible to separate the issues of ASL's legitimacy and its utility. They consider any criticism of ASL's utility to be criticism of its legitimacy—and, thus, of their identity.

Often, their unquestioning adulation of ASL is accompanied by an illogical abhorrence of spoken English.

During an Internet discussion about reading books to young deaf children, someone posted the following message:

> A parent who reads out loud to a deaf child not only encourages his later interest in reading, but also helps the child develop spoken language.

In response, an ASL extremist wrote:

> I agree with your comment about parents reading to their children encouraging interest in reading on their own.

The first person's point was that when a parent reads *aloud* it helps the child develop *spoken language*. But the militant omitted both references to speaking; in doing so, he deliberately twisted the meaning of the original comment.

Antipathy to speaking and speechreading—and, often, to the English language itself—is shared by many members of the Deaf community. They explain it as part of Deaf lore, which draws on the age-old dispute between educators who favored oralism versus those who favored sign language.

The Deaf consider an 1880 international conference in Milan to be the most disastrous event in their history. Educators of the deaf (all of whom were hearing) passed a resolution that oralism was to be the method of choice in schools, and that sign language was to be completely forbidden in the classroom.

For nearly a century, sign went underground in schools until Total Communication (usually a combination of signed, spoken and written English) began to gain favor among educators.

In recent years, with ASL being defined as a distinct language, the concept of a Deaf culture based on this language has arisen. So the Deaf view the former effort to repress sign language as an attempt to destroy what they see as their culture.

In addition, many Deaf militants reject spoken English because it is identified with the hearing people whom they view as their oppressors.

As in a tribal blood feud, they are holding a grudge long after the cause of the grudge has disappeared (along with those people who were involved). There is no organized attempt to eliminate sign language, so the militants' rejection of the language of their "oppressors" has no relation to the reality of today.

Furthermore, their version of history ignores the fact that more than 90 percent of deaf children have hearing parents.

Thus, speaking and speechreading, which some Deaf see as an attempt to destroy their culture, are actually ways for the hearing parents of deaf children to raise their children in *their* culture...to share their English language and their hearing world with their deaf children as with their hearing children.

That's what my parents did.

The main sociopolitical goal of the Deaf is to preserve and strengthen the Deaf community.

Since the community is centered on ASL, the pursuit of their goal depends on recruiting as many new deaf ASL users as possible.

This is a major reason why they advocate that ASL be a deaf child's first language, and that it be the classroom language.

But since nine out of ten deaf children have hearing parents and siblings, the norm in their families is spoken English (or some other spoken language). So how do the ASL advocates propose that a deaf child acquire ASL as a first tongue?

Their answer: by having the hearing parents and siblings of a deaf child change their normal mode of communication at home to ASL—learning and using it among themselves for the benefit of the deaf child.

The advocates see nothing at all impractical or presumptuous about this, even though it takes years of immersion to become reasonably fluent in ASL (especially for a hearing person).

So they routinely try to send parents on a guilt trip—accusing them of selfishly ignoring a deaf child's best interests if they do not turn their home into an ASL environment.

Without the easy, comfortable communication of ASL with his friends, they claim, a deaf child faces the gloom and doom of a lifetime as a frustrated social outcast.

But the reality is that in the preschool years, the deaf child of hearing parents would have no one to use ASL with—except those family members who choose to (and are able to) learn it.

Being unable to communicate with the hearing children in his neighborhood, he would be isolated from them.

The use of ASL in the preschool years precludes both written and spoken English. But the preschool years are the optimum time for language development. So the loss of these critical years will delay and discourage the child's acquisition of English even as a second language.

High on the capital-D Deaf's sociopolitical agenda is *bilingual, bicultural education.* This means using ASL as the language of instruction in the classroom, with textbooks in English (since there is no written form of ASL).

Obviously, ASL cannot be the language of instruction in a mainstream classroom with hearing students (although some advocates actually believe it can and should be).

But most of the Deaf are against mainstreaming deaf children, anyhow. What they really want is special schools (or at least classes) for deaf children, with ASL environments inside and outside the classroom.

Never mind that most parents want their deaf children to speak English, or at least use signed English.

Never mind that many children become deaf after learning to speak English.

Never mind that many of the children in special classes are hard-of-hearing, not deaf, and can speak English quite well.

The bi-bi advocates will permit no signed English in the classroom (except when English itself is being taught).

Neither will they permit speaking (unless there is enough time to squeeze in an optional, low-priority lesson in speaking and speechreading once a week or so).

Ross Stuckless, professor of education at the National Technical Institute for the Deaf (at the Rochester Institute of Technology), expressed concern about bi-bi's effects.

Its advocates, he wrote in the *American Annals of the Deaf,*

> tend to be vague or to avoid discussion altogether about how the deaf child will be taught and acquire English as a viable second language under a bilingual approach. Most assuredly, it will not occur spontaneously.
>
> The science, history, math and other textbooks will be in English. How will a child whose preschool language was exclusively ASL suddenly become proficient enough in English to read the textbooks with any degree of understanding? We may as well expect the hearing kids in American elementary schools to use science and history and math textbooks written in German or French.

As for spoken English, Stuckless pointed out that:

> under favorable circumstances, almost all children can develop a useful level of proficiency—even if it is only at the survival level—within a spoken language environment. Some proficiency in spoken language is of undeniable value to the deaf adult in most employment situations, to say nothing of the myriad of other face-to-face interactions in the community.

He objected to the fact that:

> either de facto or by intent and policy, bilingual education efforts discourage the use of voice and spoken language on the part of the deaf child and others in his or her environment, including the teacher and the parent. I believe this is wrong.

> Whatever aptitude and motivation the deaf child might
> have to develop expressive and receptive spoken language
> skills to even a moderate degree may be seriously and per-
> manently jeopardized by a practice that fosters ASL to the
> exclusion of speech.

"Time on task" is a proven factor in learning. The more time you
put into learning something, the more competent you become.

Advocates of ASL as the classroom language claim that less time
spent on English will not hurt its acquisition—because cognitive
abilities developed through ASL can be used with English.

But people do not learn English grammar without spending time
on English grammar, nor do they develop their English vocabularies
without spending time on their English vocabularies. Our family's
experience with the Hebrew language illustrates this.

When we moved to Israel, our daughters quickly became fluent
in Hebrew. They were immersed in the language in the classroom
and with their friends.

But Barbara, despite months of studying in *ulpanim* (Hebrew-
language instruction classes), lagged behind. The problem was that
as soon as she opened her mouth to speak Hebrew, the other
person, hearing her American accent, switched to English.

People wouldn't let her get much time on task in Hebrew.

Then we moved from Tel Aviv to the kibbutz.

There, nobody switched Barbara away from Hebrew. All day
long, she spoke and heard Hebrew. In a short time, she was fluent.
Today, she speaks Hebrew without the trace of an accent.

In school, our children had to read and write (as well as speak)
Hebrew for hours every day. Today, they work in the business and
academic worlds, reading and writing legal, scientific, medical and
other complicated documents in Hebrew.

Barbara, on the other hand, can just barely understand an article
in a Hebrew newspaper. Despite her fluent spoken Hebrew, she
hasn't put much time into learning to read Hebrew.

In Debby's and Laurie's homes, the language is Hebrew; their husbands are native Hebrew speakers, and their children learned Hebrew first. The schools teach eight years of English (with the help of the educational TV programs I wrote). And much of the regular television programming has English-language soundtracks with Hebrew captions.

So most people who grow up in Israel learn English, to varying degrees, in class (starting at age 10) and by watching TV.

However, our grandchildren speak English better than their peers do (and most of our grandchildren are under 10, so they haven't even started learning English in class yet).

Why the difference? Because they spend quite a bit of time speaking and listening to English with Barbara and me. Their peers don't get the time on task that our grandchildren do, and it shows.

Finally: my Hebrew sucks.

I know the alphabet, some of the grammar, and a few hundred words. But I never put much time into learning it. All my work is in English, and all my friends, coworkers, clients and suppliers are fluent in English, so I didn't push to become fluent in Hebrew. It's probably my most notable failure.

Yes, time on task is extremely important to the acquisition of a language.

The following message was posted on an electronic forum by a user of American Sign Language who was a student at a college for the deaf.

He wanted to unsubscribe from the group.

> *Please my name is no longer on that network of list as unsubsrible.*

He couldn't write a simple sentence such as "Please take my name off the list" or "Please unsubscribe me from the list."

Obviously, the structure of ASL was the cause of his butchered English grammar. Obviously, a great many jobs (not to mention promotions) are going to be closed to him because of this shortcoming. And obviously, the school made a substantial allowance for his inability to write a simple sentence in English.

The same forum debated whether a history instructor who was joining Gallaudet University should grade his students' papers on content alone, or also on the quality of the writing. Some argued that the students' command of English was none of the teacher's business, and should not figure in the history grade.

Fortunately, the teacher disagreed. He noted that an important part of a humanities education was learning how to present ideas coherently, unambiguously and effectively.

Should he expect less from his students, he asked, simply because they were deaf?

I see no reason why anyone would hire someone with a good knowledge of history and a poor command of English when there are plenty of people around with a good knowledge of history and a good command of English.

Unfortunately, however, too many teachers of the deaf look the other way—dumping their language-handicapped students into a highly competitive job market.

And that's exactly what these people are. No matter how fluent someone may be in his own language, he's language handicapped in the American job market if his English isn't up to snuff.

But the message is not getting through to many of the Gallaudet students, who are now demanding, of all things, that their exams be administered in ASL instead of in English.

Quite a few deaf students can be found in mainstream colleges and universities, including the very best schools in the country such as the University of Chicago, Stanford and MIT.

Some of them do it the way I did—by reading their teachers' lips, their classmates' notes, and textbooks.

Others take interpreters into some or all of their classes.

But regardless of how these students get *through* college, they usually get *into* college the same way: by meeting the schools' entrance requirements for SAT scores and other indications of the students' ability to do college work.

The better the school, the stiffer the admissions standards.

Gallaudet, on the other hand, accepts many students who are so deficient in reading and writing that they would not have been accepted at any other college.

The inevitable result is that the academic level of Gallaudet's undergraduate classes tends to reflect that of its student body. Many of the students cannot understand the textbooks even with their instructors' help, and their presence in the classroom pulls down the level of instruction.

The school's newspaper reported that recruiters from AT&T, speaking on campus in 1993, emphasized that the poor English skills of Gallaudet alumni are hurting them in the job market.

One recruiter said she had seen an otherwise excellent paper that had been destroyed by grammatical and spelling errors—yet the paper had received an A+ grade from a lenient instructor.

An internal study found that "employers of Gallaudet graduates are increasingly dissatisfied with the quality of many graduates' English skills."

Nevertheless, the school's public stance is that the students are getting an excellent education. The college of communication arts, for example, says it prepares its students for careers in advertising and public relations—yet many of those who receive degrees are unacceptably deficient in reading and writing.

And someone who formerly worked in the school's placement office vehemently denied that a lack of oral skills limited a deaf person's opportunities for jobs or promotions.

Some faculty members, on the other hand, decry the obvious gap between the propaganda and reality in the undergraduate schools. (Gallaudet's graduate schools, in contrast, are more or less competitive with those in other universities.)

The administration is rethinking the admissions policy. Harvey Corson, former provost and (at the time I spoke with him) vice president for pre-college programs, told me he realizes that not every deaf person who wants to go to college belongs there.

He agreed that stricter entrance requirements would raise the level of education for those who do belong there.

The trade-off, he said, is that those who are denied admission will have nowhere else to go.

I. King Jordan, president of Gallaudet, acknowledges that the students must go out into the world and earn a living.

But, according to an interview with the *Washington City Paper,* he believes the university can best prepare the students for this by providing an "empowering" environment (his term for a sheltered, signing, academically unchallenging environment) in which they may "blossom and prosper" without feeling like outsiders.

In this, he says, Gallaudet is like deaf clubs, deaf churches, deaf sporting events; it is part of Deaf culture.

But a key tenet of the culturally Deaf is a devaluation (and some-times outright rejection) of speaking and speechreading. Indeed, some of the militant Deaf faculty members are strongly in favor of not speaking at all in the classroom.

In August 1991, in the elementary and secondary schools located on the Gallaudet campus, the administrators directed the teachers to turn off their voices and communicate with their students only in American Sign Language.

Six months later, pressure from parents, the federal government and Gallaudet's board made Jordan (who had not been a party to the original decision) countermand the order.

When I spoke with Corson and Nancy Shook, principal of the elementary school, they affirmed that they recognized the value of speaking and speechreading for those who were able to acquire these skills.

While giving priority to ASL and English literacy, they said they saw a need for some oral training as well. However, the degree to which this view is actually being implemented is unclear.

In the meantime, most Gallaudet graduates are moving from one sheltered environment to another. The placement office reported that 77 percent of the class of 1989 who have jobs are employed in a place where most or all of their coworkers are deaf.

Is an academically undemanding, sign-only milieu the best form of higher education for the deaf?

The militant Deaf say yes, that it's a form of affirmative action. Some Gallaudet faculty members say no—that it is intellectually dishonest and leaves graduates unprepared for the real world.

Robert Williams was dean of the college of arts and sciences when he voiced a desire to raise the academic level and to help students develop speech and speechreading as much as possible.

When I asked if he was speaking officially for the university, Williams said that Gallaudet has no specific policy on the use or teaching of oral skills.

"We are a university," he said, "and that means a university of ideas—some of which we may agree with, and others we merely tolerate. I'm not sure if Gallaudet's president or the vice president of academic affairs would agree with me—but I believe that the more tools you can bring to a job, the better your chances are of landing the job and succeeding.

"I'm not here to say that deaf people who can speak have an easier time. I wish it weren't so, but...."

So the internal battle rages—but it is the militant Deaf who make the headlines. And, coincidentally or not, both Corson and Williams were out of their administrative positions within a year after I spoke with them, and Corson is no longer with Gallaudet.

A number of parties are interested in the outcome.

The federal government provides 80 percent of the funding for Gallaudet. The colleges and pre-college schools are supposed to be models for deaf education in the United States, and the research and other programs are supposed to benefit the 20,000,000 deaf and hard-of-hearing (HOH) people in the country.

And more than 90 percent of deaf students in America have hearing parents, most of whom want their children to become as proficient as possible in speech and speechreading.

Some faculty members and students at Gallaudet have a real-world perspective. They understand the importance of preparing students to make it outside the confines of the campus.

But the militants who want the campus to be a haven for the culturally Deaf are giving it an increasingly pervasive image of a place in which hearing, speech and speechreading—or even the mention of them—are politically incorrect.

The Gallaudet Research Institute (GRI) has long been doing noteworthy work. Its seven units collect and analyze information on a wide range of core issues relating to hearing loss—including communication, education, employment and technology.

The Center for Assessment and Demographic Studies conducts an annual survey of children, studies educational and demographic trends, tracks deaf students from school to work, and studies the effects of hearing impairment on communication at work.

Tom Allen, director of CADS, told me there are no data on the relationship between oral skills and job opportunities. Still, he said, he believes that people who can communicate with coworkers are better able to take advantage of career opportunities.

The Technology Assessment Program helps engineers develop new technologies to meet the needs of deaf and HOH people.

The outreach program holds workshops and prepares manuals to help HOH people and their families cope with hearing loss.

The Center for Auditory and Speech Sciences studies ways to help people speechread better. When it tested me, using videodisc sequences of people speaking full sentences, I identified 77 to 85 percent of the words correctly.

Tucked away in a basement, CASS receives little recognition compared to the other research units—perhaps because oral skills are, in the eyes of many at Gallaudet, abominations.

Deliberately or not, this attitude is reflected in an article by the dean of research about a committee mandated to identify broad issues for study. The issues included ASL in the classroom, cultural development, ASL interpreting skills, minority/ethnic groups, late-deafened adults, and technologies.

But there was no mention of two of the most crucial issues for deaf people—speechreading and speech.

Another part of Gallaudet, the National Information Center on Deafness, is widely known as a reputable source of information.

But its 1993 directory of organizations says the function of the Alexander Graham Bell Association for the Deaf is to promote the understanding of hearing loss.

That's like saying that the function of soap is to produce lather.

The core function of the association is actually to promote speech and speechreading (as well as the use of residual hearing) as the key to greater participation in the mainstream—which is why I gave the keynote address at its convention in 1994.

It is not Gallaudet's fault that so many applicants for admission can barely read and write English, since it has no control over what happens in elementary and high schools.

And it is unrealistic to expect a college student to improve his reading and writing by six or eight grade levels in remedial English courses and simultaneously get a decent education in his other courses (which require college-level literacy from day one).

But Gallaudet could try to attack the cause of the problem—by getting massively involved in English instruction of deaf students from preschool on up. This involvement could include:

1. Substantially increasing research into ways of teaching English to deaf students at all grade levels. The university's research institute is already somewhat involved, but the scope and resources of the current studies nowhere near match the urgency and importance of finding better methods.

2. Putting the findings into practice at the two pre-college schools on Gallaudet's campus in Washington, DC—the Kendall Demonstration Elementary School and the Model Secondary School for the Deaf. This would provide proof that the methods work, and give educators an opportunity to observe them in action.

3. Giving greater emphasis to teaching the university's education majors how to teach English skills to their future students.

4. Actively and continuously promoting these methods to the country's primary and secondary schools and teachers, to parents, to students, to local and state and federal authorities.

5. Preparing all kinds of learning aids—textbooks, workbooks, teachers' guides, teacher training materials, videotapes, etc.

6. Preparing motivational aids—as simple as posters, wall charts and certificates, as ambitious as annual Gallaudet Excellence in Reading and Excellence in Writing awards for each grade, with local, regional and national winners.

We need a full-scale, multi-pronged war against illiteracy among deaf students throughout the United States.

This approach is clearly within Gallaudet's mission as a federally funded institution—and it is just as clearly in Gallaudet's interest, because it will improve the quality of its own education.

Obviously, it will be years before a new wave of students with better pre-college English instruction has an impact on Gallaudet's student body and level of education.

But this approach attacks the disease.

The alternative is to treat the symptoms with less-than-optimal results year after year, with the same problem remaining.

But if a special committee has its way, the Gallaudet Research Institute will be disbanded and many programs phased out, such as genetic counseling and the graduate program in social work.

In the fall of 1994, the committee recommended dropping all activities that do not cater specifically to the Gallaudet community—which, to an overwhelming extent, means the ASL Deaf.

Fortunately, since the university's federal funding is predicated on the basis of its serving all 20,000,000 deaf and HOH people in the country—not just the fewer than one percent of them who use ASL—the chances of this happening are not great.

But it does reflect the attitude of a number of influential people at Gallaudet.

In the 1993 Gallaudet alumni survey, perhaps the most telling statistics were buried on page 53.

Now that they have gone out into the real world, how do the former students evaluate various aspects of their undergraduate education at Gallaudet?

The most satisfaction was with campus social life—which was rated superior or good by 88 percent of the respondents.

The least satisfaction was with preparation for a career—which was rated superior or good by only 40 percent.

Preparation for a career gets considerably more emphasis at the National Technical Institute for the Deaf, one of eight colleges at the Rochester Institute of Technology.

Like Gallaudet, NTID receives federal government funding for postsecondary education of deaf students.

But unlike Gallaudet, it is not a haven from the hearing world, nor is it dominated by an ASL-centered ideology.

William Castle, who retired as NTID director at the end of 1994, twice served as president of the Alexander Graham Bell Association for the Deaf.

So it's not surprising that he says the college takes an eclectic approach to communication. Speaking and speechreading are okay. Signed English is okay. ASL is okay.

Most instructors use simultaneous communication (SimCom), speaking and signing in English at the same time.

Unlike the isolation and insulation at Gallaudet, the 1,100+ deaf students share RIT's mainstream campus with nearly 12,000 hearing students—and about 30 percent of them take regular classes with hearing students in the other RIT colleges.

This real-world mingling lets deaf students learn and hone the social and communication skills necessary for getting along with hearing coworkers and the public, as well as for socializing with hearing friends.

While those who finish the sub-baccalaureate programs have marketable skills that qualify them for jobs, many continue their studies at the baccalaurate level in the other RIT colleges.

Between 95 and 97 percent of the job-seeking graduates find work in the fields they studied. NTID's success in preparing deaf students for the mainstream is highlighted by the fact that, in most instances, all of their coworkers are hearing.

In reaction to my emphasis on the realities of the workplace and what it takes to get good jobs and promotions, some Deaf people say that my approach is okay for someone who puts money and success above everything else—but to them, personal happiness and self-esteem are more important than material success.

They claim that success in work comes only at the expense of happiness.

It's a classic example of sour grapes.

I agree that success isn't everything, that it doesn't necessarily bring happiness, and that success without happiness can be the pits. But success and happiness aren't mutually exclusive.

Here's what makes *me* happy:

1. My family: a remarkably compatible wife who has put up with me for 39 years and strengthens my links to the hearing world; four independent daughters who haven't become neurotic despite my pushing them to do the best they could; and seven thriving grandchildren who make us prouder of them every day.

2. Our circles of friends—in Chicago, in Tel Aviv, and on the kibbutz where we lived for five years—who have stayed fairly close to us despite my driving them up the wall.

3. My work as a writer, editor, executive, computer consultant and desktop publisher.

I enjoy it so much that I'd do it for free—which I do for social and political causes I believe in.

4. Achievement. Yes, success is an important part of what makes me happy. What I have been fortunate to achieve professionally, and the accompanying financial rewards, have been tremendously gratifying.

Many non-oral deaf are underemployed.

Despite what they say, I can't see that happiness and self-esteem would be inconsistent with jobs that are more in line with their capabilities, pay them better, and enable their families to enjoy a higher standard of living.

It bears repeating that not all deaf people can acquire good speaking and speechreading skills.

But many can and do succeed in communicating orally to a usable degree, and significant numbers of them are prelingually deaf.

Those who deliberately reject spoken English are biting the tongue that feeds them.

27

Close encounters of the hearing kind

The television series "Beauty and the Beast" portrayed denizens of the underground world as warm, good-hearted human beings.

Obviously, the program was sheer fantasy.

Anyone who has dealt with an underground parking attendant knows that subterranean life brings out the beast in car hikers.

When you drive into a garage, the attendants are nowhere in sight. So you park in a spot that seems okay, and you start looking for an attendant so you can get a receipt.

Then a gorilla in grease-stained sneakers materializes from the shadows, shouting and waving his arms in self-righteous outrage.

"Whadja pucha car dere for, huh? Dincha hear me yell notta pucha car dere? Whatsa matter wicha, you deaf?"

"As a matter of fact, I am."

"Don't gimme that shit, just move that mother, whatsa matter whicha, dincha hear me yell notta pucha car dere? You deaf?"

This is an all-too-common example of the encounters between hearing and deaf people. The level of awareness and sensitivity among some hearing people is appalling. Especially when they sneer "Are you deaf?"—intending the question as a supposedly witty insult without even considering the possibility that the other person actually is deaf.

Worse, there have been times when deaf and hard-of-hearing people were harmed physically—and, yes, killed—because of such "misunderstandings."

Not long ago, a young deaf man was shot and killed by police in a southern city when he didn't hear their order to stop. A deaf Englishman was almost shot in the back by a soldier in Northern Ireland in a similar situation.

In public places such as shopping malls and airports, the security personnel—some of them armed with lethal weapons—sometimes display a cavalier, self-important arrogance. They have not yet shot an unresponding person in the back, but some encounters have been frightening for the deaf people involved.

Encounters between hearing people and those whose hearing is impaired could be less of a hassle, less awkward, less frustrating, less embarrassing, less unfair.

The handicapping nature of deafness lies partly in the attitudes and actions of hearing people. Usually, all it takes to make a big difference is a measure of awareness and consideration on the part of the hearing person.

Deaf people aren't looking for pity—just for acceptance, a little understanding, and sometimes a bit of patience.

More than 99 percent of people can hear, and about 92 percent can hear normally. So there's no reason to anticipate that someone has a hearing problem *if nothing indicates one.*

But once there *is* some evidence—if the other person doesn't respond when addressed from behind his back, or doesn't understand something said to him—then the speaker should seriously consider the possibility of a hearing problem (in addition to other possibilities, such as unfamiliarity with the language).

A popular bumper sticker reads: *I'm not deaf—I'm ignoring you.* Sometimes this is true. But often the reverse is true.

Suppose someone is blocking your path in a supermarket aisle, or your access to a bookstore magazine rack or an airport baggage carousel.

If she doesn't respond to your "Excuse me, please," don't jump to the conclusion that she is snubbing you or defying you. She simply may not have heard you.

She may be standing next to you—but if she's deaf and isn't looking at your face, she won't know you're speaking to her.

All you have to do to get her attention is raise your hand in her line of sight or touch her lightly on the arm.

Hearing losses range from mild to total. In general, it usually does no good to raise your voice when speaking to a person with impaired hearing—regardless of the amount of hearing loss, and regardless of whether he is wearing a hearing aid.

It can even be counterproductive—by distorting the sound of your words.

And if you are talking to a deaf speechreader, raising your voice not only is a waste of breath (since he can't hear it); it can also distort the movement of your lips and make it harder for him to understand what you're saying.

It is far more effective to adjust your *articulation*, your *speed* or the *pitch* of your voice.

Speaking distinctly does not mean exaggerating your lip movements; this, too, makes you harder to understand.

It means taking care not to mumble or slur your words.

If you normally talk through your teeth (as many men do), it will help to open your mouth a bit more (as many women do)—but don't exaggerate.

If you normally speak rapidly, slow down a bit. Don't speak too slowly, and don't lose the natural rhythms of speech.

When you talk to hard-of-hearing people, it often helps to drop the pitch of your voice. Many hard-of-hearing people—especially those who lost their hearing gradually—cannot understand sounds in the higher frequencies. Simply lowering your tone brings your voice within the understandable range for them.

To profoundly deaf people, the pitch makes no difference at all.

For some hard-of-hearing people, a *slight* increase in loudness may be helpful if you normally speak softly. But don't talk louder than the average voice unless they ask you to.

Sit or stand at a comfortable distance—between arm's length and six feet away. Beyond that distance, it is increasingly difficult for the hard-of-hearing to hear and for the deaf to speechread.

In a noisy place, a hard-of-hearing person may want you to stand even closer, and perhaps have you aim your words at his better ear. If so, he will position himself or turn his head to aim that ear at your mouth.

He knows what he's doing—so don't move around to face him head on. Stay there and talk to his ear.

But—a profoundly deaf person needs just the opposite. Talking to his ear is useless. He needs to see your face clearly so he can speechread you.

If someone backs off so he can see you better—especially if he's wearing glasses and trying to keep your face in focus—don't keep moving in closer to him.

Some people who want to tell me something in confidence do the James Cagney prison bit: they come close and look down at the floor while talking. I can't see a word they're saying.

Many severely and profoundly deaf people wear hearing aids although they cannot understand speech with the aids alone.

They are speechreaders—but their hearing aids provide some sensory input that helps them distinguish the vowels and some of the consonants.

So the presence of a hearing aid doesn't mean the wearer can understand you if she isn't looking at you.

And those who *can* understand speech through their hearing aids can understand you even better if they can see your lips.

Therefore, you can help *anyone* who has a hearing loss—deaf or hard of hearing, with or without a hearing aid—by keeping your face as visible as possible when you speak, unless he specifically indicates you should talk to his ear.

When a speaker is gesturing, he may inadvertently hide his lips with his hands. Even if his hand isn't near his mouth, it can get in the line of sight.

Depending on who the speaker is, I either (1) call time out and ask him to keep his hands down, or (2) reach over and push his hands down to the table without interrupting him.

In a business environment, someone may be looking down at papers on her desk while she speaks—so if I'm standing, I can't see her lips. Or she may turn her head to look for something behind her—speaking while her face is out of my sight.

I really can't blame anyone for such involuntary actions, even if they know I'm deaf. They're concentrating on what they're saying and looking for, which is the way it should be. If they remember to keep their lips in my sight, fine; if not, I remind them.

When a deaf person is talking with one or two people, the conversation is usually straightforward and easy to speechread.

But a group of six or eight people in animated conversation around a table is something else. Each person has his own train of thought, and the ball bounces all over the place—with interjections, wisecracks and questions coming from all directions.

It's easy for a speechreader to get lost each time the conversation takes a new tack. Still, with a little help from my friends and some initiative on my part, it usually works out okay.

Someone may turn to me and say "We're talking about the new bridge over the Jordan River."

Or someone will begin a story or joke and someone else will stop him and say "Start over and tell it to Lew."

Or I'll ask the person sitting next to me what's going on.

Or I'll be doing the talking myself. Or someone will start up a private conversation with me. Or I'll start one. Or I'll be wrapped up in my own thoughts.

On the other hand: sometimes, after a round of laughter, I'll ask what was so funny—and the response will be "Nothing, it wasn't important, you didn't miss anything."

This response drives a lot of deaf people up the wall. It's not a very satisfying answer.

Sometimes I push for the details. Other times, I let it go.

You can't win them all.

When a deaf person is talking to someone, it's all too easy for a third person to interrupt.

A hearing speaker may instinctively raise his voice to override an interruption. But a deaf person, unable to hear the interruption, unknowingly continues at the same level—and is drowned out.

This is one of the most offensive and demeaning experiences forced upon deaf people, and it is a widespread phenomenon.

Many hearing people have no compunction at all about walking up and breaking into a deaf person's conversation as though he weren't there.

For some hard-of-hearing people, background music can be a disaster. They can't hear the high notes; the bass tones hurt their ears; and voices get drowned out.

For a deaf person, on the other hand, background sound has no bearing on her understanding of what someone is saying.

However, she must know about the sound so that she can adjust the level of her own voice. If music or a dishwasher or a passing airplane is drowning out her words, let her know.

If you stand with your back to a window during the daytime, your face will be silhouetted against the brighter light outside— making it extremely difficult or impossible to speechread you.

Another hazard is a strong light that shines down from directly over the speaker's head; it throws distracting shadows on his face. On the other hand, too little light on his face can be worse.

A bushy mustache overhanging the upper lip is murder. If you have one, be aware that someday, somewhere, a speechreader is going to sneak up behind you with a pair of scissors.

More than 90 percent of deaf people can speak.

Approximately three-fourths of all deaf people lost their hearing in adulthood. Others lost their hearing in childhood after acquiring speech, as I did. The remainder are prelingually deaf people, and many of them have learned how to speak.

So if someone cannot hear, don't assume he cannot speak.

But if a deaf person can *speak,* that doesn't mean he can *speechread* well.

Most people deafened in adulthood retain their ability to speak, but many (especially older people) have difficulty getting the hang of speechreading. They may have to depend heavily on signed English or paper and pencil.

If someone doesn't catch what you say the first or second time, don't keep repeating it in the same words. Try rephrasing it.

In particular, tell him what the subject is—"I'm talking about a program I saw on television last night. It was about genetics."

If he asks you to spell the word he missed, spell it out. If he asks you to write it down, write it down. Don't insist on repeating the word orally if it isn't working. You don't have to write down the whole thing—just the word or words he missed.

Catching names—especially last names—is difficult enough for hearing people; it's much more so for deaf and hard-of-hearing people. Often, the only way for a me to get it is by trial and error: Cole? Cohn? Gold? Judy? Julie? Shulie?

If you change the subject abruptly, you will probably throw off a speechreader who is trying to keep up with your line of thought.

It helps to let her know you're dropping one subject and bringing up something else. To indicate this, one of my clients used to wipe the air with his palm like a teacher erasing a blackboard.

When you tell someone vital information—names, addresses, numbers—write it down. It's simply too easy to misunderstand this kind of thing. Actually, it's a good idea to do this for anyone.

And try not to be exasperated or impatient when a deaf person doesn't understand you. An attitude of annoyance is one of the most common causes of unpleasantness between hearing people and deaf people.

Deaf people who don't speak well are often reluctant to use their voices. They are sometimes met by impatience at best and ridicule at worst. Children and teenagers, in particular, can be cruel and mimicking.

Also, there's a self-fulfilling aspect among some hearing people: they expect the speech of deaf people to be unintelligible. When they find out that the speaker is deaf, his speech suddenly becomes less intelligible to them—even if they understood him before.

These forms of uncaring, rude or biased behavior are among the major reasons why many deaf people with marginal (or even good) oral skills shun the hearing world.

Understandably, rather than face the hassle of being ignored or patronized or ridiculed, they prefer the haven of a sign language community.

Whatever speaking capability a deaf person has, it's more useful than none at all. Therefore, his efforts to speak—to communicate with hearing people on their own terms—are laudable.

If he's trying his best, he should be encouraged.

Most deaf people want to be as independent as possible. Yet, although they dislike doing so, there are times when they have to ask someone to do a favor such as make a telephone call to get or convey information.

I myself have little or no reticence about asking the nearest warm body to make a call. I see it as a routine and unobjectionable necessity for a deaf person who wants to function effectively.

But such a request is inherently inhibiting, and many deaf people will simply forgo the needed help rather than ask.

You can help a deaf person overcome that inhibition by making clear that the request doesn't bother you at all.

Get the details before you dial: who you're going to speak to, and what the caller wants to know or say. This way, you can start the conversation without delay.

Also: don't hang up the phone until you're sure the conversation is finished. The response from one end may trigger a follow-up question or comment from the other end.

After you've relayed everything, ask both ends "Is that all?" before saying good-bye.

If a deaf person calls you through an intermediary, there will be time lags while the intermediary tells the caller what you said and the caller tells the intermediary what to tell you.

These dead spots can be as short as a second or two when Barbara makes a call for me (because she's doing her simultaneous translation bit).

Or they can be as long as half a minute or more through a TDD relay service, with the relay operator and the deaf person typing the words a letter at a time.

When someone says she's calling for so-and-so who is deaf, try to be patient. Especially if it's a TDD relay call, which unavoidably takes longer than a voice call.

There have been reports of hearing people hanging up on TDD relay callers—thereby denying some deaf people whatever limited access they have to the telephone.

A deaf driver can't watch the road and read your lips at the same time. If you want to say something to him, wait until the car is stopped at a traffic light.

If you're driving and a deaf person is sitting next to you, don't take your eyes off the road to face him when you speak. If he can't read lips in profile, wait until you stop the car.

Like me, most deaf people do not know sign language. If you happen to know some sign language, don't start using it with a deaf person unless you know that she signs. Ask first.

If you want to hear about how to deal with deafness (because, for example, you have a deaf child), any deaf person will be more than happy to tell you all you want to know.

But don't walk up to me and try to make small talk by saying "My 96-year-old grandmother is deaf, too."

What am I supposed to respond—"That's nice"?

Perceptions:

An old woman was living in a small village in Russia near the border with Poland. When the border was shifted eastward in 1945, her village became part of Poland.

On hearing the news, the woman wept with joy.

"Thank God!" she cried. "I don't think my old bones could have taken another one of those freezing Russian winters."

Perceptions have a strong influence on attitudes and actions, like those of the old woman.

Some employers think that deafness makes someone inherently less capable in the workplace. This common misperception is a major handicap for the deaf.

Deafness itself is rarely a problem.

Yes, there are some jobs that deaf people cannot perform simply because they cannot hear—such as an air traffic controller, or a symphony conductor, or a TV sound technician.

But almost always, if there is a problem, it's communication.

It isn't necessarily a problem, but it may be—depending on the specific person and the specific job.

Just as some creative people are, in fact, naive about business, *some* deaf people are quite unable to communicate with hearing people on the job. This is an unfortunate, undeniable fact.

But it's also a fact that many deaf people *are* very capable of communicating at the highest levels of most vocations in the mainstream—by speaking and speechreading quite fluently.

They are business executives and university professors, lawyers and engineers, doctors and journalists, scientists and government officials.

But we rarely hear about them, because there is little or nothing unusual to meet the eye. Deafness is an invisible barrier—and those who overcome it through oral skills do so invisibly.

The ability to speak and speechread doesn't *ipso facto* qualify deaf people for a particular job. It simply puts them on a par with hearing people who have similar qualifications.

They can perform as well as hearing people—as rank-and-file employees, supervisors or executives—if they have the particular capabilities required for a particular position, such as specific skills, knowledge, experience or leadership.

But this doesn't mean that only deaf people who are excellent speakers and speechreaders can make it vocationally.

Jobs vary considerably in the need for oral communication. Some require a substantial amount. Some require none at all. Most are somewhere in between.

Deaf people who have moderate or even minimal oral skills can perform many jobs competently in the hearing workplace.

As with hearing people, it's a matter of matching up a person's capabilities with the requirements of a job.

Perhaps someone can speak and speechread well enough to communicate with his coworkers, but not with strangers who may not understand him and whose unfamiliar lips he cannot read. His inability to deal with the public is no bar to his performing a job which does not require contact with the public, but which does require communication with his coworkers.

Furthermore, traditional concepts about the ways in which jobs are performed and the ways in which people communicate are being swept away by a combination of technological advances (such as electronic mail) and human ingenuity.

The reality is that deaf people can perform a vast array of jobs just as competently as hearing people can (and, quite often, more conscientiously and reliably).

The key is for an employer to take an unbiased look at the capabilities of a specific deaf person and focus on how she *can* match the requirements of a specific job—instead of looking for reasons *not* to hire her.

When you analyze the purposes and functions of a job, you'll often find that hearing *per se* has nothing whatsoever to do with getting the job done as effectively and efficiently as possible.

An open-minded reassessment of job functions may well reveal unnoticed opportunities for giving more deaf people better access to better jobs—including promotions to supervisory and executive levels.

And an open-minded evaluation of a deaf person as a unique individual, with her own particular strengths and capabilities, may well reveal a suitably qualified candidate.

However, it's a two-way street, This open-mindedness is *not* a substitute for a deaf person doing the best he can to communicate with hearing people.

I can't see that an employer has any obligation to make an effort for deaf people who don't make an effort themselves.

When some people introduce me, they say "Lew is deaf. He reads your lips."

They mean well, of course. They're simply trying to avoid a communication problem.

But I prefer that they not do it.

First is a matter of ego: I feel that I'm being treated like a child who is not capable of taking care of himself.

Second is a matter of practicality: I find it easier to converse with someone if he doesn't know I'm deaf. If I have a problem—if he covers his lips, for example—*then* I ask him to move his hands away from his mouth or whatever because I'm deaf.

I bring up my deafness only as an explanation, and only after the other person has experienced the fact that communicating with me is no big deal.

If I'm introduced as a deaf person, the other person tends to be startled or intrigued. So he tends to focus on the fact that I'm deaf instead of on what I'm saying, and he automatically exaggerates his lip movements and otherwise makes it more difficult for me to speechread him. So it's counterproductive.

If he learns about my deafness beforehand rather than during the introduction, it's not so bad. The initial impact of the news will have worn off before he meets me, and he may not be so hung up on my deafness. And my ego can live with that, because it's not like holding my hand during the introduction.

About the only time I tell anyone up front that I'm deaf is in places like medical clinics or government offices where people are called by name or number over a PA system.

Bottom line: if there's a need to tell someone I'm deaf, I want to do it myself.

You are not going to believe this, but it really happened to me.

We were at the airport seeing our daughter off. Some friends happened to be there at the same time.

Passing the time while waiting for our daughter to check in, we browsed around the terminal. I was looking at some books at a bookstand. The others were about 200 feet away.

Several young people with backpacks were sitting on the floor near me. One of them got up, came over to me with a camera in his hand and asked if I would take their picture.

Sure, I said.

Our friend saw me talking to the boy and walked toward us.

The boy went back to the group. I took their picture. The boy returned to get his camera and thanked me. Then the group picked up their backpacks and started toward the gate.

Our friend intercepted them about 20 feet away from me and spoke to the boy. I could easily see what he was saying.

"He's deaf. He needs to see your lips."

Sheesh.

I bashed him for that, hard. On the spot.

"I was just trying to help."

"I appreciate your concern. But I don't want you to do that again, ever. Anyhow, what good could it possibly do to tell them that when we were already finished talking?"

"Hey, I came over here as fast as I could."

A deaf adult doesn't need someone to hover protectively over her. She is perfectly capable of letting people know when there's a communication problem—and what to do about it.

To repeat: deaf people aren't looking for pity. All they ask for is acceptance, understanding, and a bit of patience.

And maybe a *little* help from their friends.

28

Onward

The telephone rang on a quiet April evening in 1991.

It was Laurie's husband, calling from the emergency room of a hospital just outside Tel Aviv.

The news was shattering:

Our 31-year-old daughter had meningitis.

As we rushed to the hospital, I saw my life coming full circle—51 years after spinal meningitis had taken away my hearing.

My thoughts were instinctive, inevitable and depressing:

Would Laurie, too, lose her hearing?

In the subdued lighting of Laurie's room, I stood as my parents must have stood—looking down at the motionless figure huddled unconscious on a hospital bed.

I felt the roaring, turbulent river of emotions that my parents must have felt half a century earlier and half a world away.

I felt helpless in the face of the known and the unknown.

I knew what it meant to be deaf.

I didn't know whether that would be Laurie's fate.

No, I thought, don't let it happen again.

Fortunately, it didn't.

After a few rough days, Laurie left the hospital with nothing worse than a lingering weakness and recurring headaches. In a few weeks, even those went away.

We were very, very lucky.

On the other hand: many culturally Deaf people actually hope that their children will be born deaf.

They rejoice when a baby is found to be deaf. They celebrate not only the birth, but the deafness.

I find this attitude to be incredible.

There is a world of difference between loving a deaf child and wanting a child to be deaf.

Hearing parents can love their deaf child just as they love their hearing children.

The fact that hearing parents don't *want* the child to be deaf, that they aren't *happy* that the child is deaf, does not mean that they don't want and love the child.

I simply cannot understand how any parents would wish for their child to face the lifetime of struggle, frustration, deprivation, discrimination, isolation, underachievement and other painfully real disadvantages encountered by the average deaf-born child.

Life is tough enough without the added burden of deafness, despite all the Humpty Dumpty definitions and denials that it is a disability.

I wouldn't wish that on anyone—least of all my own child.

Disease-prevention techniques and medical research can keep people from becoming disabled, or being born with disabilities.

But disability rights activists (including Deaf militants) think this is wrong. They think that people who are in favor of preventing disabilities are, in effect, saying that it's not okay to be disabled, that it would be better if disabled people did not exist.

The activists declare that it *is* okay to be disabled. They say, quite correctly, that a disability is nothing to be ashamed of.

The problem with their position is that it makes no distinction between acceptability and desirability, nor between what is and what will be.

Yes, the disabilities of those who have them today should be accepted. Disabled people are okay.

No, it is not *desirable* for others to have disabilities in the future. That's *not* okay.

In no way do I perceive the efforts to eliminate deafness to be a rejection of me as a person. On the contrary, I am enthusiastic about the progress that will benefit future generations.

Culturally Deaf people say they are proud of their deafness. They take pride in the fact that they cannot hear.

I, on the other hand, am not proud of my deafness.

I am proud of myself as a person, and I am proud of what I have accomplished in spite of my deafness.

But I see nothing about my lack of hearing—the condition of deafness itself—to be proud of.

Many Deaf people don't understand that there is a neutral ground between pride and shame.

If I'm not proud of my deafness, they say, then I must be ashamed of it.

As far as I'm concerned, my deafness is just there, like my skin—a source of neither pride nor shame.

When I tried to explain this on the Internet, someone who still didn't get it said that I could acquire pride in my deafness by joining the Deaf culture.

I am no more interested in doing so than I am in acquiring pride in my white skin by joining a white supremist organization.

The capital-D Deaf invoke the worthiness of cultural diversity in order to legitimize their concept of cultural deafness. Society should accept them the way they are, they say, precisely because they are different.

Yet many of the Deaf themselves tend to be clannish in the extreme—belittling and rejecting those who do not subscribe to their norms. They do not look favorably on diversity among deaf people.

When Marlee Matlin won an Academy Award, she was widely criticized among the Deaf for speaking her acceptance instead of signing. And when Heather Whitestone took the Miss America crown, there was an even greater expression of dismay from the Deaf that an oral deaf person had won.

Why were they unhappy?

Partly because they abhor the sight of oral deaf people as high-profile role models; they don't want parents to get the idea that perhaps their deaf children, too, may be taught to speak and speechread. And partly because Whitestone said publicly, in so many words, the blasphemy that ASL is limiting.

Even *Time* was taken in by the Deaf point of view.

Its two-page article on Whitestone doubted the applicability of her example no less than four times, took a negative view of oral communication for the deaf, and, predictably, said that Harlan Lane "talks grimly of their 'drowning in the mainstream.'"

So I responded with a letter to the editor, which wasn't printed. It said, in part:

> *Time* erred in belittling the import of Heather White-
> stone's functioning in the mainstream by speaking and
> reading lips. In questioning the applicability of her example,
> you ignored a number of facts:
>
> 1. The deafness of those who make it in the mainstream
> through oral communication tends to be invisible—and un-
> countable—precisely because we are integrated. Whitestone
> is a valid example of what many people can do.
>
> 2. Significant numbers of prelingually deaf children are
> being taught to speak and speechread. While the process
> is indeed difficult and success varies, some proficiency is
> more useful than none.

3. Employers report that the primary obstacle to hiring and promoting deaf people is an inability to communicate well enough. Despite the sheltered, feel-good environment of the Deaf community, ASL is useless in the hearing workplace. For many of the better jobs—especially managerial and executive positions—oral communication is essential.

4. Harlan Lane admits that his major concern is not for the individual deaf child, but for cultural diversity.

Shame on *Time* for concluding that Whitestone's motivational program involving "positive attitude," "a dream," "hard work," "knowing your problems but not letting them master you" and "a support team" shouldn't apply to young deaf people. Those who can manage the tougher task of communicating orally have broader horizons, both socially and professionally.

With revolutionary rhetoric, the militant Deaf and their hearing supporters accuse me of deep denial.

They say that I deny my deafness, that I am pretending to be a hearing person, that I am being deceitful by trying to "pass" as hearing, that I am deluding myself—because I choose to speak and speechread, to meet the hearing world on its own terms.

And they try to lay a similar guilt trip on the hearing parents of deaf children.

For me to accept my deafness, say the Deaf militants, I must reject speech and speechreading instead of trying to be like my hearing "oppressors," and embrace ASL.

The fact is, though, that it is they who deny reality—even though I am a living, breathing affirmation of what they continue to deny, a contradiction of what they claim.

They deny that a deaf person can belong to and be accepted by the hearing world.

They deny that a deaf person can be happy without the support of the Deaf community.

They deny that a deaf person can achieve self-esteem without American Sign Language.

They deny that speech and speechreading are necessary at all, let alone of immeasurable value.

They deny that a deaf child can take the oral route without forever hating and resenting his parents and teachers for "forcing" him to speak and speechread.

And they use semantic contortions to deny that deafness itself is a disability.

I know that the extremists do not represent the views of all culturally Deaf people (or, I hope, even most).

Many (perhaps most) members of the ASL community believe, as I do, in different strokes for different folks.

Someday, perhaps, there may be an accommodation between the oral deaf and the ASL Deaf.

If the Israelis and Arabs can start making peace, then almost anything is possible.

Yes, things are moving in the Middle East—although there are differences of opinion on where they are heading.

Concurrently with the peace process, Israel and some of the Arab countries are meeting in working groups to plan cooperation in areas such as water, economic development, public health, arms control and the environment.

I wrote some of the swords-into-plowshares proposals and speeches that the Israelis presented at the Morocco discussions on regional cooperation in agriculture. The assignment came to me from the Ministry of Foreign Affairs.

We have a lot of know-how that we're ready, willing and able to share with our neighbors.

Israel is far from perfect, but we have succeeded in building a secure, economically viable democracy that subscribes to progressive Western values—using brainpower and technology to compensate for the lack of natural resources.

As for the Palestinians, it's in our interest that they raise their standard of living (already higher than those of most people in the Arab world), that they run their own lives.

But Arafat is an unreliable partner in the peace process, and he doesn't really have control. In particular, he is unable or unwilling to control the murderous Hamas and Islamic Jihad factions.

To live with the situation, we put our faith in the Israel Defense Forces and compartmentalize our minds.

Every couple of months, the boulevard in front of our building is blocked off for half an hour while a police sapper examines a package found by a bus stop. So far, it hasn't been a bomb.

But we can't let terrorism dominate our thoughts. So people go about their business as normally as possible, until a suicide bomber blows up a bus in Tel Aviv.

National outrage and mourning follow the tragedy, but life goes on. Despite the high-profile incidents, the fact is that Israel is one of the safest places in the world.

Peace with Jordan is going more smoothly. The contrast is as striking as the disparity between Arafat and King Hussein.

In a matter of months, Hussein and Yitzhak Rabin worked out the major details, signed a treaty, and opened the borders with unprecedented speed.

The bridge across the Jordan River down the road from our kibbutz has been in ruins since the 1948 War of Independence. Even before the treaty was signed, engineers spanned the river in a few hours with a prefabricated steel bridge so we won't have to wait until the new concrete bridge is built.

We stood there and watched prefab buildings for customs and passport control being trucked in. A few days later, the ministers of transportation from Israel and Jordan cut the ribbon.

At the top of our agenda was a visit to the ancient city of Petra. Looking like huge Roman temples carved into the red sandstone cliffs, the rows of ornate tombs are a world-famous attraction.

For decades, including the years we were kibbutzniks on the border, Israelis were denied access to the rock city. It was a perfect example of Tennyson's lament: so near and yet so far.

And then, virtually overnight, the gap was bridged.

For a deaf person, likewise, the hearing world is so near and yet so far.

But technology is gradually bridging the gap. Cochlear implants, for example, are having unpredictable but often dramatic results in giving deaf people some usable hearing.

A decade ago, the primitive single-channel implants would have been of little or no help to me.

Today, the state of the art is vastly improved. The 22-channel implants come closer to simulating voices and other sounds.

The most successful implantees (about 20 percent) are able to hear over the telephone. And almost all implantees are able to speechread and speak better with the help of the auditory input.

Earlier, I mentioned that computers have been great for deaf people because everything is shown visually on the screen.

Today, the hottest new computer technology is multimedia on CD-ROM. It combines text and graphics and video and...

...*sound.*

Technology giveth, and technology taketh away.

Switching from high-tech to low-tech:

Today, a relatively new technique helps young speechreaders differentiate among similar-looking sounds as they are spoken— such as those in bad/ban/bat/mad/man/mat/pad/pan/pat.

Cued speech, developed at Gallaudet in 1966, uses eight hand-shapes in four locations around the speaker's mouth and face to represent sounds. The easy-to-learn system is useful in helping teachers and parents communicate with children and expose them to the English language at the earliest possible age.

Some studies show that when cued speech is used for teaching, the children tend to surpass signing and oral children in language comprehension and expression; to read at the same levels as do children with normal hearing; and to use spoken English that's as grammatically correct as that of hearing children.

Barbara instinctively uses this approach for one particular sound when saying an unfamiliar (to me) word in Hebrew. She holds her Adam's apple with her thumb and forefinger to indicate that the word has the gutteral "ch" sound, not the look-alike "k."

A different tack is taken by the auditory-verbal approach. It trains a deaf child to use whatever residual hearing he has, maximized by hearing aids—or a cochlear implant—without the visual input of lipreading during the training.

Under the guidance of a therapist, the parents work intensively with the child to help him learn to discriminate the sounds of speech by hearing alone. The child acquires speech and language the natural way, by hearing and repeating it.

Most deaf children have some residual hearing that could be usable with the proper technology and training. This method is quite challenging, but it has had outstanding results in preparing children for the mainstream.

It has been gratifying to break out of the mold that casts the deaf in manual occupations such as carpentry and typesetting.

But the irony of it is, I really do love to work with my hands.

In every one of our homes—three in Highland Park, two in Tel Aviv, two on the kibbutz (not to mention our daughters' homes)—we have remodeled extensively.

I have done much of the work myself as architect, carpenter, electrician and plumber—breaking down walls, building additions, always opening up and expanding.

It's the physical counterpart to my lifelong assault on the social, educational and vocational barriers presented by deafness.

As a memento of the walls that have come tumbling down, we have a well-used sledgehammer in the den.

Today, desktop publishing enables me to do almost everything on my computer, including writing, design, graphics...

...and, yes, typesetting, which I did for this book.

There's probably a moral in there somewhere.

I have been extremely fortunate to have a healthy family, good friends, and a multifaceted professional career that has been very satisfying and rewarding—both emotionally and financially.

Our relative prosperity has enabled us to live well, to educate our four daughters and buy homes for them, and to fly back and forth often to be with our far-flung family in Israel and America—which, as of this writing, includes seven grandchildren (including Laurie's third boy, Assaf).

I say this not to boast, but to acknowledge a profound debt to speaking and speechreading—which helped me make it in the hearing world without being able to hear—and to my parents, who chose the oral route for me.

It shows that deafness itself is not the problem, so long as I can communicate efficiently and effectively with hearing people.

ASL advocates say that being in the Deaf community enables deaf people to feel good about themselves.

That may be so for some people, and that's fine.

But here in the mainstream, I feel good about myself.

Very, very good.

Although my life has been atypical, I am not alone.

There are thousands of other oral deaf people like me in the professions, in business, in industry, in academe, doing just fine in the mainstream by speaking and speechreading.

From a statistical point of view, however, it's difficult to find and count us as deaf people. Those of us who took the oral route tend to go unsurveyed.

Research samples consist of people who attended schools for the deaf and people who are members of deaf social associations.

Nowhere do any records associate my socioeconomic status or mainstream activities with my deafness. The same holds true for other successfully mainstreamed deaf people.

Since we speak and speechread, our deafness is invisible to most people—so most people don't know about us.

Perhaps it's about time they did.

It would give more encouragement to the kids who are busting their buttons to learn to speak and speechread.

It would give more hope to parents who have no idea what may be possible for their deaf children.

It would give more examples of oral successes to educators of the deaf, proving that there are more of us than they think.

And it would give more employers a more enlightened view of the capabilities of those who cannot hear—especially those who can speak and speechread.

After I delivered the keynote at the biennial convention of the Alexander Graham Bell Association for the Deaf, I spent three days talking with the parents, professionals and oral deaf teenagers and adults.

I was tremendously impressed by the people and the scope of their achievements, as well as by their extraordinary commitment and motivation.

It was a delight to see so many oral deaf people (including many who are prelingually deaf) doing so well in mainstream universities, mainstream occupations and mainstream social groups.

Inevitably, I volunteered to set up an international affiliate of the Bell Association in Israel.

I do not claim that all deaf people can achieve the levels that I and many others have reached.

All the pieces fell into place for me.

There's no question that the mainstream is more challenging, and that it isn't for everyone. For those with multiple handicaps, in particular, it may well be impossible.

And the early going during childhood and adolescence can be rough at times.

But those who do succeed in communicating with the hearing world on its own terms, by speaking and reading lips, will have many more doors open to them.

The payoff in the expanded horizons and opportunities of the mainstream can be well worth the effort.

This discriminatory situation may not be right.

But that's the way it is today in a world where most people can hear—despite technologies and federal laws designed to help the hearing impaired.

It is 9:30 a.m. when we reach the synagogue in Highland Park, two hours before Lisa's wedding.

During the preceding weeks, Barbara and I and our three other daughters had flown in from Tel Aviv.

For the next eight hours, I talk with people almost nonstop—meeting many of them for the first time.

Barbara and I talk with the caterer about the food and the crew. I ask for some of the tables to be moved away from the wall.

I ask the video cameraman, shooting down the aisle from the doorway of the sanctuary, to show me a test of someone's face under the *chupah*, the wedding canopy. No good—it's silhouetted against the bright white background of the *bima*. We talk about how to solve the problem without disrupting the atmosphere.

The photographer is outside, shooting people under the oak trees while other members of the two families wait to be called. I ask the custodian to take some chairs out there.

My brother and nephew arrive with their violins to tune up. I ask the piano player whether he can stick around after the wedding and accompany my nephew on a piece at the reception.

The guests start arriving. Some of those from the groom's side come up to me and introduce themselves; to others, I say "I'm Lisa's father. Who are you?"

The groom's guests give no indication that they notice anything unusual about me. But my friends and relatives spot the difference immediately and rib me unmercifully about my wearing a suit and tie for the first time in 11 years.

The band arrives and sets up its equipment in the reception hall. I talk to the leader about inserting my nephew's performance into the program—where and when.

The rabbi and the cantor arrive. We go into the library for the signing of the *ketubah*, the symbolic marriage contract.

The processional music starts, played by two of the country's finest violinists—and I can't hear a note of it. I am consoled by the thought that at least I didn't have to pay them.

The bride is beautiful, of course, and the ceremony is relaxed and pleasant.

Facing the rabbi, I get almost everything he says. When there is a round of laughter, I raise my eyebrows at Barbara.

"He forgot Larry's name," she mouths.

The groom breaks the glass with his foot, and the celebration begins.

For four solid hours, I talk with the 150 guests.

When it is my turn at the microphone, I thank the guests for coming—and give special thanks to the people who loaned me the suit, the tie, the shirt, the socks and the belt I am wearing.

Instead of making a traditional toast, Debby, Julie and Laurie join Barbara in singing a parody I wrote of a children's Hanukkah song about spinning a *dreidl* (a four-sided top).

The final stanza:

> *We have a little daughter*
> *But it won't be the same*
> *Oh Lisa, Lisa, Lisa*
> *Now it's you and what's-his-name*

It is a wonderfully joyous and satisfying occasion—all the more so because the ability to communicate freely and spontaneously in the hearing world lets me be a central participant in the fun.

A few hours ago, I passed the screening process for a cochlear implant. The surgery is scheduled for next month, in January 1995.

It looks like I may regain some hearing, albeit of low quality.

My chances of reaching the top level of success—being able to hear on the phone—may not be too good if my auditory nerves have degenerated too much from non-use.

At first, all I'll hear will be confusing noise. At best, after months or years of therapy and teaching myself to listen, someone talking to me will sound like Donald Duck with a sore throat.

Getting an implant began as a passing thought (as did moving to Israel), but now the adrenaline is starting to flow.

The possibility of having some hearing again is appealing—but what *really* turns me on is facing a new challenge with the odds stacked against me.

Having the hardware implanted is just the first step. They tell me that the make-or-break factor is my attitude—how hard I work at learning to discriminate spoken sounds.

If I learn to hear on the phone after 55 years of total deafness, it will make a great story for my next book.

If I don't, I'll lie—and sell the story to the *National Enquirer.*

Do I really need the implant? Ask my grandson.

Debby was reminding Dor, then 5 years old, that I can't hear him when he speaks to me.

He replied: "Well, Saba Lew is just deaf in Hebrew. He can hear okay in English."

Onward.

Acknowledgments

Thanks to David James, Bosco Keown, Bill Peter, Katie Schmitz, Tilak Ratnanather and Paula Tucker for answers to my questions.

To Erwin Atwood and Miriam Clifford on the distinct issues of hard-of-hearing people; to Jozie Eisner on the auditory-verbal method; to Kimberly Laird on library resources; to Ann Major on employment issues; to Roy Miller on late-deafened adults; to Ronald Mitchell and Emilie Quast on TDDs; to Donna Morere on cued speech.

To the many participants in the deaf-l discussion group on the Internet, whose support for and opposition to my postings helped me crystallize thoughts I never knew I had.

And to my family and friends, my teachers and coworkers, and all the other people who helped me make it in the mainstream.

This is their story, too.

Index